AF740163

Infringement of the United States Patent Right

Infringement of the United States Patent Right

A Guide for Executives and Attorneys

Richard T. Holzmann

QUORUM BOOKS
Westport, Connecticut • London

Library of Congress Cataloging-in-Publication Data

Holzmann, Richard.
Infringement of the United States patent right : a guide for executives and attorneys / Richard T. Holzmann.
p. cm.
Includes bibliographical references and index.
ISBN 0-89930-864-3 (alk. paper)
1. Patent laws and legislation—United States. 2. Patent suits—United States. I. Title.
KF3114.H64 1995
346.7304'86—dc20
[347.306486] 94-39342

British Library Cataloguing in Publication Data is available.

Copyright © 1995 by Richard T. Holzmann

All rights reserved. No portion of this book may be reproduced, by any process or technique, without the express written consent of the publisher.

Library of Congress Catalog Card Number: 94-39342
ISBN: 0-89930-864-3

First published in 1995

Quorum Books, 88 Post Road West, Westport, CT 06881
An imprint of Greenwood Publishing Group, Inc.

The paper used in this book complies with the Permanent Paper Standard issued by the National Information Standards Organization (Z39.48-1984).

10 9 8 7 6 5 4 3 2 1

CONTENTS

PREFACE

The purpose of this work is to introduce the manager and technologist, the student, and the foreign patent practitioner to the United States Law of Patent Infringement. It should also be a refresher to those patent agents or attorneys who devote their time exclusively to prosecution rather than to litigation. But it should be mentioned that the highly respected Judge Hand, in 1950, noted, "... when the question is whether there is a patentable invention. The issue is as fugitive, impalpable, wayward, and vague a phantom as exists in the whole paraphernalia of legal concepts"—indicating the difficulty in determining when an invention is a patentable one.

Effort has been made to illustrate the development of that law from its historical perspective to the recent decisions of the Court of Appeals for the Federal Circuit (CAFC), the premier patent appellate tribunal. Creation of the CAFC in 1982 was a landmark in the evolution of patent law and policy. With the withdrawal of patent jurisdiction from the twelve regional Courts of Appeal, the CAFC is the court with primary responsibility for interpreting and developing the rules and principles of patent law.

Particular emphasis is placed on the large number of recent opinions on the question of equivalents in an infringement context. Many practitioners feel that several of the opinions in the 1987–1994 period are revolutionizing the scope of claims that define the invention in the means-plus-function format. It would appear that the battle in the courts, and within the CAFC itself, over the essence of the infringement analysis (i.e., the interpretation and construction of claims with the subsequent application to the accused device) has finally peaked, although many problems remain.

In most respects, the mission of the CAFC to unify the Patent Law seems to have been fulfilled to the pleasure of most and the dismay of some. The Doctrine of Equivalents is another matter, however. This court is in a period of rapid change, with major divisions among the judges themselves. It has been considered necessary to include an Epilogue since several important cases, especially *Hilton Davis,* are before this entire court and will probably be decided as this volume goes to press.

This work is not intended to be encyclopedic in nature, with a host of footnotes and citations to case law; rather its purpose is to be a monograph or handbook on the subject of enforcement. While one will find many quotations from cases, only those references from the more important cases are named. The others are provided to give a feeling for the problems and the various judicial viewpoints.

Throughout, reference is often made to Title 35 of the United States Code, and less frequently to Title 28. Title 35, entitled "Patents," was codified and enacted into positive law by Act of the Congress on July 19, 1952. This codification simplified and clarified language and arrangement, and eliminated obsolete and redundant provisions. Title 28 is entitled "Judiciary and Judicial Procedure." These codes are officially cited as "Title 35, United States Code, Section ——," or more conveniently as 35 USC 271, for example. These titles are legal evidence of the general and permanent laws, and recourse to the numerous volumes of the United States Statutes at Large for this purpose will no longer be necessary. Of course, more recent decisions and legislative enactments must be continually researched. Extensive use has also been made of the U.S. Code Annotated, which sets out the essence of court opinions construing federal legislation relating to patents.

1

TYPES OF LITIGATION IN GENERAL

The right which a party may have to institute a judicial proceeding is known as a *cause of action.* "Action" refers more peculiarly to the legal procedure of a controversy; "cause" to its merits or the state of facts involved. *Litigation* generally means a contest between parties having adverse interests, which is resolved in court.

The term *patent litigation* encompasses causes of action involving patent rights which call into question the scope or validity of a U.S. patent. Since patent rights are the exclusive province of the federal government, such cases are brought before the federal courts. Causes of action which involve patent rights but which do not call into question the scope or validity of a U.S. patent are generally not considered to be encompassed by the term patent litigation. Questions arising under contracts, such as licensing agreements or employment agreements, and testamentary disposition of patent rights may be tried in the various state courts.

The causes of action which arise under the patent laws of the United States and which are thus recognized by the federal courts include actions:

1. for damage caused by patent infringement [35 USC 281 and 284];
2. for injunction and other relief because of infringement [35 USC 281 and 283];
3. by the United States to cancel a patent for fraud [a Suit in Equity];
4. in the United States Claims Court for the unlicensed use of an invention by the United States [28 USC 1498];

5. *Qui Tam:* to recover for the unauthorized marking of patented articles and for the fraudulent marking of unpatented articles [35 USC 292];
6. to prohibit importation of products made using patented processes [19 USC 1337(a)] (Title 19 has to do with customs duties);
7. under the Federal Declaratory Judgment Act [28 USC 2201], affording relief in cases that could not be brought under existing forms of procedure;
8. to obtain a patent and actions to decide questions of priority in interferences [35 USC 145 and 146]; and
9. for relief against an interfering patent [35 USC 146 and 291].

At this point it would be helpful to provide definitions of some of the above terms.

Infringement of Patent [35 USC 271] states, "whoever without authority makes, uses or sells any patented invention, within the United States during the term of the patent therefor, infringes the patent.... Whoever actively induces infringement of a patent shall be liable as an infringer.... Whoever sells a component... knowing the same to be especially made or especially adapted for use in an infringement of such patent, and not a staple... shall be liable as a contributory infringer." In other words, knowledge of the existence of a patent is not necessary for what is known as *direct infringement* (i.e., to make, use, or sell).

Qui Tam (Who as well). A suit in which the plaintiff sues for the state as well as for himself. An action brought by an informer under a statute which establishes a penalty for the commission or omission of a certain act, and provides that the same shall be recoverable in a civil action; part of the penalty to go to the plaintiff and the balance to the state or some other institution.

Equity. In the general juristic sense, equity means the power to meet the moral standards of justice in a particular case by a tribunal having discretion to mitigate the rigidity of the application of strict rules of law so as to adapt the relief to the circumstances of the particular case. It was grounded in the precepts of conscience, not in any sanction of positive law, and thus was administered by the ecclesiastical courts, not the common law courts. In Anglo-American law, equity means the system of legal materials developed and applied by the Court of Chancery in England (as a successor to the ecclesiastical courts) and the courts succeeding to its powers in the British Empire and the United States. The first great principle of equity jurisdiction was that it could act only when the remedy in the common law courts was not adequate. By codes or practice acts adopted in a majority of the states purporting to abolish the formal distinctions between actions at law and suits in equity, and by the judicature acts in England, the administration of both common law and equitable remedies was combined into one system of procedure, in the same system of courts. New York was the first to do so, in 1848.

Reexamination. As used in this context, this means that any person at any time, during the period of the enforceability of a patent, may file a request for reexamination by the Patent Office of any claim of a patent. The request must be accompanied by a statement pointing out each substantial new question of patentability based on prior art patents and printed publications.

Injunction. An injunction is a typical order *in personam;* it purports to accomplish nothing of itself, but imposes on the party enjoined a duty to do, or to refrain from doing, some act.

The U.S. Patent and Trademark Office (PTO) has exclusive jurisdiction over all applications for U.S. patents; once a patent has been granted, however, the PTO has no further power. While an *interference* usually is resolved before the PTO and does involve adverse parties, it is not normally encompassed under the term litigation. Congress early provided procedures for resolving the question of priority of right of invention, which applied to an application interfering with a patent as well as interfering applications, within the Patent Office. Consequently, an interference procedure is used to determine the first and true inventor; that is, the one who conceived the invention, was diligent, and reduced it to practice first.

The primary adversary proceedings which call into question the scope and validity of the patent right are suits for:

1. cancellation, which can only be brought by and in the name of the United States;
2. declaratory judgment of invalidity, which can be brought by an alleged infringer; and
3. infringement, wherein the owner of the patent must be a party.

This work is concerned almost exclusively with suits for infringement. But first, cancellation and declaratory judgments will be discussed.

CANCELLATION OF A PATENT

Suits seeking the cancellation of a U.S. patent may be brought only by and in the name of the United States. Once a patent has been granted, the PTO has no power to cancel, revoke, or annul that patent. While cancellation is a special action as explained below, the terms *annul* and *revoke* are often used loosely and interchangeably when patents are granted through mistake or fraud.

When a patented invention fails to meet the requirements of patentability as determined by a court, the patent will be declared invalid. The conditions of patentability are that the invention: (1) involve statutory subject matter; (2) be novel; (3) be useful; (4) be nonobvious; (5) does not involve any statutory bars; (6) be original; and (7) be adequately disclosed in the application. However, upon appeal to another or higher court this decision may be reversed.

Unclean hands in the prosecution of the patent application in the PTO, once known as *fraud on the Patent Office* and now referred to as *inequitable conduct,* makes the patent resulting therefrom unenforceable. The party with "unclean hands" has no relief in equity.

When the government sues for cancellation and succeeds, however, the cancellation prevents the bringing of any other suits; in other words, the patent no longer exists. Action for cancellation can only be maintained by the United States under the general principles of equity, invariably for fraud. Such actions are very rare.

A patent cannot be revoked or cancelled by the president of the United States or any other officer of the government. A decree holding a fraudulently procured patent invalid between the parties to the suit does not operate to cancel it but only amounts to *res judicata* (i.e., once judicially decided, the matter is finally decided) between the actual parties to the suit. Third parties may still have a cause of action on an invalid patent. The law now provides that the commissioner may institute reexamination proceedings under certain conditions.

In beginning and prosecuting a suit in equity to repeal a patent, the United States acts through the U.S. District Attorney of the district in which the suit is brought, and he acts under the direction of the attorney general, who may be prompted by the commissioner of the PTO or any private person. But no citizen has any power to compel the attorney general to begin such a suit, or to control its prosecution after it is begun.

In addition to fraud, the Department of Justice may also sue patentees on the grounds that the manner in which they are exploiting their patents constitutes a violation of the antitrust laws. While the Federal Trade Commission Act does not invest the commission with power to invalidate patents, commission action may in fact emasculate patents procured or exploited in a manner violative of the FTC Act, such as engaging in practices which amount to unfair competition. The FTC has required patentees to grant licenses at a royalty rate set by the commission.

FEDERAL DECLARATORY JUDGMENT ACT

In the usual case, the patent owner involved in litigation has been placed in the role of plaintiff, with the alleged infringer as defendant. The Declaratory Judgment Act [28 USC 2201 and 2202], however, makes it possible under certain circumstances for an alleged infringer to take the initiative by suing a patent owner for a declaratory judgment of patent invalidity and/or noninfringement. Recent decisions permit counterclaims by the defendant (patent owner) where there are no complications, such as bringing in another patent or perjury in related litigation. The patent owner may interpose as a counterclaim a declaratory judgment for patent infringement.

In declaratory judgment suits involving patents, the court must first determine whether the action arises under the patent laws (i.e., 28 USC 1338). It is well settled that declaratory judgment suits asserting invalidity and noninfringement of a patent arise under the patent laws. On the other hand, suits seeking to enforce or declare rights arising from a patent license are considered contract questions, and thus not arising under the patent laws.

Second, there must be an existing and continuing *actual controversy* between the parties. Actual controversy has the same meaning as *case or controversy* or *justiciable controversy,* and the terms are used interchangeably by the courts. For patent controversies the regional circuit courts concluded that a declaratory judgment complainant had to satisfy a two-prong test to establish existence of an actual controversy. First, one (the alleged infringer) had to show a legally sufficient adverse interest in the patent. This was typically demonstrated by facts showing that he had "actually produced the accused device" or had "prepared to produce such a device" and his right to continue would either be lost or materially affected by the judgment. Second, one had to show a reasonable apprehension of being sued for patent infringement.

The actual controversy language in the Declaratory Judgment Act restates the requirement of Article III of the Constitution that federal court jurisdiction be limited to cases and controversies. The federal courts cannot give advisory opinions or pass upon hypothetical, abstract, or academic controversies.

At least one court has stated the prerequisites to the finding of an actual controversy as follows:

> First, plaintiffs must establish that defendant patentee has charged them with infringement or threatened them, either directly or indirectly, with a patent infringement suit.... Second, plaintiffs must have begun to produce and sell their allegedly infringing apparatus or must at least have made some substantial preparations to do so.

While declaratory judgment proceedings are still considered equitable in nature in a number of jurisdictions, the modern view is that such proceedings are neither legal nor equitable, but *sui generis* (i.e., of its own kind or class). In fact, it has been suggested that the declaratory judgment was adopted at least in part to fill the gap between law and equity, or as a step toward the obliteration of the line which has separated law from equity. The declaratory judgment has an ancient history going back to the Roman law.

The federal Declaratory Judgment Act is only an authorization, not a command. It gives the federal courts competence to make a declaration of rights, but does not impose a duty to do so; and it confers a discretion on the courts rather than an absolute right upon the litigant. Nor is it the purpose of the Act to draw into federal courts causes properly cognizable by state courts. Since the Act is limited to cases which, from their nature or from diversity of citizenship, are actual controversies over which the federal courts have jurisdiction, the mere fact that a declaratory judgment is sought is not of itself a ground for federal jurisdiction.

The propriety of declaratory relief must defer to the District Court's exercise of discretion in balancing such factors as:

1. the likelihood that the declaration will resolve the uncertainty of obligation which gave rise to the controversy;
2. the convenience of the parties;
3. the public interest in a settlement of the uncertainty of the obligation; and
4. the availability and relative convenience of other remedies.

In a declaratory judgment action alleging invalidity and noninfringement, *venue* jurisdiction is controlled by 28 USC 1391(c) and not by 28 USC 1400(b) (i.e., by the general venue statute and not by the special patent venue statute).

The only rights which the Act empowers the federal courts to declare are those "of any interested party petitioning for such declaration" and not for "all persons similarly situated." Where the interest transferred is deemed to be a license, the patent owner is a necessary party, because the patent owner is still the real party in interest with respect to the validity of the patent. The same pleadings standards are applied as in other federal civil actions. The burden of proving that a controversy exists rests with the declaratory judgment plaintiff.

While violations of the antitrust laws may be used as an equitable defense in an action brought by a patentee charging infringement, they may not be used as part of an affirmative case in an action seeking declaratory relief under this statute. Although the Act establishes a new procedure and enlarges the range of remedies available in the federal courts, it does not enlarge their field of jurisdiction. Appeals from judgments in declaratory actions are governed by the same principles as in other federal actions.

28 USC 2201: Creation of Remedy

In a case of actual controversy within its jurisdiction, except with respect to Federal taxes, any court of the United States, upon the filing of an appropriate pleading, may declare the rights and other legal relations of any interested party seeking such declaration, whether or not further relief is or could be sought. Any such declaration shall have the force and effect of a final judgment or decree and shall be reviewable as such.

28 USC 2202: Further Relief

Further necessary or proper relief based on a declaratory judgment or decree may be granted, after reasonable notice and hearing, against any adverse party whose rights have been determined by such judgment.

The purpose of declaratory relief is to liquidate uncertainties and controversies which might result in future litigation. Consequently, the patent owner must have done something to enforce, or attempt to enforce, his patent, so that a real controversy exists. A mere threat by the patentee to enforce his patent rights is usually adequate.

It should be noted that prior to the passage of the original Act in 1934, the patentee enjoyed unfair privileges in that he could publicly and privately charge infringement without actually bringing suit. In this way, he could intimidate dealers and customers or even sue for infringement, delay the trial, and move to dismiss at the last minute, the alleged infringer being virtually helpless.

The new remedy found almost immediate application in patent controversies. Since the suit is essentially one for patent infringement with the parties reversed, the courts had no difficulty in concluding that the action arises under the patent laws: "It is of no moment, in the determination of the character of the relief sought, that the suit is brought by the alleged infringer instead of by the owner." Examples of situations where the declaratory judgment remedy is most helpful include:

1. where a suit for infringement is made but not pressed;
2. where multiplicity of suits is to be avoided;
3. where relief is to be afforded against the peril and insecurity of defying an injunctive decree in a patent suit;
4. where a party desires to prevent an invalid patent from remaining in the art as a *scarecrow;*

5. where a party desires to avoid being held as a contributory infringer; and
6. where a party desires to avoid the accrual of damages.

Factors or circumstances frequently relied upon include:

1. a history of litigation between the same two parties;
2. threats or statements to customers;
3. suit against customers;
4. suits against others based on broad interpretation of patent;
5. general announcements published in trade papers;
6. an opinion by counsel by patent owner;
7. assertions made during license negotiations or arbitration; and
8. suits abroad on analogous foreign patents.

There are also many cases finding the absence of a sufficient charge. A person must have a legally sufficient adverse interest in order to maintain an action for a declaratory judgment of invalidity and/or noninfringement. The mere existence of a license agreement between two parties does not prevent the creation of a justiciable controversy. "Legal rights may only be adjudicated under the Act precisely as only legal rights may be adjudicated in any other form of civil action . . ."; "[t]he operation of the Declaratory Judgment Act is procedural [remedial] only."

A declaratory judgment is only binding on the real parties before the court. The Act did not create new substantive rights or legal relationships but added to the remedies previously existing an additional one for relief in the form of a judgment declaring the rights of the parties. If a proper basis has been laid in the pleadings and proof, a defendant in a declaratory judgment suit can be enjoined from instituting or sending notices of infringement suits to plaintiff's customers.

A declaratory judgment is *res judicata* in the matters at issue, as between the parties and their privies, even where it is a consent or default judgment. A declaratory judgment is not *res judicata,* however, as to matters not at issue and not passed upon, and only the parties to the action in which it is rendered are bound by such a judgment; as to others, it is effective only as a precedent as to the matters declared by it. Appeals from judgments in declaratory actions are governed by the same principles as in other federal actions.

Before inception of the Court of Appeals for the Federal Circuit (CAFC), there was conflict in the circuit courts as to whether a licensee had a reasonable apprehension of suit while the license was still in effect, some holding that the license must have terminated in order to bring suit.

The two cases which follow illustrate how the CAFC has handled some declaratory judgment problems.

C. R. Bard, Inc. v. Schwartz (August 1983): The CAFC noted that the Supreme Court has simply required that the disagreement not be nebulous or contingent. The Federal Circuit indicated that these conditions may be met where there is a license agreement in effect and, therefore, held that "an examination of the *totality of the circumstances* must be made to determine whether there is a controversy arising under the patent laws." The Federal Circuit enumerated several factors which provided Bard with a reasonable apprehension of suit:

1. Bard had committed a material breach of the license agreement by ceasing to make royalty payments.
2. The state suit brought by Schwartz to recover royalties shows a willingness on his part to enforce his patent rights.
3. Schwartz sought future royalties in the state court.

Goodyear Tire v. Releasomers Inc. (July 1987): Releasomers brought suit in state court for misappropriation of certain trade secrets concerning its techniques. Upon the issuance of Releasomers' patents while the state action was ongoing, Goodyear filed suit for a declaratory judgment. The District Court granted Releasomers' motion for summary judgment for lack of an actual controversy because Releasomers had made no express threat to sue Goodyear for patent infringement. The Federal Circuit reversed. The following factors provided Goodyear with an objective reasonable apprehension of an impending patent infringement suit in this case:

1. the parties were already embroiled in a protracted dispute in the state court;
2. Releasomers was seeking $18 million in damages in the state court, certainly thinking the disputed technology to be valuable;
3. Releasomers not only informed Goodyear of the allowance of the patents; and
4. counsel for Releasomers candidly stated that he would have no hesitation to sue once it was determined that Goodyear was infringing the patents.

The Federal Circuit stated that it "cannot read the Declaratory Judgment Act so narrowly as to require that a party actually be confronted with an *express* threat of litigation to meet the requirements of an actual case or controversy." The court concluded by observing that, "from the underlying facts in this case, it is a compelled inference that Goodyear had an objective apprehension of an impending law suit."

In the few declaratory judgment suits involving patents decided by the CAFC, the court has established a number of important principles:

1. It has chosen the better view by holding that repudiation of a license agreement should not be a precondition to a declaratory judgment suit.
2. It has established the totality of the circumstances test as a guide to the District Courts for determining whether a declaratory claimant has a reasonable apprehension of being sued for patent infringement.
3. An actual controversy must be established on a claim-by-claim basis and not just on the basis of the patent in suit.
4. An admission of infringement is not a precondition to establishing an actual controversy.
5. So long as the requirements of an actual controversy are met, a patentee is as entitled to seek a declaration of infringement under the Declaratory Judgment Act as a potential infringer is to seek a declaration of invalidity and noninfringement.

It is well settled in construing 28 USC 1338(a) that the Declaratory Judgment Act does not confer any additional subject matter jurisdiction but merely provides an additional remedy. If an accused infringer simply files an action seeking a declaratory judgment that the patent owner's patent is invalid or not infringed, Section 1338(a) clearly provides a basis for jurisdiction. Such a case is in essence an infringement suit with the parties juxtaposed. On the other hand, if the party bringing the suit is a licensee, the suit might be viewed as one arising under the license contract, rather than the federal patent laws. The cases are apparently in conflict as to whether Section 1338 covers such a declaratory judgment action by a licensee.

What follows to the end of this work on *enforcement of the patent right* is concerned with *infringement.*

2

THE PATENT RIGHT: WHAT IT DOES AND DOES NOT CONFER

A patent confers the right to exclude others from making, using, or selling an invention. *Direct infringement* is the doing of any of these acts of making, using, or selling during the term of the patent within the United States with respect to the invention defined by the claims without authority of the patent owner.

> It has long been settled that the patentee receives nothing from the law which he did not have before, and that the only effect of his patent is to restrain others from manufacturing, using or selling that which he has invented. (Sup. Ct. 1917)

The issuance of a patent is constructive notice to the world of its existence. One may therefore infringe without knowledge of the patent or intent to infringe.

> If what the defendant is doing infringes, plaintiff should have its decree no matter whether defendant thought it up independently or got the idea from plaintiff's patent.

Knowledge, however, is relevant to liability for inducement or contributory infringement, as well as to the question of damages.

> **35 USC 154: Contents and Term of Patent**
>
> Every patent shall contain . . . a grant to the patentee . . . for the term of seventeen years . . . of the right to exclude others from

making, using, or selling the invention throughout the United States.

35 USC 271: Infringement of Patent

(a) Except as otherwise provided in this title, whoever without authority makes, uses or sells any patented invention, within the United States during the term of the patent therefor, infringes the patent. . . .

(b) Whoever actively induces infringement of a patent shall be liable as an infringer. . . .

(c) Whoever sells a component of a patented machine, manufacture . . . constituting a material part of the invention, knowing the same to be especially made or especially adapted for use in an infringement of such patent, and not a staple article or commodity of commerce . . . shall be liable as a contributory infringer.

A U.S. patent does not grant the right to make, use, or sell the invention; it only grants the right to exclude others from performing these acts. Thus, the patent grant is not absolute; there are a number of limitations on this right to exclude.

1. State or federal safety, health, or other laws may prohibit or control this right.
2. Another may have a dominating or blocking patent which would exclude the inventor from making, using, or selling his own invention without a license.
3. The patented product, once sold, entitles the buyer to use and resell, but he cannot remake the patented invention. The right to use confers a right to repair but not to reconstruct.
4. A making or using may be excused if for experimental or other nonprofit purposes.
5. Finally, there are temporal, spatial, and agency limitations.
6. The Doctrine of Patent Misuse as well as the antitrust laws will severely restrict the patent right. This subject is discussed more fully below.

It was not until the 1952 Patent Act that Congress expressly provided for this right of exclusion rather than the right to make, which latter right, though statutory, was oftentimes clouded in Supreme Court decisions. Despite the prior statutes, the Court in one case in 1923 stated, "[a] patent confers a monopoly. . . . The idea of monopoly held by one in making, using and vending connotes the right in him to do that thing from which he excludes others."

1. Protection of the public interest may limit the patent right. The manufacture, sale, or use of hazardous products such as toxins and explosives are within the regulatory power of the states regardless of whether the product is patented. There is no immunity granted against false or misleading advertising, or the violation of trade secrets for example.

2. As early as 1793, the Patent Act contained an express provision on dominating or blocking patents which prohibited the inventor of a patented improvement from making, using, or selling his own invention. This provision was not carried forward in later statutes. Despite the fact that there is a patentable distinction between an improvement patent and a basic patent, this in no way necessarily avoids the ability of the latter to read on the former (i.e., whether properly construed claims encompass an accused structure or process).

3. There is an implied license for the purchaser of a patented invention from the patent owner or a licensee to use or resell the product free of control. Such a sale "exhausts" the patent right; the patentee has parted with the monopoly. However,

> The sale of an element of a patented combination does not necessarily imply license to use the whole combination. There is always a question of what is a fair inference from the transaction.

The line between permissible repair and impermissible reconstruction is a difficult one to draw and has been the subject of many cases. Quotations from several decisions will aid in understanding.

> The license granted to a purchaser of a patented combination is to preserve its fitness for use so far as it may be affected by wear or breakage. Beyond this there is no license.

> Thus, if the new parts so dominate the structural substance of the whole as to justify the conclusion that it had been made anew, there is a rebuilding or reconstruction.

Judge Hand, in 1945, stated,

> In order to call the monopoly, conferred by the patent grant, into play for a second time, it must, indeed, be a second creation of the patented entity. . . . Mere replacement of individual unpatented parts, one at a time, whether of the same part repeatedly or different parts successively, is no more than the lawful right of the owner to repair his property.

Whereas in 1961, Justice Brennan wrote,

> Appropriately to be considered are the life of the part replaced in relation to the useful life of the whole combination, the importance of the replaced element to the inventive concept, the cost of the component relative to the cost of the combination, the common sense understanding and intention of the patent owner and the buyer of the combination as to its perishable components, whether the purchased component replaces a worn-out part or is bought for some other purpose, and other pertinent factors.

4. The defense to a charge of infringement of experimental use is limited to its not being coupled with a commercial use. In 1832, Justice Story noted,

> [I]t could never have been the intention of the legislature to punish a man, who constructed such a machine merely for philosophical experiments, or for the purpose of ascertaining the sufficiency of the machine to produce its described effects.

However, this defense is a very restricted one; any commercial purpose will negate it unless *de minimis non curat lex* (i.e., the law does not concern itself about trifles). "[I]n the law of patents as elsewhere there comes a point where what may be literally a wrong, is of too trifling importance to justify the intervention of a court."

5. In addition to the above limitations on the patent right, there are temporal, spatial, and agency limitations as well.

The temporal limitation is for the seventeen-year term of the statutory grant measured from the date of issuance and inclusive of the date of expiration as interpreted by modern authorities. Until the patent is issued, a suit for infringement may not be brought. Damages for preissuance activity cannot be sought under federal patent law but may be had under some other theory such as a breach of confidentiality or a trade secret violation.

Use of a patented invention after issuance of the patent constitutes infringement if manufacture or sale prior to issuance was unauthorized. On the other hand, "a sale by an inventor prior to issuance of a patent carries an implied license to use after the patent has issued."

After expiration, there can be no infringement; however, articles produced by an infringer may not be sold after the expiration of a patent if they have in fact been made prior to the expiration of the patent. Furthermore, one may make preparations to make, use, or sell prior to expiration provided that one does not actually make, use, or sell.

Many countries measure the term of the patent from the application date, laying open (i.e., publishing) the application eighteen months thereafter, thereby destroying its secrecy. While any right for recovery may not be implemented until issuance, an *inchoate* right arises upon the laying-open, inchoate meaning imperfect or begun but not completed. In patent law the inchoate right refers to the right of an inventor to his invention while his application is pending which matures as property when the patent issues. A system such as this is under consideration in the United States to bring our laws more in harmony with international practice.

The spatial limitation, of course, is throughout or within the United States, which includes its territories and possessions as well as U.S. ships at sea. The territory embraced by the grant of a patent is coextensive with the borders of the government which granted it. 35 USC 272 exempts (under certain circumstances) the use of a patented invention on a vessel, aircraft, or vehicle entering the United States temporarily or accidentally, so long as the invention is used exclusively for the needs of the vessel, aircraft, or vehicle and is not sold in or used for the manufacture of anything to be sold in or exported from the United States.

Making in the United States, even though only for use or sale abroad, infringes because making in itself is an act of infringement. Importing a product made or purchased abroad for use or sale in the United States infringes because using or selling in the United States is an act of infringement.

The agency limitation basically means that the patent grant does not confer on the owner the right to go after an agent, acting within the scope of his employment, for infringement. In other words, patent infringement is a tort and the courts apply the general principles of the law of agency as to the liability of a principal for the acts of a servant or agent.

As a general rule, corporate officers and directors are not liable absent some special showing, such as deliberate use of a corporation as an instrument to infringe. The corporation law doctrine of piercing the corporate veil is usually applied. It is only when the officers act outside the scope of their official duties that they become liable, although there is much case law on this subject. A number of decisions evoke the concept of inducement or contributory infringement codified in 35 USC 271(b) and (c).

As to the United States and its contractors, a patent owner's exclusive remedy when his invention is used or manufactured by or for the United States without authority is in the new U.S. Claims Court. Prior to 1910, a patent owner could not sue for infringement since this sounds in tort and the federal government had sovereign immunity. This is no longer the case and since there are many relevant decisions, these should be consulted rather than covering these very special circumstances in a work of this type.

With respect to states, sovereign immunity presents many difficulties in a federal court action against a state, a state agency, or a state officer. However, such immunity in general does not apply to city, county, or other political subdivisions for patent infringement arising from its activities.

The Foreign Sovereign Immunities Act of 1976 abolishes this defense with respect to commercial activity carried on in or directly affecting the United States.

3

ACTS CONSTITUTING INFRINGEMENT

The word *infringement* suggests an encroachment or trespass on a right or privilege. Unlike a trespass on real estate, patent infringement is a statutory wrong and is governed by federal law. 35 USC 271 of the present Patent Act was the first congressional effort (1952) to codify the common law doctrines of patent infringement. U.S. law recognizes two kinds of infringement: direct and indirect infringement. "Infringement of a patent is an erroneous phrase; what is infringed is a *claim,* which is the definition of invention, and it is the claim which is the cause of action."

DIRECT INFRINGEMENT

35 USC 271: Infringement of Patent

(a) Except as otherwise provided in this title, whoever without authority makes, uses *or* sells any patented invention, within the United States during the term of the patent therefor, infringes the patent.

(b) Whoever actively induces infringement of a patent shall be liable as an infringer.

The Patent Act grants to the patentee the right to exclude others from making or using or selling the claimed invention. The making, using, or selling of a patented invention outside the United States thus is not proscribed unless it induces or contributes to a domestic infringement.

In 1859 the Supreme Court held, "It is well settled that the mere *making* of a patented machine, though it is neither used nor sold, is an infringement of the right of the patentee," and in 1972, "The right to make can scarcely be made plainer by definition, and embraces the construction of *the thing invented.*" The thing must be actually associated in an operable assembly. A manufacturer of unassembled parts could be guilty only as a contributory infringer.

> Where defendants manufacture a device capable of an infringing use and sell it with the intent that it shall be so used, they infringed the patent, even though their device is capable of a noninfringing use, and even though they go through the form of instructing that it shall be used in a noninfringing way.

The question of what constitutes using of an invention has rarely arisen. Mere possession absent threatened or contemplated use or sale has been held to not constitute infringement. However, use for a sales demonstration has constituted infringement. Furthermore, use of a patented invention for a purpose not disclosed or even contemplated by the patentee does not escape infringement.

The 1952 Patent Act codified the right of the patentee to exclude others from the selling of the claimed invention even without their use or manufacture.

> Just as the manufacture of one machine by an infringer is sufficient to make the manufacturer liable, regardless of use or sale . . . so *one sale* is sufficient.
>
> The sale . . . is an act of infringement, although it may be made under such circumstances that complainants cannot recover damages for it.

To wit, sale to the patent owner or his agent may not itself be an infringement due to the common law maxim *volenti non fit injuria* (i.e., he who consents cannot receive an injury).

Normally, one does not use or sell a process or a machine by dealing in products made by the process or machine. However, recent revisions of the Patent Law (1988) have made the importation of a product made from a patented process and its subsequent use or sale [35 USC 271(g) and 35 USC 154], under certain conditions, liable for infringement.

With respect to direct infringement, knowledge that what is being made, used, or sold is covered by a subsisting patent is not an element necessary in establishing infringement. That is, one is an infringer even if he is in total ignorance of the existence of a patent. *Motive* or *intent* is immaterial. Intent to infringe, however, may make one liable for enhanced damages up to treble the amount of actual damages. By contrast, some degree of knowledge or intent is necessary to constitute indirect infringement. Willful patent infringement may give rise to a violation of the Lanham Act.

No infringement, either direct or indirect, can occur until the patent is issued. Consequently, damages cannot begin to accrue until the patent is issued. Issuance of the patent constitutes constructive notice to the world of its existence. A patentee may appropriately mark patented articles to the effect that the same are patented. In the event of failure to so mark, no damages will be recoverable by the patentee in any action for infringement, except on proof that the infringer had actual knowledge of the infringement and continued to infringe thereafter, in which event damages may be recovered only for infringement occurring after such notice.

35 USC 287 requires that notice of patent infringement be given an alleged infringer before an infringement suit can be brought. Filing of an action for infringement shall constitute such notice. 35 USC 287 is inapplicable where there has been no authorized manufacture or sale under the patent, but the statute does apply to a nonmanufacturing patentee who has licensed or authorized others to produce or sell the patented article.

Tests of Infringement

While the patent statute is silent about experimental use, it has been held that not every unauthorized construction of a patented article constitutes an infringement, and "the use of a patented machine for the sole purpose of gratifying a philosophical taste or curiosity or for instruction or amusement" does not constitute an infringing use.

The Drug Price Competition and Patent Term Restoration Act of 1984 now exempts testing solely for the purpose of securing marketing approval from the FDA.

Infringement is not avoided by the addition of steps or embellishments to a patented process or by imperfect practice of a patented invention, such as weak rather than strong embossing. Imperfect infringement is nonetheless infringement. Using a single means to perform some function in some manner as two separate means does not avoid infringement. There can be no infringement by one who deals exclusively with the patent owner.

Where a manufacturer carried out all but the last steps of the claimed process, the manufacturer's customer carrying out the last step, the court held the manufacturer liable as a direct infringer by in effect treating the manufacturer's customers as the agents of the manufacturer.

The literal infringement of a patent is rarely found in litigated cases. Literal infringement meaning that the claims read on and, therefore, encompass the patented product or process.

> [T]he transition may be gradual between literal infringement by substantially identical structures and infringement by equivalent structures.

Literal infringement is not conclusive, as infringement is not a mere matter of words or phraseology. The structures must do the same work in substantially the same way and accomplish substantially the same result. Every element is conclusively presumed to be essential and therefore every element, or its functional equivalent, must be found in the accused device or there is no infringement.

Interchangeability is an important test in determining the question of infringement. Noninterchangeability of parts tends strongly to negative infringement.

One may not escape liability for infringement by:

1. adding to a patented device,
2. changing its form, or
3. making it more or less efficient, while it retains its principle and mode of operation and attains its result by the use of the same or equivalent mechanical means.

UNITED STATES CODE ANNOTATED [35 USCA ——]

The United States Code Annotated is the Official Revision and Codification of the Laws of the United States with Annotations from Federal and State Courts. What follows in this and other sections wherein USCA is referenced are quotations from the USCA without the use of quotation marks for the sake of convenience. These quotations have been selected from the thousands of cases presented therein in order to provide a sense of the judicial decisions. Complete and up-to-date (1984) court opinions construing federal legislation relating to patents are also set out in these volumes.

> It is not an infringement to make various parts of a patented combination within the United States and ship the parts outside the United States for assembly and use.
>
> Another means of avoiding infringement is to show that the claims include elements for which there are no equivalent counterparts in the accused structure.
>
> Infringement is also avoided where one element of a claimed combination is missing.

The sale of a product made from a process does not infringe a patent on that process.

A change of form does not avoid infringement of a patent, unless the form shown in the patent is necessary to the functions which the patent ascribes to the invention, or is a distinguishing characteristic or essential to patentability, or is a specified particular form.

Immaterial variations in an accused device will not avoid infringement.

Structures which are designed merely for the purpose of evading the *spirit of the invention,* but which contain all the elements of the claims, are infringements of the patent.

Changes of the proportions of the ingredients of a *composition of matter* will not avoid infringement of a patent for such a composition, where those changes do not affect its essential character in any way more important than to increase its bulk more than they increase cost.

Infringement is not avoided merely because the infringing substance is outside the preferred range.

One who appropriates and manufactures or uses a patented invention or the substance thereof without the consent of the patentee does not escape or avoid infringement by *improving* upon the invention, or using an improvement made by another.

An embellishment made possible by technical advances may not permit an accused device to escape the "web of infringement."

Two patents may both be valid when the second is an *improvement* on the first, in which event, if the second includes the first, neither of the two patentees can lawfully use the invention of the other without the other's consent.

An *addition* to a patented machine or manufacture does not enable him who makes, uses, or sells the patented thing with the addition to avoid a charge of infringement. But the same authorities teach that if the addition results in a new combination, invention exists. ("There must be similarity of elements which perform the desired functions before infringement is shown.")

Omission of one element or ingredient of a combination covered by any claim of a patent averts any charge of infringement based on that claim.

A combination is an entirety. Every element of a combination claim for an apparatus and every step or operation of a combination claim for a process is conclusively presumed to be material.

The patentee makes all the parts of a combination material when he claims them *in combination* and not separately.

In determining infringement of a patent for a process, every step in the process claimed is conclusively presumed to be material. The *omission of one step* of the process avoids infringement of that claim, whether or not the omitted step was essential to the combination, unless some equivalent step or act is substituted.

This *rule of omission,* however, has no application to anything which, for convenience, may be made in several sections; for example, a shoe last, even if made in only two sections, may infringe a patent for a last of the same shape, but which is made in three sections instead of two.

Changing the relative positions or reversal of the parts of a machine does not avert infringement, where the parts transposed perform the same respective functions after the change as before, unless the machine acquires a substantially different mode of operation thereby.

No one is permitted to evade a patent simply by constructing the patented thing so *imperfectly* that its utility is diminished. On the other hand, a defendant's machine may be better than that covered by the patent in suit and may be an improvement upon it; if that superiority resulted from some *addition* to the latter, it will have no tendency to avoid infringement. And it matters not that the addition or improvement is patentable or patented.

When a *combination of old elements* is relied upon for patentability, there will be no infringement if any one of the material parts is omitted, and the patentee will not be heard to deny the materiality of any element included in his combination claim. It is immaterial whether there be advantage or disadvantage in such omission, but the change of location of an element of a combination, if the function remains the same, will not avoid infringement.

On the other hand, the superiority of the defendant's machine may be due to the fact that he has discovered an entirely different mode of construction and operation in which event it does not infringe.

A patent for a process is infringed by one, who, without ownership or license, uses substantially the process which the patent claims, whether or not the apparatus used is substantially that which the patent describes and whether materials prescribed by the patent are used, or equivalents thereof.

A mere sale of the *product of a process* does not constitute infringement of the process, nor does manufacture of a machine which might be used in infringement of a process patent.

Addition to a patented composition of matter of an ingredient which the patent purposely avoided and which when added substantially changes the character of the composition also avoids infringement. The ascertainment of the character of a composition of matter is a work for chemists; and that work consists in the application of proper tests to each particular case.

Chemical equivalency is not necessary to legal equivalency between substances in respect to a nonchemical use of those substances. The term *equivalent means equally good* when it refers to ingredients of compositions of matter. The fact that two substances are classified by chemists in the same reaction will not necessarily make them legal equivalents.

A *substituted* ingredient may perform the required function *better* than the patented ingredient, and may perform that function in a somewhat different manner, and still be an equivalent for the latter.

One ingredient is an equivalent of another in the composition of matter if it performs the same function, even though it also performs another function, which that other is wholly incompetent to accomplish.

A patentee may disclaim a particular equivalent if he chooses, and where a particular equivalent is disclaimed, that disclaimer is binding even if it was unnecessary; the use of that equivalent avoids infringement even though the two perform the same function in that composition of matter.

The respective results of a machine or manufacture covered by the claim of a patent and of a machine or manufacture alleged to infringe that claim do not furnish a criterion by which to decide the question of infringement. Those results may be identical, while the mode of operation and the means by which the result is secured are different. Any person may accomplish the result performed by a patented thing without infringing the patent, if he uses means substantially different from those of the patent. To hold the contrary of this rule would be to retard and not to promote the progress of the useful arts.

However, it is an infringement of a patent to use any machine

> or manufacture claimed therein, though such use is for a purpose which is not mentioned in the patent.

> [T]he court or jury, as the case may be, are not to judge about similarities or differences by the names of things, but are to look at the machines or their several devices or elements in the light of what they do, or what office or function they perform, and how they perform it.
>
> That two machines produce the same effect will not justify the assertion that they are substantially the same, or that the devices used by one are therefore mere equivalents for those of the other.

Mode of operation is a criterion of infringement on one side of that question, but not on the other. If the mode is substantially different, infringement must be negatived. If substantially the same, additional criteria or tests must be evaluated. The best way to investigate the subject is probably to reason by analogy from precedents.

> [A]n infringement involves a substantial identity, whether that identity be described by the terms "same principle," same "*modus operandi*" or any other.
>
> [I]f, in *the eye of the ordinary observer,* giving such attention as a purchaser normally gives, two *designs* are substantially the same, if the resemblance is such as to deceive such an observer, inducing him to purchase one supposing it to be the other, the first one patented is infringed by the others.
>
> The essence of a design resides, not in the elements individually, nor in their method of arrangement, but in their *tout ensemble*—in that indefinable whole that awakens some sensation in the observer's mind.

The infringement of a design involves a two-part test: (1) if "in the eye of the ordinary observer two designs are substantially the same . . .", and then (2) if "the accused device must appropriate the novelty in the patented device which distinguishes it from the prior art. . . . It is quite possible that infringement of a *plant patent* would occur only if stock obtained from one of the patented plants is used, given the extreme unlikelihood that any other plant could actually infringe."

The grant of a subsequent patent raises a legal presumption of a patentable difference from an earlier patented invention, but there is no presumption that the subsequently granted patent does not infringe the earlier patented invention.

> [A] very considerable portion of the patents granted are in a field covered by a former relatively generic or basic patent, and are tributary to such earlier patent and cannot be practiced unless by license thereunder.

One court has said that the presumption that a later patent does not infringe an earlier patent, even when the Commissioner of Patents has held that no interference existed between the two patents, is not conclusive. Patentable difference does not of itself tend to negative infringement. It might just as well be based upon infringement plus improvement; an improvement may lie in addition, simplification, or variance.

If a party does not possess any valid patent property rights, there can be no trespass and no infringement. Both contributory and direct infringers are liable as tort-feasors for the infringement. In order to prevail in an action for contributory infringement, plaintiff must not only establish infringement of a claim, but must first establish the validity of the patent.

Equivalents

No substitution of an equivalent for an ingredient of a combination covered by a patent can avert a charge of infringement of the claim, whether or not the equivalent is mentioned in the patent. But substitution of something which is not an equivalent will have that effect. The Doctrine of Equivalents (much more on this below) is an exception to the rule that patent claims are limited to what they claim.

A patent which effects a true advance in the art, a pioneer or primary patent, is entitled to liberal treatment and protection by a liberal application of the Doctrine of Equivalents. The claims must be interpreted not literally *in vacuo,* but rather in the light of the specification. Only in this manner will the doctrine be elastic enough to catch the evil practitioner who copies the thought and omits only the unimportant and nonessential features of a patented invention.

The Doctrine of Equivalents may not be relied upon to recapture broad claims that have been surrendered by amendments which explicitly abandoned before the PTO the cancelled subject matter.

> A patentee having deliberately taken a position in the PTO proceedings to induce the grant of the patent to him, is not thereafter permitted to repudiate that position.
>
> [I]f two devices do the same work in substantially the same way, and accomplish substantially the same result, they are the same, even though they differ in name, form or shape.
>
> Equivalence, in the patent law, is not the prisoner of a formula and is not an absolute to be considered in a vacuum.

> An important factor is whether persons reasonably skilled in the art would have known of the interchangeability of an ingredient not contained in the patent with one that was.
>
> The wholesome realism of this doctrine is not always applied in favor of a patentee but is sometimes used against him. [The Reverse Doctrine of Equivalents.] Thus, where a device is so far changed in principle from a patented article that it performs the same or similar function in a substantially different way, but nevertheless falls within the literal words of the claim, the Doctrine of Equivalents may be used to restrict the claim and defeat the patentee's action for infringement.

The inventor is entitled to a range of equivalents commensurate with the scope of his invention: broad if his invention is broad; narrow if his advance is a small one in a crowded field.

The purpose of the Doctrine of Equivalents is to give a patent claim a somewhat broader scope than it literally has. There are two tests of equivalency: (1) identity of function and (2) identity of way of performing that function; the test is whether the accused device does the same work in substantially the same way and accomplishes substantially the same result. The Doctrine of Equivalents requires that the function performed be assessed rather than the form alone.

One thing may accordingly be an equivalent of another, though it does more than another, but it cannot be such an equivalent if it does less: "a 'pioneer' ... patent covering a function never before performed, a wholly novel device, or one of such novelty and importance as to mark a distinct step in the progress of the art." The range of equivalents covered by the patent corresponds with the character of the invention. Where the prior art has forced the patentee to accept claims that are narrow in scope, the range of equivalents may be limited under the Doctrine of File Wrapper Estoppel.

If a patent is not put into commercial use, it is not entitled to construction of any broader scope than it is clearly required to be given, and a paper patent is generally strictly construed. However, where a patent is involved with a revolutionary new concept, the fact that it has not been built and operated is not a proper basis for describing the patent as a paper patent.

Reissue Patent Infringement

The statutory basis for reissue is set forth in 35 USC 251 and 252. Reissue practice is governed in the PTO by 37 CFR1.171–1.179. It is generally agreed that the purpose of reissue is remedial, and the statutory provisions are to be interpreted liberally to achieve the statute's remedial purpose to correct defects.

Any person who commences to infringe a reissue patent at any time after it is granted is subject to the same liability as a person who infringes an original patent subsequent to its issue date: "every reissued patent shall have the same effect . . . as if the same had been originally granted in such amended form."

Liability for the infringement of a claim appearing in a patent as originally issued and as reissued is unchanged, regardless of when the infringing action commenced. Damages for infringement of the common claim can accrue from as early as the issue date of the original patent.

Dependent claims in the original patent rewritten in independent form in the reissued patent, and claims in the original patent amended to remove minor flaws under the second paragraph of 35 USC 112 have long been believed to be identical within the meaning of 35 USC 252.

Intervening Rights

Equitable considerations arise when a person's previously lawful activities suddenly become infringements because the patentee has changed the scope of the claims of the original patent. For example, an original patent claims A + B + C and therefore a person who makes, uses, or sells a combination including only the elements A + B will not infringe. A reissued patent with broadened claims covering the subcombination A + B filed within two years of the issuance of the original and patentable over the prior art and supportable by the original disclosure would be infringed by continued use or sale of the A + B device.

There is an inference of abandonment associated with the original patent because it disclosed but did not claim the A + B subcombination. This inference was rebutted when the patentee filed a broadening reissue application within the required two-year period. Until the original patent is actually reissued, however, the patentee remains bound by the limited manner in which the invention was originally claimed. Intervening rights attach to any A + B devices that are manufactured or purchased before the reissue patent is granted.

Statutorily created intervening rights represent a compromise between two competing considerations. In essence, the statute provides for the compulsory, royalty-free, nonexclusive licensing of certain activities that would otherwise constitute infringement of claims appearing in the reissue patent but not in the original patent. The license granted is limited in scope; it grants the nonexclusive, royalty-free right to use and sell anything patented by the reissue patent that was made or acquired before the granting of the reissue and that did not infringe any claim in the reissued patent that was also in the original patent.

Additional equitable considerations arise where the infringing manufacturer has expended substantial funds for facilities and equipment either to manufacture a product or to use a process encompassed by claims appearing in the reissue patent but not in the original. 35 USC 252 also provides for the conditional creation of an intervening right to continue manufacturing a product or to continue using a process covered by broadened reissue claims. The right to continue manufacturing is not guaranteed under the statute. The intervening manufacturer must invoke the equity powers of a court, and the manufacturer may be required to compensate the reissue patentee in some manner for the continued use of his invention. The Federal Circuit has adopted a very liberal construction of intervening rights in favor of the infringer, even where the infringement was willful.

In *Scripps Clinic and Research Foundation and Revlon v. Genentech, Inc.*, a District Court in California held on February 24, 1989 that plantiffs' reissue claims in issue to be invalid for: (1) violation of the best mode requirement, (2) inequitable conduct, (3) lack of reissuable error, and (4) for attempting to reissue plaintiffs' '509 patent to recapture subject matter intentionally deleted by the inventors prior to filing.

Recapture Rule: A patentee is barred from securing, through reissue, claims to subject matter of the same or broader scope than those deliberately cancelled from the original application. Relatively few reissue patent cases brought the interpretation of the reissue statute under judicial scrutiny before the CAFC came into existence in October 1982. Nevertheless, it is fair to say that the paucity of decisional authority, in combination with some questionable CCPA (the Court of Customs and Patent Appeals) precedent, created some uncertainty in the administration of the reissue statute by the PTO and the courts.

Intervening rights under 35 USC 252 is an affirmative defense that must be raised at trial.

Seattle Box v. Industrial Crating I (1984): An original patent cannot be infringed once a reissue patent has issued, because the original patent is surrendered. In Section 252, Congress expressly limited claim continuity to claims in the reissued patent identical to claims in the original patent. The statute permits the claims of the reissue patent to reach back to the date the original patent issued, but only if those claims were identical to claims in the original patent. With respect to new or amended claims, an infringer's liability commences only from the date the reissue patent issued.

The only question to ask under the intervening rights test is whether claims of the original patent which are repeated in the reissue patent are infringed. If valid claims in the original patent appear unaltered in the reissue patent, the Doctrine of Intervening Rights affords no protection to the alleged infringer.

The reissue statute was not enacted as a panacea for all patent prosecution problems, nor as a grant to the patentee of a second opportunity to prosecute *de novo* an original application. Error is limited to inadvertence, accident, or mistake.

While the few reissue cases decided by the Federal Circuit have achieved a certain measure of uniformity, it is less clear that they have removed uncertainty in the interpretation of the reissue statute consistent with its remedial purpose. In the twenty or so significant cases decided until this time, there have been some strong concurring and dissenting opinions. This divergence of opinion in so few cases suggests that a more consistent approach to Sections 251 and 252 remains to be developed by the Federal Circuit. Inasmuch as the number of reissue cases is relatively small, it may be some time before the court speaks to the issue of intervening rights and, more particularly, what constitutes substantial preparation.

In one case, the CAFC purports to interpret Rule 175(a)(3), yet the opinion does not do so, but merely alludes to Rule 175 as a whole and Section 1444 of the MPEP (the Manual of Patent Examining Procedure). While stating that the MPEP is not binding on the court, Section 1444 nevertheless was used against applicant in affirming the board's decision.

INDIRECT INFRINGEMENT

In the section above, our concern was with the person who directly infringes the patent right by making, using, or selling under 35 USC 271(a). In this section we are concerned with the person who indirectly infringes by inducing infringement by another or one who contributes to infringement [35 USC 271(b) and (c) and (d)]. 35 USC 271(b) is concerned with active inducement of infringement; 35 USC 271(c) deals with the question of contributory infringement; 35 USC 271(d) includes three acts which are declared not to be misuse. It has also been held that absent direct infringement of the patent claims, there cannot be liability for inducement of infringement. Nevertheless, circumstantial evidence of such direct infringement that occurs as a result of defendant's acts will normally be sufficient. In fact, direct infringement may be inferred from evidence that a particular component has no practical use other than in an infringing system.

35 USC 271(c) provides that one shall be liable as a Contributory Infringer who sells:

> a component of a patented machine, manufacture, combination or composition, or a material or apparatus for use in practicing a patented process, constituting a material part of the invention, knowing the same to be especially made or especially adapted for

use in an infringement of such patent, and not a staple article or commodity of commerce suitable for substantial noninfringing use.

Infringement by inducement involves urging, encouraging, or aiding another to engage in the making, using, or selling of the patented invention coupled with knowledge by the inducer that such conduct will likely constitute infringement. To reach an indirect infringer, direct infringement must first be proved and at least one direct infringer must be joined in a suit against an indirect infringer.

A Minnesota District Court in 1988 concluded that "[n]o difference in remedy exists for violations of subsections [271(a) and (b)]. That is, one who induces infringement is treated for liability purposes as exactly as one who directly infringes."

Types of Inducing Acts

What follows are extracts from many judicial decisions concerning what are and what are not considered to be inducing acts.

> Licensing others may constitute active inducement if the licensor provides instructions, plans, or the like enabling the licensee to practice the patented product or process. However, there must be some connection between the license and the act of direct infringement.
>
> A standard agreement to indemnify another for liability for patent infringement does not normally constitute active inducement.
>
> Active inducement by repair and maintenance is clearest when performed by the manufacturer or seller of the item on a continuing basis or pursuant to contract.
>
> Design of an infringing apparatus or system for another may constitute active inducement.
>
> Purchase for use or resale of a product made by an infringing process or machine does not normally constitute active inducement.
>
> Numerous decisions find active inducement where a defendant selling products capable of either innocent or infringing use provides through labels, advertising, or other sales methods instructions and directions as to the infringing use.
>
> Publication of information about a patented product or method does not constitute active inducement unless accompanied by other activity, such as sale of material capable of an infringing

use. The patent itself is published and must contain a full disclosure of how to make and use the invention.

Apparently, liability for indirect infringement can be based on activities occurring prior to the issuance of the patent, one condition being that the eventual direct infringement occurred within the seventeen-year life of the patent. Prior to the issuance of a patent, there can be no infringement.

Activities constituting infringement prior to amendment in reissue remain an infringement if the pertinent claims emerge from reissue without substantial change.

The monopoly did not exist at common law, and the rights, therefore, which may be exercised under it cannot be regulated by the rules of the common law. It is created by the act of Congress; and no rights can be acquired in it unless authorized by statute, and in the manner the statute prescribes.

Any infringement must be committed during the life of a patent since the exclusive property rights of a patent commence with the grant and terminate with its expiration.

Where an act was commenced before the expiration of a patent, which was not to be completed until after the expiration thereof, it was held not to constitute infringement. But infringing articles made during the life of a patent cannot lawfully be sold or used after its expiration. And it is to be noted that there is no such thing as partial infringement.

An unauthorized appropriation of an invention, prior to issuance of a patent to the invention, may be actionable as a common law tort, but it is not an infringement capable of redress under the Patent Law.

[W]here, in advance of the granting of a patent, an invention is disclosed to one who, in breach of the confidence thus reposed, manufactures and sells articles embodying the invention, such person should be held liable for the profits and damages resulting therefrom, not under the patent statutes, but upon the principle that equity will not permit one to unjustly enrich himself at the expense of another.

One who purchases from the inventor prior to the application for a patent has an implied license to make, use, or sell without liability therefor.

Infringement within the scope of 35 USC 271(b) [Inducement] includes only activity performed by a third person that causes another to directly infringe a patent. A corporate officer may be held personally liable for actively inducing his corporation to infringe.

Contributory Infringement

Many patents are directed to a combination of elements which are individually old, the invention residing in a particular manner of combining these elements. Ordinarily, one who makes, uses, or sells less than the complete combination, as this has been claimed, is not an infringer. However, if infringement were limited to the manufacture, use, or sale of the total combination, it would be easy for manufacturers to evade liability by merely making something less than the entire combination and instructing purchasers thereof how to complete the combination. To obviate such situations, the courts developed the Doctrine of Contributory Infringement, which has been codified in 35 USC 271(c) of the present Patent Act.

The Supreme Court recognized the concept of contributory infringement only after it had been developed by the lower courts. It began as a judicial doctrine to prevent injustice, since there was no such statutory provision. In the early days of this century, it became a very viable cause of action for the patentee.

Extracts from the dissents in some case law decisions emphasize the nature of the problem:

> doctrine that one who furnishes materials, knowing their proposed use, becomes thereby a tort-feasor, if the proposed use is a tort, is certainly novel as applied to most kinds of torts.
>
> Privity with a wrongdoer is not to be inferred from the exercise of a legal right. The man who sells a gun or a knife would be guilty of an impertinence if he should inquire of the purchaser whether he intends to use it legitimately, and is under no duty to do so.

Nevertheless, decisions did find contributory infringement where the sale of components capable of innocent use was accompanied by active inducement in the form of instructions, advertising, or the like, or other steps indicating an intent by the defendant that the component be used in an infringing fashion. The 2nd Circuit extended the concept of intent to cover mere knowledge or even indifference by the defendant as to the consequences of his acts: "One who makes and sells articles which are only adapted to be used in a patented combination will be presumed to intend the natural consequences of his acts."

In 1871 appeared the first case clearly recognizing that a person can be held to infringe by making or selling an unpatented element for use in a patented combination or process. While the defendant relied on early case law holding that a combination cannot be infringed by a device omitting one element, the court held that this rule would not protect the defendant in view of the common law principles as to joint tort-feasors.

In *Morgan Envelope Co. v. Albany Perforated Wrapping Paper Co.* (1894), the Supreme Court first addressed the issue. The patentee had a patent on a toilet paper dispenser and the defendant manufactured paper rolls specially adapted to be used in the dispenser. While acknowledging contributory infringement as a cause of action, the Court denied the patentee relief, since to do so would give him the benefit of a patent on ordinary articles of commerce.

In *Leeds & Catlin Co. v. Victor Talking Machine Co.* (1909), the Court upheld an injunction against a contributory infringer who manufactured unpatented phonograph records especially designed for use in the patentee's record and stylus combination. The Court noted that the record was essential to the patented invention and had no other commercial use outside the patentee's invention. Contributory infringement now was the law.

In *Henry v. A. B. Dick Co.* (1912), the Court found that even though the patentee required his licensees to purchase unpatented paper and ink as a condition of using his patented mimeograph machine, it was not monopolistic and did not exceed the patentee's rights; the theory being that, since the patentee could lawfully preclude all infringement, there was nothing wrong with letting him take his income from the direct infringement via his profits on supplies and parts for the direct infringement rather than royalties. After all, the invention created the market for the ink and paper. In later decisions, the attitude of the Supreme Court hardened against such tying arrangement. Employment of such license restrictions constituted a misuse of the patent that would disable the patentee, at least temporarily, from enforcing his patent against anyone.

Before the 1952 Patent Act, the Supreme Court applied the Doctrine of Patent Misuse to limit control by patent owners over unpatented materials. Lower courts continued to find contributory infringement where the unpatented component was useful only in an infringing process or combination or where its sale was accompanied by active inducement of infringement. However, the sale of a standard article of commerce, even with knowledge that the defendant would use it to infringe, cannot constitute contributory infringement.

However, in *Motion Picture Patents Co. v. Universal Film Mfg. Co.* (1917), the Court looked not to the existence of infringement by the defendant, but rather to the inequitable conduct of the patentee who was attempting to enforce a tying arrangement whereby purchasers of a patented motion picture machine were required to use only a certain unpatented film in the projector, which was also purchased from the patentee. Relief was denied to the patentee solely based on his conduct, not that of the accused infringer. It noted that due to prior rulings, conditional licensing agreements had increased to the point of favoritism and oppression. This opinion departed drastically from that of *A. B. Dick*, and this new view began the erosion of the Doctrine of Contributory Infringement which protected the patentee and enhanced the defense of patent misuse.

The next important case heard by the Supreme Court was *Carbice Corp. of America v. American Patents Dev. Corp.* (1931), wherein the Court appeared to be uninterested in whether or not the defendant was guilty of infringement, and barred the suit solely due to patent misuse. Here the patent covered a cooling system for transporting ice cream and used dry ice as its cooling medium. The patentee required all users of its combination patent to purchase dry ice from the patentee's exclusive licensee.

By this time, some people thought that by the use of conditional licenses and tying arrangements patentees extended the monopoly beyond what their patent granted. By the 1940s, the defense of patent misuse became the alleged infringers' preferred defense to the claim of contributory infringement. The mere filing suit for contributory infringement in many courts constituted misuse of the patent, making it unenforceable.

In the *Mercoid* decisions in 1944, the Supreme Court's constraints against tying seemed to jeopardize the existence of any remedy for contributory infringement. To dispel possible implications of *Mercoid,* Congress in 1952 enacted Sections 271(c) and (d).

In *Mercoid Corp. v. Mid-Continent Investment Co.* (1944) and *Mercoid Corp. v. Minneapolis-Honeywell Regulator Co.* (1944), Mid-Continent, the patentee, owned a combination patent for a domestic heating system and had an exclusive licensing agreement with Minneapolis-Honeywell, which could make, use, sell, and sublicense others to make, use, or sell the patented combination. Honeywell manufactured and sold nonpatented switches that were a vital component of the machine and had no substantial use other than in the patented heating system. The patentee only granted rights to construct the patented system if the customer purchased the switches from Honeywell, which, in turn, paid royalties to the patentee based on the number of switches sold.

Mercoid manufactured the unpatented switches but was not a licensee, and, consequently, its customers did not receive a license to use the patented machine and directly infringed the patent. Since Mercoid knowingly supplied its customers with the switches to be used in the machine, the patentee brought suit against it for contributory infringement. Mercoid raised the defense of patent misuse and argued that the patentee was attempting to extend its patent monopoly to cover unpatented components. The Supreme Court reaffirmed the misuse doctrine and frankly acknowledged that the "result of this decision, together with those which have preceded it, is to limit substantially the doctrine of contributory infringement.... The patent is for a combination only."

Justices Black and Murphy seriously questioned the existence of a remedy for contributory infringement: "If the present case compelled consideration of the morals and ethics of contributory infringement, I should be most reluctant to conclude that the scales of moral values are weighted against the right of producers to sell their unpatented goods in a free market."

The 6th Circuit in the same year held,

> The result [of *Mercoid*] may be that only he is an infringer who furnishes all of the elements of the patented combination and integrates them into operating embodiment and so in many cases, the only infringers . . . are the ultimate consumers whom it would be fruitless to pursue in the enforcement of patent rights.

The majority of decisions, however, viewed *Mercoid* as essentially a misuse case that did not affect the remedy against straight contributory infringement.

> [T]he Supreme Court has not, so far, rejected the doctrine as applying to a "straight" contributory infringement suit where there are no licenses or other tie-ins and no evidence of intention to extend the grant in violation of the Antitrust laws.
>
> [T]he precise holding of *Mercoid* is that contributory infringement liability may not be asserted by the patentee where he, himself, comes into court with unclean hands and where he has attempted to misuse his patent grant.

Although the Court presumed that *Mercoid* was a contributory infringer, they nevertheless decided, in a 5-to-4 opinion, to deny relief stating that the patentee had misused its patent. There were five separate opinions written in this case which threw the patent bar into a state of confusion as to whether anything remained of the doctrine of contributory infringement. Justice Black, in a concurring opinion, stated,

> If there is such a wrong as contributory infringement, it must have been created by the federal patent statutes. Since they make no direct mention of such a wrong, its existence could only be rested on inferences as to Congressional intent.

Following this decision, some lower courts even held that the mere bringing of an action for contributory infringement was patent misuse. Other lower courts held the defendant liable for "selling machines with the knowledge, purpose and intent that it shall be used in a combination which will infringe."

It was clear that the Supreme Court was more concerned with the antitrust aspects of patent misuse than it was with protection of the patentee. After all, the end user would still be a direct infringer in these cases, but the patentee would have to now go after every direct infringer leading to a proliferation of lawsuits.

Leaders in the area of patent law decided to propose legislation to Congress to reform the patent statutes which had been last revised in 1870, and contributory infringement and patent misuse was the driving force behind this movement. Finally, in the 1952 Patent Act, Section 271 addressed these problems. Paragraph (a) of this section was concerned with direct infringement, (b) addressed "inducing infringement" without regard to staple commodities of commerce or the like, (c) "contributory infringement" with a number of limitations, and (d) three acts which are declared not to be misuse. It is worth restating paragraph (c) here:

> (c) Whoever sells a component of a patented machine, manufacture, combination or composition, or a material or apparatus for use in practicing a patented process, constituting a material part of the invention, knowing the same to be especially made or especially adapted for use in an infringement of such patent, and not a staple article or commodity of commerce suitable for substantial noninfringing use, shall be liable as a contributory infringer.

Thus, a potential defendant that manufactures a component part of a patented device does not contributorily infringe if the part is a staple article of commerce that can be used in a noninfringing manner. However, if you induce infringement with a staple article of commerce, you may still be liable under Section 271(b).

The Senate and House Reports on the 1952 Act stated,

> The doctrine of contributory infringement has been part of our law for about 80 years. . . . The purpose of this section is to codify in statutory form principles of contributory infringement and at the same time eliminate this doubt and confusion. . . . The last paragraph of this section [271(d)] provides that one who merely does what he is authorized to do by statute is not guilty of misuse of the patent.

In 1961, Justice Black cited congressional hearings and committee reports as indicating that Section 271(d) "was designed specifically to prevent the *Mercoid* case from being interpreted to mean that any effort to enforce a patent against a contributory infringer in itself constitutes a forfeiture of patent rights."

Aro Mfg. Co. v. Convertible Top Replacement Co. (1961) (Aro I) presented the Supreme Court with its first opportunity to interpret Section 271. In a split opinion, four separate opinions were rendered by the Court. The plaintiff had a patent on a convertible top mechanism, and the defendant only sold replacement fabric which the purchasers of the automobiles were using to repair their worn convertible tops. The plaintiff brought suit for contributory infringement. Since the defendant did not directly infringe, the Court held that there could be no contributory infringement and the defendant was not liable since, in their opinion, Section 271(c) defined contributory infringement in terms of direct infringement.

The plurality held that no component of a combination patent was entitled to a monopoly regardless of whether it was essential to the patented combination and regardless if it was costly or difficult to replace this component. Extensively cited was *Mercoid* for several propositions, the main one being that a patent monopoly may not be extended to cover components in a combination patent. By relying on *Mercoid,* it was implied that Section 271 had not overruled *Mercoid* and its legal principles concerning the extension of a patent monopoly over component parts. One commentator on this case not only believed that this interpretation of 271 was blatantly incorrect, but that the majority of the Court was misled by the Department of Justice's brief. It should be noted that the department wanted the entire concept of contributory infringement to be abandoned; probably due to its sole concern with antitrust. It is surprising that such heavy reliance was placed on *Mercoid,* when later in the opinion the decision was based upon patent misuse which was not an issue before the Court in this case.

Using this argument, unless an alleged infringer manufactures the entire invention, he will not be guilty of contributory infringement. Yet, neither the language of Section 271 nor the legislative history places such a requirement on the alleged contributory infringer; all he must do is manufacture an element constituting an essential part of the patented machine. In Aro I, the Court reached its holding based upon the fact that General Motors had a license to use the patent on the convertible top, and the activity here was merely noninfringing repair of fully authorized convertible tops.

In *Aro Mfg. Co. v. Convertible Top Replacement Co.* (1964) (Aro II), the facts were different. Ford had no license under the convertible top patent. Consequently, when Ford manufactured and sold automobiles with the patented top, it directly infringed the patent, and its customers received no implied license to repair its tops, so it too directly infringed when it repaired its worn tops. Now that there was direct infringement, the Court could look to see if Aro contributorily infringed the patent by supplying the material with which to repair the tops. The Court found that Aro was guilty of infringing because it knowingly supplied its customers with material and supplies, to infringe the patent.

> Here, as was not the case in Aro I, the direct infringement by the car owners that is a prerequisite to contributory infringement by Aro, was unquestionably present....
>
> If the owners' use infringed, so did his *repair* of the top structure, as by replacing the worn out fabric component. Where use infringes, repair also does, for it perpetuates the infringing use.

The majority's opinion appears still to be the law today.

Probably the most definitive decision (5 to 4) on this subject of the 1952 Patent Code contributory infringement, patent misuse, and its effects on *Mercoid* came as a result of the *Dawson Chem. Co. v. Rohm & Haas Co.* (1980) case. This case is still good law today and is cited for the proposition that although patent misuse remains a viable defense, a patentee is not *per se* guilty of misuse merely because he extends his patent to cover unpatented goods.

Rohm & Haas had a patent on a process for weed control by spraying rice fields with an unpatented chemical that had no other substantial use outside of the patented process. It produced the chemical and sold it in containers that had directions stating how to use the chemical to practice the weed control process, and kill the weeds but not the rice crop. The customers who purchased this chemical from Rohm & Haas received a license to use the patented process, expressed on the product's label and hence called a "label license."

Competitors also manufactured and marketed the chemical in containers that had directions on how to perform the process. Their customers, of course, received no license to practice the patented invention and were direct infringers. Dawson did not dispute that it was guilty of contributory infringement, and its only defense to liability was that the patentee was guilty of misuse. The Court was forced to focus its analysis on patent misuse and its effect on 271(d).

Justice Blackmun, writing for the majority, reasoned that the distinction between staples and nonstaples was the key element considered by Sections 271(c) and (d) to adjust two antithetical doctrines: (1) that of contributory infringement which exists to protect patent rights from subversion; and (2) that of patent misuse which exists to prevent the extension of patent rights to suppress competition in unpatented matter. Thus, the Court held that the owner of a patent claiming a process of using a certain chemical compound was not guilty of patent misuse through tying by selling the compound and refusing to issue licenses to competing manufacturers of the compound because the compound was a nonstaple, that is, was not suited for commercial use other than in the patented process.

The 5th Circuit, affirmed by the Supreme Court, found that propanil was a nonstaple article and that Section 271(d) so altered the Doctrine of

Patent Misuse and *Mercoid* as to allow a patent owner to sell unpatented components that are not staples within the meaning of 271(c) [on contributory infringement] while refusing to license others to do the same conduct.

Justice Blackmun went on to say,

> Proponents of contributory infringement defend this result on the grounds that it is necessary for the protection of the patent right, and that the market for the unpatented article flows from the patented invention. They also observe that in many instances the article is "unpatented" only because of the technical rules of patent claiming. . . . If both the patent misuse and contributory infringement doctrines are to coexist, then, each must have some separate sphere of operation with which the other does not interfere.

It should be noted that contributory infringement requires: (1) a sale (2) of a material component of a patented invention, (3) with knowledge that such component has been especially made for use in an infringement of such invention. Only the seller of such component is liable as a contributory infringer; the buyer becomes liable as a direct infringer when he uses the overall patented combination.

That an item, though a component of a patented invention, is a staple article or commodity of commerce suitable for a substantial noninfringing use constitutes a defense, precluding liability for contributory infringement.

Knowledge is a necessary element; intent is a necessary element of contributory infringement. To incur liability, the seller must, in addition, actively aid or abet actual infringement, as by instructing a purchaser how to use the item he sells in the patented invention.

Direct and contributory infringers are joint tortfeasors.

These limitations on contributory infringement in Section 271(c) are

> counterbalanced by limitations on patent misuse in Section 271(d).
>
> First, . . . this provision clearly signifies that a patentee may make and sell [i.e., derive revenue] nonstaple goods used in connection with his invention.
>
> Second, . . . this provision's use in the disjunctive of the term "authoriz[e]" suggests that more than explicit licensing agreements is contemplated.
>
> Finally, . . . this provision plainly means that the patentee may bring suit without fear that his doing so will be regarded as an unlawful attempt to suppress competition.

> The statute explicitly states that a patentee may do "one or more" of these permitted acts, and it does not state that he must do any of them.
>
> In our view, the provisions of 271(d) effectively confer upon the patentee, as a lawful adjunct of his patent rights, a limited power to exclude others from competition in nonstaple goods.

Justice Blackmun noted that "the policy of stimulating invention that underlies the entire patent system runs no less deep . . . in our legal system than . . . the policy of free competition."

To understand the import of 35 USC 271(d) one must appreciate the distinction between contributory infringement and a tying arrangement which involves the conditioning of a patent license upon the purchase from the patentee of goods, which, though usable in or with the patented invention, are themselves unpatented. Tying arrangements are illegal and constitute patent misuse. The crux of the distinction between the two is that in tying arrangements an attempt is made to create a monopoly in what is not patented.

The Court held:

> In our view, the provisions of [paragraph] 271(d) effectively confer upon the patentee, as a lawful adjunct of his patent rights, a limited power to exclude others from competition in nonstaple goods. A patentee may sell a nonstaple article himself while enjoining others from marketing that same good without his authorization.

The fact that Dawson was inducing infringement under 271(b) was ignored. It was most important to the Court that this chemical was a nonstaple product with no substantial noninfringing use and that it was at the heart of Rohm & Haas' invention. "The legislative materials demonstrate a clear intent to both change the law and give patentees more power to protect their rights against contributory infringers."

The dissent, in a very lengthy opinion, did not believe legislative history showed an intent to allow tying in a patent context. The 1988 amendments to 271 resolved this dispute.

In 1984, Congress added two subsections (e) and (f) to Section 271. Subsection (e) states that it is not infringement to manufacture a patented invention and collect data on safety and efficacy, if the purpose is to submit information under a federal law which regulates the manufacture, use, or sale of drugs. This allows a company to prepare for commercial activity after a patent expires by getting governmental approval for its product prior to a patentee's patent expiring. If competitors are forced to wait until the patent expires, the patentee gets an effective extension of the monopoly due to the time the FDA takes to approve the device or drug for marketability. This new subsection enhances quickened entry of generic drugs onto the market.

Subsection (f) was also added in 1984 to make an act of infringement the manufacture of a substantial number of the parts of a combination patent in the United States and then to ship them overseas for assembly there. Congress did not believe that an alleged infringer should be permitted to make the infringement in the United States and bypass the U.S. patent laws by postponing the assembly of the patented combination to the buyer's place in a foreign country.

In 1988, Congress again amended Section 271(d) by adding paragraphs (4) and (5) to the list, thus reinforcing *Rohm & Haas.* Section 271(d) had listed three acts that were explicitly stated not to be misuse; new paragraph (5) is most important:

> (5) conditioned the license of any rights to the patent or the sale of the patented product on the acquisition of a license or right in another patent *or purchase of a separate product,* unless, *in view of the circumstances,* the patent owner has *market power* in the *relevant market* for the patent or patented product on which the license or sale is conditioned.

Subsection (5) seems to overrule both some early case law and some Department of Justice policies that saw all tying arrangements as *per se* illegal.

Congress established a rule of reason approach to tying arrangements in a patent licensing context. Much remains uncertain about Subsection (5). The legislative history expressly gives the courts wide latitude when deciding the issues of "market power" and "relevant market." Many courts remain biased to believe a patent is *per se* market power, no matter what.

Subsection 271(g) was also added in the amendment of 1988 extending the concept of infringement to importers of products made abroad by processes patented in the United States. Only importation was necessary to have a cause of action under section (g); no sale or use is necessary as interpreted by a District Court.

Some of the principles of Federal Circuit decisions emphasized are set out below.

1. Absent direct infringement there can be neither contributory infringement nor inducement of infringement. Without direct infringement, there is nothing to which the accused products could "contribute."
2. Direct infringers do not have to be parties to the suit to main-

tain an action against others for infringement under Sections 271(b) and/or (c). Proof of direct infringement may be based on circumstantial evidence.

3. Both Sections 271(b) and (c) require a showing that the contributory infringer have *knowledge* of the direct infringement.

4. Each purchaser of a patented machine has a license to replace any worn out part no matter "how essential it may be to the patented invention, . . ." unless the replacement part is separately claimed. However, replacement of a material part of the invention which is not worn out constitutes patent infringement because it is reconstruction of the patented machine.

5. To establish liability for contributory infringement, a patentee is also required to show that the defendant's components were "especially made or especially adapted for use in an infringement of" the patented combination and were not a staple article "suitable for substantial non-infringing use" [35 USC 271(c)].

6. According to the Federal Circuit, in reviewing a claim of contributory infringement the court focuses on the infringer's acts as compared with focusing on plaintiff's actions when reviewing a defense of patent misuse. However, under exception (1) or (2) of Section 271(d), a patentee is not guilty of misuse if its acts would amount to contributory infringement if committed by a third party without permission.

7. The language of Section 271(c) focuses on the material actually sold by the accused and not the uses made of it by its purchasers; a court must look at what is actually sold and whether it is a material part of the invention especially made or adapted for use in infringement of the patent.

8. Without protection from contributory infringers, owners of method patents would have no effective protection. The court noted the impracticality and undesirability of suing each individual consumer practicing the patented invention.

9. The Supreme Court has recently noted, "[w]hen a charge of contributory infringement is predicated entirely on the sale of an *article of commerce* that is used by the purchaser [allegedly] to infringe a patent, the public interest in access to that article of commerce is necessarily implicated" [*Sony Corp. v. Universal City Studios Inc.* (1983)].

Relation Between Sections 271(b) and (c)

Legislative history indicates that these two sections were intended as complementary provisions, together codifying the basic principles of contributory infringement developed by the courts prior to 1952. It should be emphasized that mere sale of a staple with knowledge of the buyer's intended use does not constitute active infringement.

> If defendant were supplying articles or commodities of commerce suitable for substantial noninfringing use, it seems clear that something more than mere knowledge of an intended infringing use would be required to make out a case of active inducement under 271(b).

Overlapping the Doctrine of Contributory Infringement is the Repair-Reconstruction Doctrine. Acquisition of an article embodying one or more patents from or through one who was authorized by the patent owner carries with it an implied license to repair such article, but reconstruction of an article embodying a patented combination would constitute infringement.

In 1988, a District Court concluded that cases "have found that replacement of even a majority of the parts of a patented device does not constitute an infringement of the patent." Also in 1988, a District Court (S.D.N.Y.) affirmed the little known or discussed fact that 35 USC 271(b) and (c) have extraterritorial effect.

> [A] product sold abroad for resale in the United States is protected by United States patents. Its seller abroad may be liable for infringement inducement or contributory infringement of the United States patent under 35 USC 271(b) or (c), even though that seller neither made, used nor sold the product in the United States.

Privilege as to Misuse—Section 271(d)

> It is well within congressional power to allow certain patentees incidental market power over items not technically within the patent grant when this is necessary to effectively market and protect the patented invention. [271(d)(1)]

Section 271(d)(2) allows the patent owner to license others to make and sell nonstaple parts or materials for use in the patented combination or process. Such acts performed by another would constitute contributory infringement under 271(c).

Finally, Section 271(d)(3) provides that a patent owner shall not be "deemed guilty of misuse . . . by reason of his having . . . sought to enforce his patent rights against infringement or contributory infringement."

Numerous decisions rule that filing of a suit in good faith to prevent contributory or direct infringement is not patent misuse. Furthermore, such suits do not violate the antitrust laws unless they are "an integral part of a conspiracy to restrain trade or to monopolize over and beyond the protection afforded by the presumptively valid patent rights."

Patent misuse is an extension of the equitable Doctrine of Unclean Hands. Since the Doctrine of Patent Misuse is equitable in nature, upon dissipation or purge of the effects of such misuse the patentee may thereafter enforce his lawful property rights granted by the patent:

> It is the established rule that a patentee who has granted a license on condition that the patented invention be used by the licensee only with unpatented materials furnished by the licensor, may not restrain as a contributory infringer one who sells to the licensee like materials for like use.
>
> The legality of any attempt to bring unpatented goods within the protection of the patent is measured by the anti-trust laws not by the patent law.
>
> It is not necessary that the defendant asserting the misuse defense has been—or would be—injured by the misuse. . . . It is a principle of general application that courts . . . may appropriately withhold their aid where the plaintiff is using the right asserted contrary to public policy.
>
> [C]lauses which tie-in the exclusive sales of non-patented items with patented items are contrary to public policy for the reason that such tie-in agreements extend the patent monopoly beyond the scope permitted by the Constitution and the Congress.

TYPES OF INFRINGERS

Any person, legal entity, or government, who, without authority from the patentee or patent owner, performs an act of making, using, or selling a patented invention, or procures such an act to be performed, or adopts it and accepts its benefits when performed, is guilty of infringement.

> Co-owners are not immune from infringement against each other.

A license transfers an interest in the invention and a party acting under the terms of the license is not an infringer.

A corporate officer is usually not personally liable when the officer acts within the duties of the office.

Several recent CAFC cases concerned the acquisition of a majority of shares, or the receipt of income from a third party, or finding a corporate officer liable for being the moving force behind the infringing action. The first two cases held no infringement, all must be decided on the facts in each case and are concerned with the degree of control exercised.

A municipal corporation is responsible for acts of infringement performed by its officers and agents for its benefit.

28 USC 1498 "authorizes the [U.S.] Government to 'take', through exercise of its power of eminent domain, a license in any U.S. patent."

[T]he U.S. have no more right than any private person to use a patent invention without license of the patentee or making compensation to him. . . . It necessarily follows that, unless expressly permitted by act of Congress, no injunction can be granted against the United States.

28 USC 1498 provides in part:

(a) Whenever an invention described in and covered by a patent of the U.S. is used or manufactured by or for the U.S. without license of the owner thereof or lawful right to use or manufacture the same, the owner's remedy shall be by action against the U.S. in the Court of Claims [now the U.S. Claims Court] for the recovery of his reasonable and entire compensation for such use and manufacture.

The statute was intended primarily to permit the government to purchase goods or services for the performance of governmental functions without the threat that the work would not be carried out because its supplier or contractor was enjoined from or feared a suit for infringement of the patent.

[W]ithout its consent, the United States may not be sued for infringement of a patent. . . . Congress has determined the conditions upon which the United States consents to be sued.

When the invention is made under a government contract, the government has a royalty-free license to practice the invention. A 28 USC 1498 action and a 35 USC 271 action "are only parallel and not identical"; the principles of claim construction are the same for either type of action.

SPECIAL SITUATIONS

Infringement under 35 USC 271(e)(1)

In *Eli Lilly and Co. v. Medtronic Inc.* (1989), the Federal Circuit held that 35 USC 271(e)(1) permits the manufacture and use of all patented inventions, including patented medical devices, for purposes relating to development and submission of information to the FDA. The patent term *restoration legislation,* which became codified in 35 USC 156, extended the patent extension benefits not only to drugs, but also to medical devices.

> The clear intent of Congress was to create an FDA *experimental use* exception for use which *Roche* had held would constitute infringement under section 271(a).

The court also noted the absence of persuasive reasoning why Congress would create an exception only for drugs, particularly when medical devices received the benefit of the companion patent term restoration legislation. The court concluded that "Section 271(e)(1) allows a party to make, use, or sell any type of 'patented invention' if 'solely' for the restricted uses stated therein."

Another question has arisen concerning whether there is now a need for a statutory exemption from patent infringement liability for research-oriented manufacture and/or use of patented technology. The present experimental use defense is judicially created and is very narrow. It has been limited to use of the invention for purely philosophical or academic reasons. The defense is not available when the use is for purposes of commercially exploiting the invention. The patent statute allows for testing of patented pharmaceutical products for purposes of regulatory approval as shown above, for example, 35 USC 271(e), but there is no general statutory defense against a charge of infringement for experimental use of patented technology. The Patent Law Committee of the AIPLA (American Intellectual Property Law Association) has formed an *ad hoc* subcommittee with members of the Chemical Practice Committee to study this topic and report to their Board of Directors.

Infringement under 35 USC 271(f)(1)

In 1984, Congress enacted 35 USC 271(f)(1) concerning export infringement which imposes liability as an infringer on one who:

> supplies or causes to be supplied in or from the United States all or a substantial portion of the components of a patented machine, where such components are uncombined in whole or in part, in such a manner as to actively induce the combination of such components outside of the United States in a manner that would infringe the patent if such combination occurred within the United States.

In *Hybritech, Inc. v. Monoclonal Antibodies, Inc.* (Fed. Cir. 1986), on the authority of 271(f), the District Court's preliminary injunction order precluded defendant Monoclonal from selling its immunoassay products abroad as well as in the United States. Requests for preliminary injunctive relief were granted to Hybritech against Monoclonal as well as against Abbott (*Hybritech, Inc. v. Abbott Laboratories* [Fed. Cir. 1986]), whereas Scripps' request against Genentech (*Scripps Clinic & Research Foundation v. Genentech, Inc.* [Fed. Cir. 1991]) was denied. The court ruled squarely that Monoclonal had based nearly its entire business on the infringement of Hybritech's patent, but this fact gave it no special legal or equitable consideration. "One who elects to build a business on a product found to infringe cannot be heard to complain if an injunction against continuing infringement destroys the business."

Given the diagnostic and pharmaceutical value of much of the new biotechnology, the public interest factor is likely to remain important.

In conclusion, it should be emphasized that the judiciary must be particularly careful in assessing biological subject matter and in interpreting claims drawn thereto. In the biologic arts, claimed subject matter may be identified but not isolated, isolated but not characterized, characterized but not fully characterized.

Infringement of Design Patents

The Federal Circuit greatly enhanced the perceived value of design patents when it affirmed a summary judgment of validity, infringement, and willfulness with respect to two separate design patents on tennis shoes in *Avia Group International, Inc. v. L. A. Gear California* (1988). The CAFC cited with approval the test for design patent infringement first expressed by the Supreme Court in *Gorham Co. v. White* (1871):

> If, in the eye of the ordinary observer, giving such attention as a purchaser usually gives, two designs are substantially the same, if the resemblance is such as to deceive such an observer, inducing him to purchase one supposing it to be the other, the first one patented is infringed by the other.

The Federal Circuit then embellished this test by noting that "[i]n addition to overall similarity of designs, 'the accused device must appropriate the novelty in the patented device which distinguishes it from the prior art'."

The CAFC rejected as a defense to infringement the argument by L. A. Gear that its shoes were intended for different customers than were the patented shoes. The Federal Circuit held that, even if that were true, to find infringement of a design patent the accused product need only appropriate the protected design, not the patentee's market as well. As with utility patents, an infringer of a design patent can be liable even if the patentee manufactures no product at all. In another case, the CAFC stressed that the designs must be equivalent in their ornamental and not their functional aspects.

Privilege as to Temporary Presence in the United States—35 USC 272

> The use of any invention in any vessel, aircraft or vehicle of any country which affords similar privileges to vessels, aircraft or vehicles of the United States, entering the United States temporarily or accidentally, shall not constitute infringement of any patent, if the invention is used exclusively for the needs of the vessel, aircraft or vehicle and is not sold in or used for the manufacture of anything to be sold in or exported from the United States.

The word *temporarily* within this section and comparable provisions of the Paris Convention for the Protection of Industrial Property of 1958 does not mean any less than entrance for the purpose of completing a voyage, turning about, and continuing or commencing a new voyage.

Patent which relates to modification introduced into JT–4 jet engines was not infringed by regular use of patented engine in air service to the United States by transoceanic commercial air carriers, which were air carriers of their national states.

The territorial protection afforded a patent is limited to the United States and it is not an infringement to make or use a patented product outside the United States. The importation of articles or their sale by the owner, importer, consignee, or agent of either may be proscribed under the provisions of 19 USC 1337 (Section 337 of the Tariff Act of 1930) whenever unfair methods of competition and unfair acts in the importation of articles—to restrain or monopolize trade—are declared unlawful and found by the president to exist—and therefore may be excluded from the United States. 19 USC 1337(a) prohibits the importation into the United

States of products made, without the authority of the patentee or his assignee, under a process covered by a claim of his unexpired patent.

WILLFUL INFRINGEMENT

35 USC 284 states that "the court may increase the damages." Prior to 1983, the realities of the patent law in action had been for the competitor to utilize the self-help license of willful infringement in confidence that there was profit to be made thereby in many situations. This attitude actually encouraged the tort of willful, even malicious, patent infringement. But there has been a sharp change since the Federal Circuit came into being. In its first five years, the Federal Circuit awarded attorneys' fees or multiplied damages some fifteen times.

In summary, the elements of willful infringement include:

1. an actual infringement;
2. knowledge of the patent;
3. awareness of the relevance of the patent which would seem to require the accused infringer also to have knowledge of:
   (a) the patent's scope vis-à-vis the product/process he makes, uses, or sells;
   (b) the validity of the patent under sections 100, 101, 102, 103, 112, etc.; and
   (c) the enforceability of the patent as against charges of patent misuse, inequitable conduct in the patent solicitation, and the like;
4. absence of infringer's honest doubt or good faith belief.

It seems clear that if, before he commences infringement, the infringer has knowledge of a patent as relevant to his activity, his burden in showing nonwillfulness will be relatively greater. And if his investments and activity in the infringement were substantial, long continuing and in innocence of any knowledge of the patent, and his first knowledge comes in the complaint in the infringement suit, that circumstance alone will go a very long way toward establishing his infringement as not willful. But any continuance of the infringing activity after effective notice of infringement seems particularly subject to a possible conclusion of willfulness, depending upon the variety of factors to be discussed below.

For unless an infringer has a belief on each of them, or a known duty to develop a belief on them, he is not recognizing or callously disregarding an infringement upon the rights of the patentee. The presumption of validity and the circumstance that a defendant has the burden of proof of invalidity or unenforceability by the clear and convincing standard appear to give rise to a duty of defendant, when once informed of a patent's relevance to his product or process, to develop a belief about validity, enforceability, and infringement.

The courts tend to speak about the totality of circumstances reflecting the infringer's honest doubt or good faith belief as to whether a right was being infringed.

1. *"Honest Doubt" or "Good Faith Belief."* Prior to 1983, under the regional Courts of Appeals, the infringer's good faith belief that his defense was sound was almost uniformly seen to be an adequate defense to a charge of willful infringement. Even an honest doubt, which is much short of a good faith belief, had been held by a few regional courts to be a defense.

Today, after a fair number of Federal Circuit decisions finding willful infringement, it appears that even a strong defense, plausible enough to merit a day in court, does not of itself disprove willfulness of the infringement at infringement time. On the other hand, the pattern of the CAFC opinions is conflicting, which makes any legal advice uncertain.

The tenor of the Federal Circuit decisions is to the effect that, before infringing activity begins, the infringer must have some honest doubt about the validity of the patent or he must have a good faith belief that his activity is otherwise proper. And that doubt or belief must have a reasonable basis, as might be found in a competent legal opinion.

2. *Attorneys' Opinions.* Failure to get an opinion is perhaps the most dramatic evidence of callous disregard of the rights of others when advised of a patent's potential relevance to his activity; to obtain a responsible legal opinion regarding the known patent with respect to his intended process/product; and to do this before initiation of his potential infringing activity. Such failure, unexplained, has often been the basis in itself for a finding of willful or deliberate conduct.

One Federal Circuit case from those of 1983, 1984, 1985, 1986, and 1987 brings home the importance of this factor. In *Underwater Devices, Inc. v. Morrison-Knudsen Co.* (1983), the Federal Circuit stated crisply that an infringer having knowledge of a patent has an affirmative duty to obtain legal advice before the initiation of possible infringing activity, that is, the infringer must exercise due care to determine whether he might be infringing the patent. Without such a determination, how can he have a meaningful doubt or a good faith belief of no infringement upon the rights of the patentee?

Nevertheless, there is no *per se* rule. Nor is there a rigorous rule even though the court has said in one case, in affirming willful infringement, that there was no evidence that the infringer asked for or received a "written legal opinion on validity, including an analysis of the file history of either [of the patents in suit] . . . or on infringement, including an analysis comparing and contrasting the [accused devices] to the [patents in suit]."

Notwithstanding that the essence of an attorney's opinion justifying the accused activity is not conclusive of willfulness, virtually the most disastrous mistake that an infringer can make is failing to obtain a competent supportive legal opinion, provided, and this is no small proviso, he can obtain such a competent opinion consistent with the difficulties expressed below. At least some courts will apparently presume pressure on house counsel to write a biased (i.e., incompetent) opinion.

Two Federal Circuit decisions in 1988 addressed the issue of whether the use of in-house counsel to render an opinion of invalidity or noninfringement is sufficient to comply with the affirmative duty of due care. In both cases, the Federal Circuit affirmed the District Court's findings of no willful infringement. An in-house attorney need not be in a superior position to outside counsel for his position to be competent. The question is whether the in-house attorney is qualified to render an opinion. If the in-house attorney is qualified to render an opinion and the client's good faith reliance on the opinion is justified, the infringement should be found to be not willful. "[C]onclusionary and unsupported remarks regarding validity and infringement are not competent."

The attorney's opinion, at a minimum, should have

> within its four corners a patent validity analysis, properly and explicitly predicated on a review of the file histories of the patents at issue, and an infringement analysis that, *inter alia,* compared and contrasted the potentially infringing method or apparatus with the patented inventions.

The court has stated under the totality of the circumstances test, the issue is whether the infringer "investigated the scope of the patent and formed a good-faith belief that it was invalid or that it was not infringed."

All the factors relating to evidence of patentability are also factors relating to the competence of an opinion and should be given serious consideration when writing the opinion. These factors include at least the following:

a. Proper consideration of interviews with workers in the art at the time the invention was made and just before, as to why they did not make the invention at that time;
b. the presence, if any, of a long-felt want;
c. the long term of the availability of all of the prior art references and tools for making the invention;
d. the commercial success of the invention;

e. acquiescence by a substantial portion of the competitors in a market in the validity of a patent, generally through acceptance of a license;

f. skepticism by those in the art even after the invention was made, as to whether it would work;

g. trials and failures in making the invention;

h. the number of patents in the same art evidencing work by other researchers seeking to solve essentially the same problem between the time the tools for making the invention were available and the time the invention was made;

i. contemporaneous professional recognition of an invention's value;

j. the ease or difficulty with which the application for a patent moved through the examination process of the PTO; and

k. deliberate copying of the patent holder's device.

Thus, it cannot be emphasized too strongly the significance of this new law which puts the competence of the lawyer's opinion, written or oral, squarely into issue, which forces us to search for propatent evidence if we want to be sure our opinion of invalidity stands up. One must be especially careful, for example, when the infringer may specifically request an oral opinion so that it can be concealed if it turns out to be adverse; or request a written opinion but withhold important facts from the attorney to ensure a favorable result. Patentees' attorneys must seek discovery of those patterns. The totality of the circumstances must be considered.

Of course, the duty to seek competent legal advice cannot arise prior to obtaining knowledge of the existence of the patent. If, however, he learns of the patent and its relevance during his activity, he then has the duty to seek counsel and he should do so within a reasonable time. If he acts within that time and he obtains a competent opinion within that time of patent invalidity or noninfringement, he should not be adjudged a willful infringer. But delay may be construed as callous disregard or failure to discharge the duty and his infringement may be found to be willful.

Ignoring the opinion of counsel can have the worst possible consequences. The existence of an opinion of counsel on patent invalidity or noninfringement will not be enough to avoid a finding of willful infringement if the infringer cannot demonstrate that he relied upon the opinion and that his reliance was justified.

In *du Pont v. Phillips Petroleum* (1987), the CAFC affirmed a District Court's finding that infringement was not willful, despite the fact that Phillip's decision to continue infringing du Pont's patent was based primarily on business considerations, not on the opinion of its counsel that the patent was invalid. Although the District Court noted that the issue was a close call, it found, and the Federal Circuit affirmed, that du Pont had not carried its burden of clear and convincing evidence to show willfulness. The District Court pointed out that if the burden of proof had been a preponderance of the evidence, du Pont would have succeeded.

In *Underwater Devices, Inc. v. Morrison-Knudsen Co.* (1983), the CAFC set down certain minimum standards for an attorney's opinion. The four corners must contain a patent validity analysis based on a thorough review of the file history and an infringement analysis that compares the accused device with the patented invention. In *Central Soya Co. v. George A. Hormel & Co.* (1983), the CAFC held that an opinion "based solely on the file history prior art" does not, of itself, raise an inference of good faith sufficient to reverse a District Court's finding of willful infringement.

In a more recent case, the Federal Circuit held that simply because the reasoning and conclusion in an opinion prove to be wrong, the opinion does not necessarily lack sufficient reasoning to establish a good faith reliance. Thus, the opinion does not need to be correct in every respect for reliance at the time the opinion is rendered to be justified.

3. *Copying the Patented Device.* The burden of proof of showing good faith belief is moved without any explanation to the infringer, once any significant element of callous disregard of the patent right is proven by the patentee, for example, copying the patented device. In two 1988 cases there was the added factor of defection from the patentee to the infringing company, a distributor in one case, and a manager in the other.

4. *Attempt to Obtain a License.* The Federal Circuit upheld an award of increased damages and attorney fees, relying on the defendant's unsuccessful attempt to obtain a license to the patent in issue to support the conclusion that the defendant was thereby made explicitly aware of the possibility of infringement.

5. *Infringer's Attempt to Patent the Invention Himself.* One difference between two leading cases of the CAFC was that in the one there was no attempt to design around the patent, while in the other, distinct modifications were made. However, the philosophy of the subject judges was surely as important as that difference in the facts.

6. *Infringer Declaratory Judgment Action.* In *Kaufman Co. v. Lantach, Inc.* (CAFC 1986), the infringer had faithfully copied the claimed invention while the application for patent was pending. After the patent issued and the infringer received notice, he obtained counsel and filed a declaratory judgment action. The court said that the infringer's position with respect to invalidity and noninfringement were untenable and frivolous. His infringing activity during pendency of the action was found to be willful and the award of damages was doubled.

7. *Prior Adjudication of the Patent.* In one case the CAFC affirmed a finding of nonwillfulness of infringement despite the fact that the infringer

had been aware of the infringement and presented no new art besides that over which several claims of the patent had been held valid in a prior litigation. However, the trial court held that the infringement was not willful because "the defenses raised had a basis sufficiently reasonable for exploration and inquiry through the trial process."

8. *Bad Faith.* Where an infringer set up an undercapitalized, judgment-proof subsidiary to make, use, or sell the infringing device or the parent corporation sold the infringing subsidiary and obtained an indemnity or hold-harmless agreement from the purchaser of the subsidiary, in both such situations, these factors were cited as evidence of a willful and deliberate nature of the infringement and an attempt by the infringer to avoid the judgment he believed would be found.

9. *Infringement Searches.* To be sure of avoidance of a finding of willful infringement, the performer of an infringement search must be prepared to follow up with obtaining a competent legal opinion and complying with it as to any patent found to present a significant question of infringement.

The Federal Circuit has declared that "[t]he jurisprudence . . . uniformly requires clear and convincing evidence in support of increased damages." After the patentee's evidence on awareness of a general relevance of a patent, the burden of proof may be found to have shifted, so that the infringer has the psychological, if not legal, burden of proving good faith belief and honest doubt, which means that the infringer will in the larger sense carry the burden of proving nonwillfulness.

On the other hand, if the infringer does get into evidence a competent legal opinion justifying his activity, his good faith belief and honest doubt appear to be presumed from that opinion. The patentee must rebut the presumption by showing that, despite the existence of that opinion, the infringer still acted without responsible good faith belief or honest doubt, as for example, because the opinion was itself not in good faith or because there were also other opinions, perhaps oral opinions, expressed along the way during work on the lawsuit, to a contrary effect. The Federal Circuit treats a finding of willfulness as a finding of fact and under present law it will be reversed on appeal only if it is at least clearly erroneous.

The best appellate strategy, then, is to win willful infringement at trial because the trial court ruling will almost always be upheld; and to win the awards of attorney fees and multiplied damages also at trial, because any explicit discretion of the trial judge is also upheld unless abused, even though it is an issue at law.

To show that the infringer relied on the competent legal opinion, the infringer must waive the attorney-client privilege protecting the substance of the communication. If the privilege is waived, the patentee may discover not only the opinion itself, but all communications relating to the opinion and relating to its competence. This waiver could even include trial attorney work product materials. The infringer is therefore placed on the horns of a dilemma, and there is Federal Circuit language implying that the opinion is adverse if privilege is claimed, this being strong discouragement for claiming the privilege through trial.

Accused infringers always urge privilege during discovery, and then often waive privilege at trial time when the patentee has no chance to obtain discovery as to its competence or as to other opinions that may have been rendered orally.

It must be remembered that essentially, every thorough opinion for an infringer that considers the evidence on both sides, contains some admissions of value to the patentee.

In its first five years, the Federal Circuit developed the law of willful infringement thusly:

1. a new frequency of awards of attorney fees and multiplied damages;
2. a new reluctance to conclude no willfulness based solely upon the defenses at trial appearing to be substantive;
3. a tremendous new pressure on the infringer to waive attorney-client privilege and offer legal opinions in evidence, which surely is in error and should be corrected;
4. a focus on there being a good faith, unequivocal belief at the time infringement commenced rather than merely at trial time; and
5. a new role for the competence of attorneys' opinions wherein a defect in the opinion presented in evidence may be the feature which destroys the client's defense against a finding of willful.

But given the bias of the Federal Circuit to affirm even flatly inconsistent trial court rulings as not clearly erroneous, there is no clear, reliable law on what is and is not a basis for multiplying damages or awarding attorney fees. In light of that bias to affirm, it would be better to win in the trial court.

The significance of a finding that an infringement has been willful is that it authorizes a court both to increase the patentee's damages up to three times the amount found, pursuant to 35 USC 284, and to award the patentee his attorney's fees, pursuant to 35 USC 285. A finding that infringement has been willful makes the case exceptional under Section 285.

Findings of willful infringement were generally based on:

1. the infringer's failure to obtain an opinion of counsel after being charged with infringement;

2. copying the patentee's product;
3. misappropriation of trade secrets in connection with the patent infringement; and
4. putting forth untenable defenses.

The District Court is obliged to determine that the infringer "acted in disregard of the patent, that is, that the infringer had no reasonable basis for believing it had a right to do the acts."

Just because a defendant's answer contains the

> entire litany of defenses commonly asserted in patent cases . . . something more in the way of vexatious acts is necessary to establish that defenses are asserted in bad faith.
>
> [W]here a potential infringer has actual notice of another's patent rights, he has an affirmative duty to exercise due care to determine whether or not he is infringing. . . . Such an affirmative duty includes, *inter alia,* the duty to seek and obtain competent legal advice from counsel before the initiation of any possible infringing activity.

Ordering the prosecution history is "a normal and necessary preliminary to a validity or infringement opinion," and an opinion containing "only bald, conclusionary and unsupported remarks regarding validity and infringement . . ." is inadequate.

***Central Soya v. Hormel* (1983)**

> Hormel's intentional disregard of its counsel's opinion negates any inference of good faith, placing Hormel in the same position as one who failed to secure the advice of counsel. . . . Hormel had not only to show an opinion from competent counsel but also that it had exercised reasonable good faith adherence to the analysis and advice therein.

Further, it is necessary to look at "the totality of the circumstances presented in the case." In the *Hormel* case, Hormel:

1. hired plaintiff's experienced staff to set up a duplicate manufacturing line;
2. would not be sued because too good a customer of plaintiff; and Hormel's
3. counsel suggested that manufacturing be done in the 8th Circuit where a patent had not been held valid or infringed in years;

4. diversion of two large accounts from plaintiff;
5. failure to seek an updated opinion when it first began production; and
6. purchase of infringing products from a third party when it discontinued its own manufacturing line.

Willfulness of infringement is a finding of fact which therefore will not be reversed unless clearly erroneous.

A reasonably prudent person will obtain a written opinion of counsel. "[T]o willfully infringe a patent, the patent must exist and one must have knowledge of it. A 'patent pending' notice gives one no knowledge whatsoever."

There is a public policy to "design around... patented products... which should not be discouraged by punitive damage awards except in cases where conduct is so obnoxious as to clearly call for them."

> [A] conclusionary account [in a warning letter to a competitor] of defense counsel's aspirations for winning an infringement suit without any supporting reasons does not amount to an "authoritative opinion" upon which a good faith reliance may be founded.
>
> [T]o willfully infringe a patent, the patent must exist.
>
> [T]he incentive to "design around" patents is a positive result of the patent system.
>
> [A] decision to continue production after notice, was clear and convincing evidence of willfulness.

Multiple damages do not require a finding that the case was exceptional [may award reasonable attorney fees], as long as infringement was willful.

All fact findings of a jury, including jury findings of willful infringement, are nonadvisory, unless made in an area expressly removed from the jury's verdict.

> [I]n respect of willfulness, there cannot be... hard and fast *per se* rules... an accused infringer's affirmative duty to obtain competent legal advice before infringing or continuing to infringe does not mean that the absence of such opinion alone requires a finding of willful infringement... totality of the circumstances.

In conclusion:

—"totality of the circumstances...."

—no hard and fast *per se* rules

—an opinion of counsel is the primary indicator of good faith

—preferably outside counsel

—preferably patent attorney

—accused must:
  (a) adhere to opinion
  (b) altering one's product in an attempt to avoid infringement is evidence of good faith

—in writing based on a review of:
  (a) prosecution history
  (b) cited references

—a factual finding, thus,

—a clearly erroneous authoritative standard; and by a jury; explain reasoning, not conclusionary and may not be treated as merely advisory.

—timing is critical, not after notice.

In *Allen Archery v. Browning* (April 1987), the District Court declined to hold that infringement was willful although the infringer, Browning, knew of the patent. The District Court found that:

1. the infringer had been represented by competent counsel;
2. it had acted in the good faith belief that the claims in suit were invalid;
3. its defense had a basis sufficiently reasonable for exploration and inquiry through the trial process; and
4. any delay in bringing the case to trial was at least in part the patentee's fault.

The Federal Circuit agreed with the patentee that the evidence could support an inference that infringement was willful, but noted that "the 'clearly erroneous' standard of Federal Rule of Civil Procedure 52(a) 'does not entitle a reviewing court to reverse the finding of the trier of fact simply because it is convinced that it would have decided the case differently'."

In *Rite-Hite v. Kelley Co.* (May 1987), the CAFC observed that "there is no *per se* rule that an opinion letter from patent counsel will necessarily preclude a finding of willful infringement . . . nor is there a *per se* rule that the lack of such a letter necessarily requires a finding of willfulness." Based on the totality of the circumstances, the court held that the District Court's finding was not clearly erroneous.

In *Spindelfabrik et al v. Schubert et al.* (September 1987), the District Court found that defendant:

1. had requested a license under the patent and was refused;
2. had been aware of the significance of the patent in the marketplace; and
3. had relied solely on the opinion of its in-house German patent counsel.

Based on these circumstances, the District Court found that defendant's infringement was willful. The CAFC affirmed this finding as not clearly erroneous and, furthermore, noted that a refused request for a license makes the accused infringer explicitly aware of the possibility of infringement and holds it to "a high degree of caution to avoid the possibility of infringement." Finally, while recognizing the absence of any good faith attempt to design around the patent in this case, the court reaffirmed its earlier pronouncements on the value of encouraging design around efforts and their role in tending to avoid a finding of willfulness.

In reviewing the CAFC's decisions on willful infringement during this period, much guidance has been provided by the court, and this is summarized below.

1. A willfulness determination should depend upon the totality of the circumstances.
2. There cannot be any hard and fast *per se* rules.
3. An opinion from counsel is the primary indicator of good faith. However, there are a number of subsidiary conditions:
   (a) preferably an American patent attorney who is not in-house,
   (b) in writing based upon an in-depth study of the prosecution history and cited references,
   (c) it must be authoritative, of course, reflecting the uncertainties of litigation,
   (d) the timing is critical, an opinion rendered after infringement has commenced or continued may not avoid a holding of willfulness.
4. Knowledge of another's patent, not patent application, can come from third parties but must be specific, that is, a specific patent and a specific product.
5. Copying of a product tends to show willfulness, although public policy favors designing around patents.
6. Other *indicia* of willfulness are:
   (a) putting forth weak infringement or validity defenses,

(b) hiring the patentee's employees,
(c) making statements evidencing disregard for the potential rights of the patentee,
(d) infringing after a request for a license has been refused,
(e) failure to conduct a patent search prior to manufacture.

7. Willfulness is a factual finding.

INTERFERING PATENTS—SECTION 291

When two or more patents claim the same subject matter, one has interfering patents. A civil action brought under 35 USC 291 is called an "Interfering Patent Suit." All but one of several interfering patents are void, as to the interfering claim or claims; though all may be valid as to the other claims which they respectively contain.

The existence of an interference is a mixed question of fact and law. Absent interference, a court has no power under 35 USC 291 to adjudicate the validity of any patent.

> When a patent has received the signature of the Secretary of the Interior [1898], countersigned by the Commissioner of Patents, and has had affixed to it the seal of the Patent Office, it has passed beyond the control and jurisdiction of that office, and is not subject to be revoked or cancelled by the President, or any other officer of the Government. . . . The only authority competent to annul it, or to correct it for any reason whatever, is vested in the courts of the United States, and not in the department which issued the patent. . . . Had the original patent been procured by fraud or deception it would have been the duty of the Commissioner of Patents to have had the matter referred to the Attorney General with the recommendation that a suit be instituted to cancel the patent; but to attempt to cancel a patent upon an application for reissue when the first patent is considered invalid by the examiner would be to deprive the applicant of his property without due process of law . . . the Patent Office had no power to revoke, cancel or annul it.

However, a patent owner or any other party having an interest may institute an Interfering Patent Action. It must be borne in mind that even a single interfering claim makes the patents interfering. The questions which may arise in an interference suit include the following:

1. The presence or absence of an interference between the patents.

2. Whether the subject of the interference was patentable at all or whether either or both of the patents is void on any ground.
3. Whether the first party to conceive the invention involved in the suit was also the first to reduce it to practice or to file an application for a patent thereon, as the case may be.
4. Whether the first party to conceive the invention, if he neither reduced it to practice nor applied for a patent thereon till after another party to the suit did one or the other of those things, was negligent of the invention before that other party conceived the invention himself.

The interfering claims of the two patents must be substantially identical. The identity of the claims is the test of the question of the existence of an interference. All owners are indispensable parties. In litigation involving interfering patents under the patent statutes, the decision of the PTO and of the appellate court on appeal from such PTO decision in interference proceedings in favor of one of the parties is not *res judicata* upon the question of priority of invention between them and is no bar to the prosecution of such a suit, but the decision of the PTO is entitled to great weight.

> A patent regularly issued, and even more obviously, a patent issued after a hearing of all the rival claimants, is "presumed to be valid" until the presumption has been overcome by convincing evidence of error.

There is a recognized *prima facie* presumption that patents are not interfering—that they do not claim the same invention. The burden is on the junior party to establish priority of invention, but the burden of going forward with evidence in support of an affirmative defense interposed by the defendant is upon the one asserting it.

When a court finds no interference between plaintiff's patent and defendant's patent, it would not pass upon the validity of the patents. In such a case the appellate court cannot pass upon the question of patentability, and the case must go back for retrial.

35 USC 271: Infringement of Patent

This section relating to contributory infringement of a patent, as construed to require a showing that alleged contributory infringer knew that combination for which his component was especially designed was both patented and infringing, is constitutional. When interpreting this section proscribing unauthorized making of patented invention in the United

States, courts must balance protection extended to patentee by patent laws with public's right to use constituent elements.

At common law, there could be no contributory infringement without an infringement to which to contribute or, in other words, without actual infringement, and, since this section making a person who actively induces infringement liable as infringer was not clearly in derogation of the common law of contributory infringement, it had to be concluded that Congress had intended the term "actively induces infringement" to cover situations in which actual infringement resulted from active inducement.

Notice to competitor that he is infringing, and to manufacturer for competitor, and to a limited number of his customers, are not to be condemned when characterized by good faith.

A suit pending to sustain validity of a patent is notice to all infringers of insistence by patentee on his claimed rights.

Even if plaintiff were owner of patent and it was valid and infringed, no recovery of damages could be had where plaintiff had failed to mark patented apparatus or give other notice of infringement.

Device which embodies principles of basic patent as well as one for improvement infringes both.

Infringement is made out where defendant has infringed any one of several claims.

One manufacturing and supplying parts to users of infringing mechanism was jointly liable with user.

Infringement of patent is tort, and all who are parties to it are liable as joint tortfeasors.

Acts Constituting Infringement Generally

Fact that alleged infringer was promoting, advertising, and soliciting orders for structure which copied that claimed by holder's patent did not constitute act of infringement unless alleged infringer manufactured or sold infringing product.

Person to whom invention is disclosed in advance of granting patent is liable for profits and damages resulting from his manufacture and sale, in breach of confidence reposed by inventor of articles embodying the invention.

Fundamental basis of patent law requires that a patent holder establish acts of direct infringement before liability for inducement or contributory infringement can be found.

Where alleged infringer had built accused device only experimentally and it had neither manufactured the device for sale nor sold any, the accused device could not be relied on to establish infringement.

There is no such thing in patent law as partial infringement.

A machine that infringes part of the time is an infringement, although it may at other times be so operated so as not to infringe.

If an accused machine is substantially identical with the prior art, there can be no infringement of patent.

Patent claiming improvement on prior art would not be infringed by device that utilized the prior art without the improvement.

In determining whether there is noninfringing repair of patented article or infringing reconstruction, the idea of reconstruction has the special connotation of those acts which would impinge on patentee's right to exclude others from making the article.

Patent monopolist cannot prevent those to whom he sells from reconditioning articles worn by use, unless they in fact make new article.

Whether an operation constitutes reconstruction amounting to patent infringement, or merely replacement, depends on whether new parts so dominate structural substance of the whole patented combination as to justify conclusion that it has been made anew.

The theory on which one may repair patented article without being guilty of infringement is that patentee intends buyer to have a longer use of article than the life of the shortest-lived part.

Patents were not contributorily infringed where defendant merely sold unpatented replacement parts, even if such replacement parts had constituted gist of invention.

Durable parts of patented device may be mended or repaired, but not replaced, and perishable elements may be replaced.

Patentee alone may supply parts for reconstruction or reproduction of patented invention.

When a patented article is sold by patentee or a licensee, it is no longer within protective range of the patent and may be resold by purchaser without infringement liability.

Unauthorized use of patented invention, without more, constitutes infringement.

Experimental use is not public use if it is conducted in good faith for purposes of testing invention and for no other purpose not naturally incidental to experimental purpose.

Contributory Infringement

Contributory infringement is "the intentional aiding of one person by another in the unlawful making or selling or using of a patented invention."

The liability of a contributory infringer of a patent is commensurate with that of the infringer himself.

Before one may be held for contributory infringement it must be shown that he had knowingly done some act without which the infringement would not have occurred.

If there is no direct infringement of claims of a patent, there can be no contributory infringement and obviously no active inducement of direct infringement.

Unlike direct infringement, which must take place within the United States, contributory infringement does not require any activity by contributory infringer in this country, as long as direct infringement occurs here.

A manufacturer who instructs users to introduce an element which makes the device an infringement is chargeable with contributory infringement.

This section prohibits the sale, whether or not domestic, of an apparatus for use in the domestic practice of a patented process where the seller knows the apparatus will reach domestic markets and will be found especially adapted for an infringement of the patent.

The supplier of an element in a valid combination embodied in a patent might be guilty of infringement, though element was not patentable, and was old.

Issue of contributory infringement will not ordinarily arise where the thing supplied is itself patented.

A nonstaple is a product the unlicensed sale of which would constitute contributory infringement of a patent covering the product; a staple component is one which does not meet that definition.

Owner of patent and method may monopolize and reserve to himself sale of unpatented nonstaple products that are materially component parts of his patented process.

Where alleged infringing device was capable of substantial non-infringing use, such use would preclude a finding of contributory infringement.

One who supplies a component which is not patented to someone else who uses the component to infringe a patented machine or process is liable as a contributory infringer.

Contributory infringement will result from the furnishing of plans of an infringing device or from designing and helping to build an infringing machine.

Inducement of infringement of a patent is found when one knowingly causes, urges, encourages, or aids another in infringement of patent claim even though he himself has not infringed patent claim by making, using, or selling invention.

Some affirmative act is necessary for patent infringement within this section providing that whoever actively induces infringement of a patent shall be liable as an infringer.

Proof of inducement of infringement requires proof of direct infringement of all of elements of claim.

Persons Liable

Owner of patent of improved rolling mill had a right of recovery against user of infringing mill as well as against manufacturer of infringing mill.

While a patentee is getting his patent sustained, he is not bound to sue everyone whom he might afterwards seek to bring within the patent or to assert his claims to fullest scope by suing every conceivable infringer, especially in view of infringer's right to declaratory judgment.

Corporate officers are not liable for patent infringement where they have not been active other than as such officers, but if they willfully and knowingly participate in, induce, and approve acts of infringement, they are liable with corporation for the wrongful acts.

Parent corporation of infringing subsidiary may be held liable.

Where a patentee has been fully compensated by an infringing manufacturer for the manufacture and sale of infringing device, patentee has no recourse against a customer who is solely a user of such device, but the patentee is not precluded from proceeding against the customer until full compensation has been received from the manufacturer and seller.

Public policy favors rule that litigation for purposes of ascertaining and sustaining alleged rights of the patentee or manufacturer should be brought against alleged wrongful manufacturer rather than against customers of the manufacturer.

Where a decree against an infringing manufacturer has been secured, the patentee may maintain infringement suits against customers of the manufacturer.

A joint owner of a patent cannot be sued for infringement by another part owner.

A tenant, occupying under a lease a building the construction of which embodies a patentable feature, is not necessarily a user in such sense as to be an infringer.

No charge of infringement can be asserted by a patentee against his licensee with respect to the licensed patents under a subsisting patent license agreement.

Patent owner's cause of action against infringing manufacturer is wholly separate and distinct from cause of action against one who resells the infringing product.

One may infringe a patent if he has the articles manufactured for him by an independent contractor.

Infringement by servant acting within the scope of his general authority is tort of the master though the master has expressly forbidden him to commit it.

Principals are responsible for infringement by agent, within the scope of his authority.

Purchaser of patented product having actual notice of limited patent license in form of written label notice attached to product restricting use to which purchaser may put product and who uses and sells such product in violation of limited patent license is infringer.

Successor corporation is not liable for liabilities of dissolved corporation for patent infringements.

4

FACTORS DETERMINING INFRINGEMENT

INTRODUCTION

Early practice in the United States was to describe the invention in the specification of the patent and then claim the invention in general terms often "substantially as herein described" (an omnibus claim). As time went on, ever-increasing emphasis was placed on the language of the claims as the measure of the exclusive rights conferred by a patent. The question of infringement moved from one of whether the defendant's device embodied the plaintiff's invention to one of whether the claims of the patent, fairly construed, read on the defendant's device. Thus, a claim is a definition of an invention. It is an abstraction of an indefinite number of physical objects. The number which the claim will read on is its scope or breadth.

Winans v. Denmead (1853) was the first decision to use the Doctrine of Equivalents to do serious damage to the literal meaning of the language of the patent claim. The defendant constructed railroad cars for the carrying of coal that were "octagonal and pyramidal" in shape, rather than "cylindrical and conical" of the invention, which were "in the form of the frustum of a cone." In a 5-to-4 decision, the Supreme Court held that the defendant substantially embodied the invention, and thereby obtained the same kind of result as was reached by the invention.

After the Patent Act of 1870, the Supreme Court placed increased emphasis on the language of the claims as the measure of the exclusive rights granted by a patent. Despite this new emphasis on claim language, *Winans* and the Doctrine of Equivalents survived as a tool of interpretation. Further, the range of allowable equivalents was said to depend upon and vary with the degree of invention. In other words, a pioneer invention was entitled to a broad range and an invention in a crowded art was confined to the specific embodiment described in the patent, with gradations in between. The Supreme Court affirmed the role of the Doctrine of Equivalents in modern patent law in *Graver Tank & Mfg. Co. v. Linde Air Products Co.* (1950). The Court early recognized that proper construction of the language of claims required consideration of both the contents of the prior art and the proceedings on the application in the Patent Office. File wrapper estoppel developed as an aspect of this general principle of interpretation.

Determination of infringement requires a construction of the meaning of the claim language and then application of the claims as construed to the accused product or process. The task is rarely easy, especially when one considers that the patentee can be his own lexicographer.

The Court of Claims, in an infringement against the U.S. in *Autogiro Co. of America v. United States* (1967), offered a "recital of this court's law of patent infringement" which is an excellent discussion of claim interpretation and application. It noted that the determination of patent infringement is a two-step process:

1. derivation of the meaning of the claims "by a study of all relevant patent documents . . ."; the language of the claims must be interpreted, and
2. reading of the claims on the accused product or process, that is whether the claimed invention is being made, used, or sold by the alleged infringer.

The first is a question of law for the court; if, however, the meaning of a term of art in the claims is disputed and extrinsic evidence is needed to explain the meaning, construction of the claims is left to the jury; the second is an issue of fact.

The absence of even one element and its equivalent function of the claimed invention places the accused device outside the claim's coverage.

> The claims of the patent provide the concise formal definition of the invention. . . . It is to these words that one must look to determine whether there has been infringement. . . . Although courts are confined by the language of the claims, they are not, however, confined to the language of the claims in interpreting their meaning. . . . In deriving the meaning of a claim, we inspect all useful documents and reach . . . the "felt meaning" of the claim. In seeking this goal, we make use of three parts of the patent: the specification, the drawings, and the file wrapper. . . . File wrapper

> estoppel serves two functions in claim interpretation; the applicant's statements not only define terms, but also set the barriers within which the claim's meaning must be kept. . . . In file wrapper estoppel, it is not the prior art that provides the guidelines, but the *applicant's acquiescence with regard to the prior art*. . . . The use of the various parts of the patent to determine the meaning of the claim is only half the process of determining patent infringement. The other half is "reading the claims on the accused structures." If the claims read literally on the accused structures, an initial hurdle in the test for infringement has been cleared. The race is not over; it has only started. . . . If the claims do not read literally on the accused structures, infringement is not necessarily ruled out. The doctrine of equivalents casts around a claim a penumbra which also must be avoided if there is to be no infringement. . . . The range of equivalents varies with each patent; however, some general guidelines can be drawn. . . . In summary, the determination of patent infringement is a two-step process. First, the meaning of the claims in issue must be determined by a study of all relevant patent documents. Secondly, the claims must be read on the accused structures. In doing this, it is of little value that they read literally on the structures. What is crucial is that the structures must do the same work, in substantially the same way, and accomplish substantially the same result to constitute infringement. This is the general approach which this court uses to determine the infringement of all the patent claims properly before it in this case.

Whether an alleged equivalent to an element of a patent claim must have been in existence and known in the relevant art as an equivalent is a long-standing problem with the Doctrine of Equivalents. The Supreme Court, early on, seemingly indicated in a number of decisions that the alleged equivalent must have been so known. However, the CCPA in 1974 held that references after filing date may not be used to show enablement but may be used to "*construe* claim language and in particular to prove the definiteness of claim terminology."

It should be noted that the Doctrine of Equivalents can work in reverse. It should also be noted that it does not necessarily follow that file wrapper estoppel applies only when the patent owner seeks to rely on the Doctrine of Equivalents, and the Supreme Court has apparently never so held. Nevertheless, some lower courts have adopted such a position.

Generally, the burden of proof as to factual issues relating to infringement rests upon the patent owner. Whether infringement is a question of law or of fact bears on the propriety of summary judgment. It is frequently stated that infringement is a question of fact. However, infringement, like validity, is really a conclusion arrived at by applying certain legal standards to facts. Thus, decisions treat the existence of infringement as a question of law when the basic facts are undisputed. A finding of equivalence is a determination of fact.

The test for direct infringement of a patent is stated in 35 USC 271(a), which provides that whosoever, without authority, makes, uses, or sells a patented invention within the United States during the term of the patent therefor infringes the patent. One of the most problematic aspects of infringement has been determining what the patented invention is. Prior to the creation of the CAFC, there was little consistency in the approaches taken by courts in interpreting claims or in applying the Doctrine of Equivalents and the Doctrine of Prosecution History Estoppel.

One area of confusion has been with respect to literal infringement and infringement under the Doctrine of Equivalents. Some courts found direct or literal infringement while in reality applying the Doctrine of Equivalents; others, the reverse. Noninfringement has been found despite the literal readability of a claim on an alleged infringing thing by reading into the claim limitations from the specification or other claims, where an accused device was not equivalent to that disclosed, or where the specification taught away from or disclosed a different use.

Graver Tank (Sup. Ct. 1950) established that direct infringement arises not only where the same thing is done in the same way to accomplish the same result, but also where substantially the same thing is done in substantially the same way to accomplish substantially the same result.

Courts have also been inconsistent in their application of the Doctrine of Prosecution History Estoppel to limit the range of equivalents to which an invention is entitled. Since its inception, the Federal Circuit has considered infringement issues frequently. Not unexpectedly, the court has evidenced a somewhat liberal, propatent point of view, and in general the court's handling of infringement issues has been rather consistent and uniform, that is, until very recently.

CONSTRUCTION AND INTERPRETATION OF CLAIMS IN INFRINGEMENT LITIGATION

Claim Interpretation

The statutory basis for infringement can be found in 35 USC 271(a) which provides that:

> Except as otherwise provided in this title, whoever without authority makes, uses or sells any patented invention, within the United States during the term of the patent therefor, infringes the patent.

35 USC 112, last par. with respect to "means for" clauses: "... and such claim shall be construed to cover the corresponding structure, material, or acts described in the specification and *equivalents* thereof."

While it is plainly no excuse for infringement that new technology falls within the proper scope of a claim to older technology, the crux of the matter becomes appropriate claim interpretation. The thousands of judicial attempts to determine the proper scope and fair meaning of the patented invention, consistent with the policies underlying the patent system, gave rise to the case law addressing the issues of: claim interpretation, Doctrine of Equivalents, "Reverse" Doctrine of Equivalents, and Doctrine of Prosecution History Estoppel.

Both validity and infringement involve construction of patent claims, and the construction must be the same in determining both. Even though there is a difference between the range of equivalents afforded a claim in (a) litigation and in (b) during prosecution in the PTO, there is no difference afforded a claim in (a) litigation and (b) for purposes of validity, when comparing the claim to the prior art.

The claims must be read as a whole and without first referring to the accused matter; the invention is construed not only in light of the claims, but also with reference to the file wrapper, the prosecution history, the other claims, and offered extrinsic evidence such as the testimony of experts and evidence of how those skilled in the art would interpret the claims. It is equally well established that the restrictions of narrower claims cannot be read into broader claims either to avoid invalidity or to escape infringement; some believe that the courts, nevertheless, do so routinely.

There are a number of limitations on claim scope which must be evaluated when interpreting the claims. The threshold test of patentability under 35 USC 101 is simply whether the subject matter is made by man and has utility. The criteria for determining whether patentable subject matter is new within the meaning of Section 101 are no different from the criteria for determining whether that subject matter possesses the novelty expressed in Section 102. In the context of infringement, while microorganisms, plasmids, vectors, antibodies, proteins, sequences of nucleic acids, and so on are routinely claimed, the definition of those subjects must be undertaken with careful deliberation. Proving infringement, or noninfringement, of the patented invention can be quite difficult. The problem consists of the two interrelated aspects mentioned.

Both aspects should be kept in mind during claim drafting such that the accomplishment of the first gives rise to the second. A court can too readily make a conclusion of infringement based upon a loose definition or interpretation of broad claim language. That situation may result from a failure to properly construe the claims prior to determining infringement, for example, when an infringement analysis is undertaken without a concomitant investigation into validity. Thus, a court looking only at the similarity between an accused product and a product claim may fail to properly first construe the accuser's claims in light of the specification, the prior art, the file history, and other evidence. In the biologic arts particularly, the result can be that claims are given a breadth that is entirely beyond the scope of the invention, was not intended by the patentee at the time of filing, and is not enabled by the specification.

The enablement requirement is, of course, a limitation on the claim scope. A patentee's failure to supply an enabling disclosure is always a defense to validity in an action for infringement. "The relevant inquiry . . . [is whether] the scope of enablement provided to one of ordinary skill in the art by the disclosure is such as to be commensurate with the scope of protection sought by the claims."

The elements of the enablement requirement have been stated as follows: "A patent application must, (1) when filed, (2) contain a disclosure sufficiently clear and complete to enable (3) one skilled in the art to which the invention pertains to make and use the invention (4) as claimed, (5) without undue experimentation. . . . If the description is so vague, that no one can tell, except by independent experiment, how to construct the patented device, the patent is void."

If a claim as issued unquestionably and intentionally covers material which is not enabled by the specification, the patent is invalid. Thus, for example, claims to protein isolate preparations which recite only a lower limit in defining their purity must be supported by a specification which demonstrably permits the production . . . without undue experimentation or further invention . . . of a completely or nearly pure protein, virtually free of any other contaminants. Rejection of open-ended claims having a lower limit but no upper limit will be sustained. Although enablement is essentially a question of law, it can include questions of fact.

The definiteness requirement of 35 USC 112, 2nd par., may also have a bearing on the determination of infringement. However,

> if the claims, read in light of the specification, reasonably apprise those skilled in the art both of the utilization and scope of the invention, and if the language is as precise as the subject matter permits, the courts can demand no more.

The claim format can also impose limitations. For example, a product may be claimed by the process of making it. Classically, this type of claim was used only where the product could not be described in any other manner than by the process through which it was made. Now, a product claim in which at least one element is described by the process used to make it may be presented under any circumstance. While it is settled that the patentability of a product claimed in product-by-process format must reside solely in the product, not the process, it has been held that a product-by-process claim is infringed *only* by a product made following the same process defined by that claim. Courts have refused to apply the Doctrine of Equivalents in this situation; the same process must have been used for infringement to lie.

One further limitation on claims scope is that related to pioneer inventions. Pioneer inventions mark "a distinct step in the progress of the art, distinguished from a mere improvement or perfection of what had gone before." Pioneer inventions, as such, are entitled to a liberality in the determination of infringement, the courts are generous in finding infringement by equivalence. This liberal view flows directly from the relative sparseness of prior art in nascent fields of technology.

> Since the purpose of this doctrine is to give the inventor the opportunity to secure a just reward for his invention . . . the degree of protection afforded beyond the language of the claims will vary directly with the value of the inventor's contribution to the art. As the principle is commonly put, the inventor is entitled to a range of equivalents commensurate with the scope of his invention: broad if his invention is broad; narrow if his advance is a small one in a crowded field.

In general, if the words of a claim read on an allegedly infringing device or method, then there is said to be literal infringement of that claim. An infringement analysis is fundamentally a determination of whether a claim *covers* an accused device. The analysis begins with a reading of the claims, but always includes an analysis of the specification, prosecution history, prior art in some cases, and the accused device. A claim is not infringed by an accused structure or method unless that structure or method contains all of the elements of the claim, or an equivalent thereof.

A determination of literal infringement cannot be made until the meanings of the words of the claim are understood. Begin with: (1) ordinary meanings as in a dictionary or relevant field of technology; then we must (2) refer to drawings, specification and prosecution history; expert testimony may also be used.

By using means-plus-function (MPF) language, a claim can be literally infringed by a product which does not use the specific devices or apparatus described in the specification of Section 112, last par., "equivalents thereof." For example, instead of restricting the attachment of one thing to another by stapling, one might say "means for fastening," which is much broader and would include equivalents not described in the specification.

There is a difference between PTO and court interpretation in an infringement context. The foregoing discussion of the range of equivalents afforded MPF language by Section 112, last par., is applied in litigation, not in the PTO. In pending applications, the PTO examiner construes an

MPF clause in its broadest reasonable interpretation consistent with the scope of enablement in the specification, and does not look to equivalents, because the applicant can then amend his claims (not possible with a patent at trial). This long-accepted rule has not been acknowledged by the CAFC, however.

Nota bene: Recent CAFC cases have held that the PTO broadest reasonable interpretation standard applies in reissue and reexamination proceedings, as well as *ex parte* (on the application of one party only) patent prosecution. Thus, the MPF clauses, typically used in electronic cases, could be given a significantly broader interpretation in reissue/reexamination proceedings, possibly resulting in rejection of claims which otherwise might have withstood an attack on their validity in litigation. Also, if claims are amended or added during reexamination, intervening rights may arise under 35 USC 307.

Where some claims are broad and others narrow, the narrow claim limitations cannot be read into the broad, whether by the patentee to avoid invalidity or by the alleged infringer to escape infringement. If there be literal infringement, the Doctrine of Prosecution History Estoppel is inapplicable. While an invention should not be struck down because a patentee has misconceived the scientific principle involved, such error cannot be overlooked when that misconception is embodied in a claim. When an incorrect or questionable theory of operation is included in a claim, or when a claim requires a means for accomplishing an unattainable result, the claimed invention must be considered inoperative as claimed and the claim must be held invalid under either Section 101 or Section 112.

Resort must be had in the first instance to the words of the claim, which defines the metes and bounds of the invention, and that words in a claim will be given their ordinary and accustomed meaning unless it appears that the inventor used them differently. It is improper to read limitations into a claim for any purpose, either to save the claim from invalidity or to escape infringement. There have been dissents saying that the majority ignored clear precedent of the Court of Claims, which held that the claims should be construed to preserve their validity. Construing some of the claims to include limitations found in other claims is error as a matter of law; this is a fixed, long- and well-established rule and enjoys immutable and universally applicable status comparatively rare among rules of law.

In determining patent infringement, the two inquiries involved are:

(a) the scope of the claims, a question of law. If the language of the claims is undisputed, a court could interpret or construe the undisputed claims as a matter of law. If, however, the meaning of a term of art in the claims is disputed and extrinsic evidence is needed to explain its meaning, construction of the claims could be left to a jury.

In construing or interpreting claims, a host of factors may be considered:

(1) prosecution history may be used not only in an estoppel context, but also as a claim construction tool;

(2) words defined in the specification must be given the same meaning when used in a claim;

(3) if a dependent claim limits a feature set forth in a broader claim, it is improper to read the narrower limitation into the broader claim; and

(4) expert testimony may be considered as to the manner in which the claims would be construed by those skilled in the art.

(b) whether the claimed invention has been infringed. Proper claim construction precedes determination of whether the claims in suit read on the accused devices, and generally involves examining the specification, prosecution history, and other claims.

The court has cautioned against limiting a claimed invention to preferred embodiments or specific examples in the specification and has reviewed the process of claim interpretation:

> A claim is construed in the light of the claim language, the other claims, the prior art, the prosecution history, and the specification, not in light of the accused device.... It is only after the claims have been construed without reference to the accused device that the claims, as so construed, are applied to the accused device to determine infringement.

The word *comprising* when not used in a transitional phrase has no legal effect, and that reasonably interpreted means *having*. Where key terms in the claim are disputed, resort to certain extrinsic evidence such as the specification, prosecution history, and other claims is always necessary to interpret disputed claims. While recognizing that the use of experts is generally within the discretion of the trial judge, the Federal Circuit has noted that this discretion is not unlimited, and stated that in a patent case involving complex scientific principles, expert testimony is particularly helpful, since the test of claim interpretation is directed to one skilled in the art. Since the determination of the scope of claims is a question of law, a dispute respecting that legal issue does not preclude summary judgment where there are no genuine issues of material fact.

In *Howes et al. v. Medical Components* (March 1987), the CAFC noted that claim construction is a question of law, and that the mere existence of a dispute as to that legal issue does not preclude summary judgment, although underlying factual disputes may arise which would preclude summary judgment. When a claim is in dispute, it is always necessary to look at certain extrinsic evidence such as the specification, the prosecution history, and the other claims, and that if complex scientific principles are involved or if expert testimony is needed to explain a disputed term, then an underlying factual question may arise which makes summary judgment improper.

In *Fonar Corp. v. Johnson & Johnson* (June 1987), the CAFC noted that in order for it to reverse the District Court's grant of J & J's motion for JNOV (judgment *non obstante veredicto*—notwithstanding the verdict) on infringement, Fonar must show that there was substantial evidence to support the jury's findings. The court noted that substantial evidence is such relevant evidence from the record taken as a whole as might be accepted by a reasonable mind as adequate to support the finding under review. It also noted that while inventors may be their own lexicographers, they must use words in the same way in the claims and in the specification.

The use of some expressions can result in limiting the scope of the claims; "optionally," for example. In two recent decisions, the board refused to condemn as indefinite the presence of the use of *optionally* to describe a limitation in a claim.

> Situations may arise in which the expressions "such as" and "particularly" render a claim indefinite as to whether such expressions introduce exemplary or limiting detail. However, the use of the term "optionally," as employed in [the] claim [in question] is akin to expressions such as "up to" and "0 to . . ." [and "not more than"]. Such alternative language does not normally render claims indefinite under the 2nd Para. of 35 USC 112.

The *preamble* is the initial part of a claim, the purpose of which is to name or define the thing being claimed. *Corning Glass Works v. Sumitomo Electric U.S.A.* (CAFC 1989):

> To say that a preamble is a limitation if it gives "meaning to the claim" may merely state the problem rather than lead one to the answer. The effect preamble language should be given can be resolved only on review of the entirety of the patent to gain an understanding of what the inventors actually invented and intended to encompass by the claim.

The District Court correctly interpreted the preamble to the claim in suit—"an optical waveguide"—as a structural limitation on the scope of the claim rather than a statement of purpose.

> To read the claim in light of the specification indiscriminately to cover all types of optical fibers would be divorced from reality. The invention is restricted to those fibers that work as waveguides as defined in the specification. . . . The claim requires, in addition, the particular structural relationship defined in the specification for the core and cladding to function as an optical waveguide.

In *Ex parte Hoffman* (1989), it was held that although *consisting essentially of* is typically used and defined in the context of compositions of matter, there is nothing intrinsically wrong with the use of such language as a modifier of method steps. In the board's view, when used as a modifier of method steps, the claim is rendered open only for the inclusion of steps which do not materially affect the basic and novel characteristics of the claimed method.

Late Claiming. In *Kingsdown Medical Consultants, Ltd. v. Hollister, Inc.* (1988), the CAFC noted:

> [T]here is nothing improper, illegal or inequitable in filing a patent application for the purpose of obtaining a right to exclude a known competitor's product from the market; nor is it in any manner improper to amend or insert claims intended to cover a competitor's product the applicant's attorney has learned about during the prosecution of a patent application. Any such amendment or insertion must comply with all statutes and regulations, of course, but, if it does, its genesis in the market place is simply irrelevant and cannot of itself evidence deceitful intent.

The broadest protection under the Doctrine of Equivalents is reserved for pioneer or generic patents, which cover a function never before performed, a wholly novel device, or one of such novelty and importance as to mark a distinct step in an art's progress as distinguished from a mere improvement or perfection of what had gone before. Liberality is the keynote of construction of a pioneer patent. The claims of a patent whose language specifically teaches away from the method employed in the accused structure is not infringed by such accused structure under the Doctrine of Equivalents.

The court has rejected the view that virtually any claim amendment creates a file wrapper estoppel, now known as prosecution history estoppel, effective to bar all resort to the Doctrine of Equivalents and to confine the patentee strictly to the letter of the claims granted. Amendment of claims is a common practice in the prosecution of patent applications, and there is no reason for limiting application of the Doctrine of Equivalents to those comparatively few claims allowed exactly as originally filed and never amended. When a patentee relies on the Doctrine of Equivalents to extend the scope of his claims, he opens the door to rebuttal based upon prior representations made by him to the PTO which appear in the file history.

The Doctrine of Equivalents is designed to avoid the necessity for an inventor being required to predict all future developments which would enable the practice of his invention in substantially the same way. For example, DuPont argued that so long as direct infringement is lacking, the grant of a patent to an accused infringer constitutes a *prima facie* determination of nonequivalence and, accordingly, noninfringement. The court disagreed, holding that where the material features of a patent had been appropriated, infringement will be found even when those features have been supplemented and modified to such an extent that the defendant may be entitled to a patent for an improvement.

The Doctrine of Prosecution History Estoppel is an equitable tool for determining the permissible scope of patent claims as against a specific structure accused of infringement. Further, amendment of claims during prosecution does not necessarily bar all benefit of the Doctrine of Equivalents to restrict a patentee to the literal language of the claims; it depends upon the nature and purpose of the amendment, the reasons therefor. Where a patentee's amendment was not required in response to a rejection or critical to the allowance of claims, no estoppel is created. Similarly, an estoppel is not necessarily created by an amendment designed only to remove a Section 112 indefiniteness rejection.

Infringement under the Doctrine of Equivalents raises material issues of fact, therefore, there should be no summary judgment. Infringement, either literal or by equivalents, must be determined by comparing the accused device with the claims in suit, not with the preferred or commercial embodiment.

Literal Infringement

Although literal infringement of a properly interpreted claim is a fact question, its determination may be rendered clearly erroneous through an improper interpretation and application of the governing law. Further, infringement requires a comparison between the asserted claims and the product or process accused of infringement, not a comparison between parts of the description in the patent and the accused product or process, or a comparison between commercial products. Modifying an accused device by merely adding elements or functions cannot negate infringement.

The construction of a claim is a question of law, and if the language of the claim is not disputed, then the scope must be construed as a matter of law. An underlying factual issue exists, however, when the meaning of a term in a claim is disputed and extrinsic evidence is necessary to explain the term. The second inquiry, which is the ultimate determination of infringement, is a fact issue, and a motion for summary judgment on that issue should be approached with great care.

To interpret means-plus-function claims, it is necessary to resort to the last paragraph of Section 112, which expressly states that a patentee is entitled to a claim covering equivalents of the specified structure, material or acts, and that such a patent claim is construed to cover both the disclosed structure as well as equivalents thereof. In construing means-plus-function claims, a number of factors may be considered, including the language of the claim, the specification, the prosecution history of the patent, other claims in the patent, and expert testimony.

Oftentimes, confusion has resulted where courts have mistakenly held Section 112 literal infringement equivalents when the Doctrine of Equivalents should have been relied on; this latter comes into play only when literal infringement is not found. Once the accused device is found to be equivalent under Section 112, a question of fact, then literal infringement has properly been established. As an aid to ascertaining equivalents under Section 112, last par., the specification, prosecution history, and so on, may be considered.

On November 6, 1987, the Federal Circuit issued its decision in *Pennwalt Corp. v. Durand-Wayland Inc.* The court made an effort to clarify the analytical framework that it thought should guide the trial courts in assessing infringement:

1. Read the literal language of each element of the asserted claim on the accused device. If the literal language does not read on the accused device, the literal infringement inquiry ends, and infringement can only be found under the Doctrine of Equivalents.
2. If the literal language of the claim does read on the accused device, determine whether any of the elements are expressed in means-plus-function language in accordance with Section 112, 6th par.
3. If the claim literally reads on the accused device, and an element of the claim is written in means-plus-function language, determine whether the structure in the accused device which performs the function is the same as or an equivalent to the structure in the specification for performing that function. If the structure in the accused device is not equivalent to that disclosed in the specification for performing the function of any

element of the claim written in means-plus-function language, the literal infringement inquiry ends, and infringement can only be found under the Doctrine of Equivalents.

4. If the claim literally reads on the accused device, and all means-plus-function elements find equivalent structure in the accused device, a *prima facie* case of literal infringement is established. To rebut that *prima facie* case, it must be shown that the accused device is so far changed in principle from the claimed invention that it does not achieve substantially the same result, does not perform substantially the same work, or performs the same or similar work in a substantially different way. That rebuttal is commonly known as the Reverse Doctrine of Equivalents.
5. Under the Doctrine of Equivalents:
   (a) Determine whether the accused device achieves substantially the *same result* as the claimed invention. If the accused device does not, the infringement inquiry is ended.
   (b) Determine whether the accused device performs substantially the *same work* as the claimed invention. If the accused device does not, the infringement inquiry is ended.
   (c) Determine whether the accused device operates in substantially the *same way* as the claimed invention. In so doing, compare each element of the claim with the accused device to determine whether the accused device contains each element or its substantial equivalent. A substantial equivalent is one that causes the accused device to operate in substantially the same way as the claimed invention, considering the nature, purpose, and quality of the element and its corresponding structure in the accused device.

This analytical framework can be set forth schematically as follows, as shown in Nieman, "The Federal Circuit Resolves Ambiguities in the Doctrine of Equivalents," 70 JPTOS, 153–158 (1988) (see page 81).

While the scope of claims under Section 112 is a legal determination, it is not devoid of equitable considerations, particularly when determining the breadth of means claims on complex and evolving technologies.

In *Texas Instruments v. U.S. ITC* (November 1986), the accumulated differences distinguished the accused calculators from that contemplated in the patent and transcended a fair range of equivalents, considering the invention as a whole. Thus, even where one has literal infringement, in this case, the technological changes transcended equitable limits and propelled the accused devices beyond a just scope of the claims.

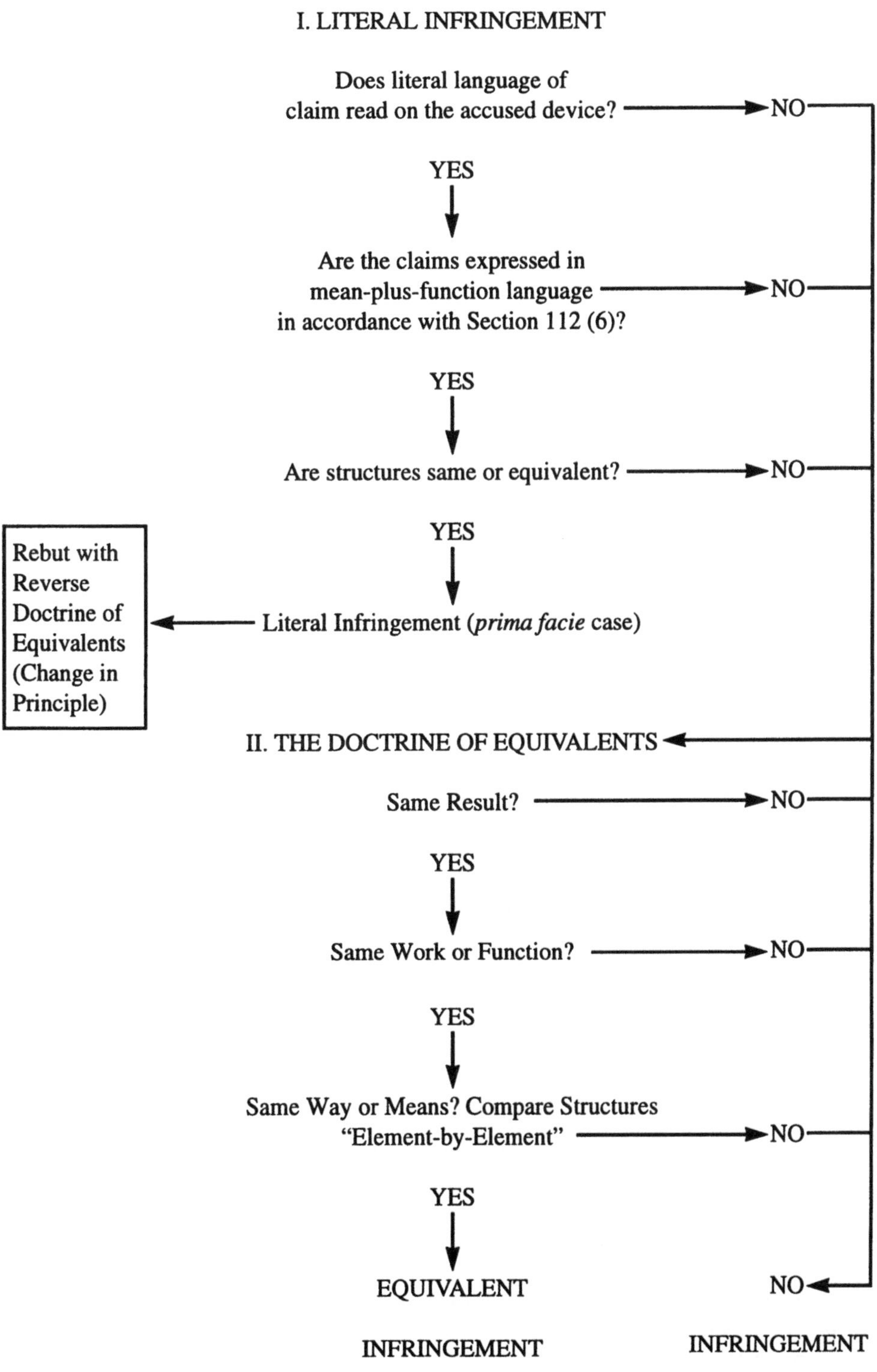
I. LITERAL INFRINGEMENT
Does literal language of claim read on the accused device?
NO
YES
Are the claims expressed in mean-plus-function language in accordance with Section 112 (6)?
NO
YES
Are structures same or equivalent?
NO
YES
Rebut with Reverse Doctrine of Equivalents (Change in Principle)
Literal Infringement (*prima facie* case)
II. THE DOCTRINE OF EQUIVALENTS
Same Result?
NO
YES
Same Work or Function?
NO
YES
Same Way or Means? Compare Structures "Element-by-Element"
NO
YES
EQUIVALENT
INFRINGEMENT
NO
INFRINGEMENT

In *Data Line v. Micro Technologies* (March 1987), the court noted that construction of a means-plus-function limitation in a claim is governed by 35 USC 112, last par., and covers the corresponding structure, material, or acts described in the specification and equivalents thereof. If all the other limitations in a claim are literally met and the accused device is shown to contain an equivalent of a structure which was identified in means-plus-function language and disclosed in the specification, infringement is literal, as distinguished from infringement under the Doctrine of Equivalents. In yet another case, the court noted that the specification, other claims in the patent, prosecution history, and expert testimony, may all be considered in ascertaining the scope of a claim under Section 112.

In *Spindelfabrik et al. v. Salzer* (September 1987), the Federal Circuit noted that a finding of literal infringement of a claim expressed in terms of a series of means for performing particular functions requires interpreting the claim to define the recited functions. If, as a threshold matter, the recited functions are not performed by the accused device, then there can be no literal infringement. On the other hand, if the recited functions are performed, it must be determined whether the means by which the accused device performs each function is the same as or equivalent to the means disclosed in the specification for performing each function.

In *Tandon v. U.S. ITC* (September 1987), the CAFC explained that claim interpretation is a question of law having factual underpinnings, and that when the meaning of key terms is disputed, extrinsic evidence may be adduced, including testimony of witnesses, and reference may be had to the specification, the prosecution history, prior art, and other claims.

Pennwalt v. Durand-Wayland (November 1987), Section 112, last par., rules out the possibility that any means which performs the function specified in the claim literally satisfies the invention, and that while such means encompass equivalents of those disclosed in the specification, Section 112 nevertheless acts as a restriction on the literal satisfaction on a claim limitation. The court pointed out that if the required function is not performed *exactly* in the accused device, there is no infringement under Section 112, last par.

What constitutes infringement of a patent of course varies with the nature or scope of the invention on which the patent is based; and depends upon the language of the claims, judicial interpretation of the language of the claims, specification and file history, and on the Doctrine of Equivalents. In determining infringement, the initial inquiry is whether the structural features of an accused device embody each and every element of a patent claim as properly construed in light of the specification and the prosecution history.

A 1984 Federal Circuit decision in the *Atlas Powder Co. v. E. I. DuPont de Nemours & Co.* case is important for reemphasizing a basic tenet of infringement law:

> DuPont concedes that, if Atlas patents A + B + C and DuPont then patents the improvement A + B + C + D, DuPont is liable to Atlas for any manufacture, use or sale of A + B + C + D because the latter directly infringes claims to A + B + C. DuPont urges, however, that it is not liable for manufacture, use or sale of patented improvement A + B + C', even though A + B + C' is "equivalent" to A + B + C. We reject DuPont's attempted distinction. Whether DuPont makes A + B + C + D or A + B + C', DuPont has used the gist of Atlas' invention to devise a patentable composition. There is no compelling reason to hold DuPont liable for infringement in one instance but not the other.

In another case, the Court of Appeals, in holding literal infringement, would not consider arguments concerning infringement pursuant to the Doctrine of Equivalents.

The Federal Circuit has also held:

> a patent holder was not precluded from taking a position in a subsequent action inconsistent with a position taken in a prior action if the opposing party in the subsequent action fails to demonstrate either
> (1) personal reliance on the decision granted in the prior suit,
> (2) prejudice to its litigation of the issues in the present suit by reason of the decision in the prior suit, or
> (3) the patent holder's apparent misuse of the court.

The question of infringement in *Hormone Research and Hoffmann La Roche v. Genentech* (1990) was decided against the patent holder on Genentech's motion for summary judgment. A number of important rulings were made in this suit; but, first it should be noted that the Federal Circuit has upheld the granting of summary judgment motions in favor of accused infringers, where the claims do not read on the accused structure and a prosecution history estoppel makes clear that no actual infringement under the Doctrine of Equivalents can be found. As to some of the holdings:

1. The court recognized and stated that literal infringement can only be found after properly interpreted claims are determined to read on the accused product or method.
2. The court stated that "in chemical structures as sensitive as these the literal infringement showing must be exacting."
3. The court remarked that, while infringement under the Doctrine of Equivalents is a question of fact, application of the

Doctrine of Prosecution History Estoppel to limit application of that doctrine is a question of law.

4. The court focused on the requirement that a patent must enable one skilled in the art to make and use the claimed invention, stating that "the problem was that HGH could not, given the state of scientific knowledge at the time the application was filed, be produced by the solid phase process in a homogeneous form which could be used as HGH."

The court granted Genentech's motion for summary judgment of invalidity.

Doctrine of Equivalents

Background. Direct infringement of a patent claim is either literal or via the Doctrine of Equivalents. Since literal infringement is rare, almost all judicial decisions involve the doctrine in one way or another. Consequently, this section is quite lengthy in order to provide the reader with a "feeling" for its development over the years. Unless one has this understanding, it will be difficult to protect one's rights when challenged by the doctrine.

The Doctrine of Equivalents was first declared by the Supreme Court in 1853 in *Winans v. Denmead,* wherein the Court stated that "the exclusive right to the thing patented is not secured, if the public are at liberty to make substantial copies of it, varying its form or proportions." It brought equity into the determination of infringement.

A more specific characterization of the doctrine came in 1877 in *Machine Co. v. Murphy,* wherein the Court stated: "If two devices do the same work, in substantially the same way, and accomplish substantially the same result, they are the same even though they differ in name, form or shape." This has become known as the *function-way-result* test, or the so-called "tripartite" test.

Other quotations from the early cases are:

1880 "attempted evasion by infringers who adopted substantially similar process"; and

1892 "use of an old and well-known mechanical equivalent... obviously intended to evade the wording of the claims."

This was followed in 1929 by *Sanitary Refrigerator Co. v. Winters,* in which the Supreme Court repeated essentially the same language, again expressing distaste for the practice of copying the essence of a claimed invention.

The Supreme Court, in *Graver Tank v. Linde Air Products Co.* (1950), summarized the historical basis of the doctrine, including its equitable nature, as follows:

> [C]ourts have also recognized that to permit imitation of a patented invention which does not copy every literal detail would be to convert the protection of the patent grant into a hollow and useless thing. Such a limitation would leave room for—indeed encourage—the unscrupulous copyist to make unimportant and insubstantial changes and substitutions in the patent which, though adding nothing, would be enough to take the copied matter outside the claim, and hence outside the reach of the law. One who seeks to pirate an invention, like one who seeks to pirate a copyrighted book or play, may be expected to introduce minor variations to conceal and shelter the piracy. Outright and forthright duplication is a dull and very rare type of infringement. To prohibit no other would place the inventor at the mercy of verbalism and would be subordinating substance to form.... The doctrine of equivalents evolved in response to this experience. The essence of the doctrine is that one may not practice a fraud on a patent.

According to recent commentary, "No single issue has sparked more controversy in patent law over the last few years than the doctrine of equivalents." It is one of the most difficult concepts in the law of patents and currently one of the most hotly debated at both bench and bar. As the doctrine evolved from *Graver Tank* in the modern era, its typical application was in cases in which, overall, the products or processes did the same thing to get the same result as the patented invention. Often lost was the third leg of the *Graver Tank* test, getting there in "a substantially different way." The application of the Doctrine of Equivalents became uneven.

The question can be stated simply: When would an accused infringer be liable for patent infringement even though technically avoiding the literal language of the claims? The difficulty in answering this question has caused a division among the judges of the Court of Appeals for the Federal Circuit and arguably inconsistent decisions between panels. Major changes, including a philosophical shift by the U.S. Court of Appeals for the Federal Circuit, are in progress. Concepts such as the function, way, and result of an invention are not easy to resolve in any given factual situation, and the factual situations vary considerably. In the last few years, however, the Federal Circuit has begun to focus on equitable considerations such as copying in applying the doctrine.

Especially noteworthy is the fact that early in December 1993, the Federal Circuit in a pending case, *Hilton-Davis Chemical Co. v. Warner-*

Jenkinson Co., requested *sua sponte* (voluntarily) the briefing of certain procedural issues that have significant substantive consequences for the doctrine. It is hoped that a decision on this appeal will be available shortly; further guidance is critical.

The doctrine did not originate strictly as a way to catch infringers who avoided the literal language of patent claims. The doctrine was primarily an equitable one, to be applied against copyists who made only slight changes in the form of the invention. In *Winans,* for example, the Court specifically identified "copying" in its reasons for giving a scope of coverage beyond that disclosed in the patent. Thus, from its origination and into the twentieth century, application of the doctrine generally required more than just a simple comparison of function, way, and result of the invention to the accused device. Equitable considerations, such as copying by the infringer, also were used to justify its application.

Graver Tank is first and foremost a *copying* case. Specifically, the Court held only that a patentee "may invoke" the doctrine to "prevent an infringer from stealing the benefit of an invention," and that the doctrine was "available for utilization when the *proper circumstances* for its application arise." The opinion does not spell out what the proper circumstances are for applying the doctrine. The Court posed the question to be answered, however, as to whether under the circumstances the change was so insubstantial that the trial court's invocation of the doctrine was justified. Therefore, the doctrine would clearly not apply unless the change in the accused product from the patented invention is insubstantial.

Another circumstance in which the doctrine would not apply is where its application is barred by prosecution history estoppel. Furthermore, the Court in *Graver Tank* noted that the range of equivalents varies with the circumstances. Finally, the one circumstance in *Graver Tank* that cannot be ignored is the lack of independent development by the infringer.

In the three decades following the decision in *Graver Tank,* the courts were generous in their application of the doctrine. The Court has often noted the equitable nature of the doctrine, but rarely have equitable factors come into play. Instead, the focus in the Federal Circuit has largely been on the tripartite test for equivalency clearly set forth in *Graver Tank.* Since how equivalency to a specific claim limitation is met necessarily varies from case to case and is not subject to a rigid formula, it is not surprising that confusion and contradiction have resulted. But this is not entirely the fault of the Federal Circuit. The problem seems to be inherent with trying to give meaning to such an amorphous test.

Perhaps in recognition of the fact that the court has gone as far as it can with the function-way-result, the Federal Circuit has looked for new ways to decide how and when the doctrine should be applied. Ironically, the court has returned to the equitable origins of the doctrine that seem largely forgotten since *Graver Tank.* The following discussion traces this trend in the recent cases of the Federal Circuit.

In 1987, the Federal Circuit decided *Perkin-Elmer v. Westinghouse Electric Corp.* Chief Judge Markey, writing for the majority, found the accused Westinghouse lamp did the same thing to get the same result as the claimed lamp, but not in the same way when viewed against each of the specific elements or limitations of the claims. The majority concluded that the element Westinghouse substituted in the lamp for the corresponding element in the claim was so different as to change the way the element performed; therefore, no infringement. In *Perkin-Elmer* a hypothetical modification of an accused device in order to make it more nearly equivalent to a claimed invention argued against a finding of infringement under the doctrine.

Judge Newman, in strong dissent in *Perkin-Elmer,* argued that the element-by-element approach adopted by the majority ignored the underlying basis for the doctrine, by which appropriation of the "gist" or "essence" or "heart" of the patented invention constitutes infringement under the doctrine. Thus, she charged, the majority had departed from *Graver Tank* and invoked a "new interpretation of the principles of physics and law."

Pennwalt. The issue of overall versus element-by-element analysis thus was clearly joined, and later that year sitting *en banc* in *Pennwalt Corp. v. Durand-Wayland Inc.* (1987), the majority in a 7-to-4 decision again emphasized the importance of an element-by-element claim analysis as the starting point in determining equivalence, as in assessing literal infringement. The result was no infringement and a strict application of the mechanistic test of the All Elements Rule.

The Federal Circuit began its discussion of infringement under the Doctrine of Equivalents by noting that in applying this doctrine each limitation in a claim must be viewed in the context of the entire claim, that it was well settled that each element in a claim is material and essential, and that in order for a court to find infringement the plaintiff must show the presence of every element or its substantial equivalent in the accused device. To be a substantial equivalent the element substituted in the accused device for the element set forth in the claim must not be such as would substantially change the way in which the function of the claimed invention is performed.

There were dissenting opinions in this case which are important. According to Judge Newman, the sweeping rule which treats all functions mentioned in a claim as being essential simply because they are there and bars consideration of the significance of any function in the overall invention or in any part thereof is an incorrect application of the Doctrine of Equivalents and is contrary to the precedents of the Supreme Court and Federal Circuit. She stated further that the requirement that every part of a function must be discretely performed in an accused device, one-to-one, whatever significance to the invention as a whole, was contrary to overwhelming body of precedent.

Another dissent said that a court is required to consider each element of a claim on an element-by-element basis and look for correspondence in the alleged infringing device. If an accused device does not contain at least an equivalent for each claim limitation, there can be no infringement because a required part of the claimed invention is missing.

There often can be no clear line between literal and substantive infringement under the Doctrine of Equivalents. It is

> well settled that each element of a claim is material and essential, and that in order for a court to find infringement, the plaintiff must show the presence of every element or its substantial equivalent in the accused device.
>
> [I]n applying the Doctrine of Equivalents, the fact finder must determine the *range of equivalents* to which the claimed invention is entitled, in light of the prosecution history, the *pioneer/non-pioneer status* of the invention, and the prior art. It must then be determined whether the entirety of the accused device or process is "substantially the same thing, used in substantially the same way, to achieve substantially the same result . . ." as to fall within that range.

The Federal Circuit has clearly held that improvements based on post-patenting state-of-the-art can give rise to infringement under the Doctrine of Equivalents. Even if a device is recognized as being similar to another as described in a valid patent claim, it does not mean that the device necessarily infringes under the Doctrine of Equivalents. The entire device must also be substantially equivalent. For two devices to be substantially equivalent, "the element substituted in the accused device for the element set forth in the claim must not be such as would *substantially change the way* in which the function of the claimed invention is performed."

Once the court answers affirmatively the threshold question of whether the doctrine applies to a particular situation, it next addresses the critical question with regard to infringement under the doctrine, that is, do the substituted elements perform substantially the same work or function in substantially the same way to obtain substantially the same result?

The Doctrine of Equivalents can be applied in reverse so that even where literal infringement is found, the infringer will be relieved of liability if it can be shown that the "device is so far changed in principle from a patented article that it performs the same or a similar function in a *substantially different manner,* but nevertheless falls within the literal words of the patent."

Pennwalt, therefore, has adopted the requirement that the Doctrine of Equivalents be applied on an element-by-element basis as opposed to application by looking at the invention as a whole.

Pennwalt cited *Prouty v. Draper* (1841) for the precedent that where a part of the claimed invention, that is, a limitation of the claim, is lacking in the accused device exactly or equivalently, there is no infringement. The *Pennwalt* decision has been the subject of criticism that the Federal Circuit had, in effect, overruled its own decisions in *Hughes Aircraft v. United States* and *Texas Instruments v. United States International Trade Commission.*

The use of an as-a-whole test in *Hughes* was later sought to be clarified by Chief Judge Markey in his subsequent opinion in *Perkin-Elmer,* where the court took the position that the application of an as-a-whole test in *Hughes* was not error since *Hughes* concerned a Doctrine of Equivalents inquiry involving an entire claim and not a Section 112, 6th par. literal infringement inquiry involving only a means-plus-function clause.

Nota bene: The word *equivalent* in the Doctrine of Equivalents and in Section 112, 6th par., obviously do not mean the same thing, as is explored further below.

There still appears to be a major split in the Federal Circuit if one looks at some of the dissenting opinions. The CAFC has also said,

> In determining equivalence under section 112 . . . "[T]he court must compare the accused structure with the disclosed structure and must find equivalent *structure* as well as identity of claimed *function* for that structure."

In *Sun Studs v. ATA Equipment* (CAFC 1989):

> An apparatus claim describing a combination of components does not require that the function of each be performed by a separate structure in the apparatus. The claimed and accused devices must be viewed and evaluated as a whole.

In another 1989 case, the CAFC commented that there is no legally recognizable or protected essential element, gist, or heart of an invention in a combination patent.

Texas Instruments Inc. v. U.S. International Trade Commission (1986), rehearing denied *en banc* (Fed. Cir. 1988): In denying the TI petition for rehearing, the Federal Circuit discussed points raised by the parties and an *amicus* brief, including infringement of pioneer patents, literal infringement and the Reverse Doctrine of Equivalents.

In 1986, the Federal Circuit had affirmed the ITC's finding of no patent infringement for TI's pioneer patent relating to hand-held calculators. The prior decision construed the claims pursuant to 35 USC 112, 6th par., because all of the elements of the claims are in means-plus-function form. The court held that

> though every function of the claimed combination was performed in the accused devices, the structures performing those functions were not equivalents of the structures disclosed in the patent.

Regarding pioneer patents, the court stated that there

> is not a discontinuous transition from "mere improvement" to "pioneer" . . . The judicially "liberal" view of both claim interpretation and equivalency accorded a "pioneer" invention, is not a manifestation of a different legal standard based on an abstract legal concept denominated "pioneer." *Rather, the "liberal" view flows directly from the relative sparseness of prior art in nascent fields of technology.*

The court then held that the pioneer status of the TI patent did not change the way infringement is determined, and that the scope of the claims is determined by considering the patentee's disclosure, the prosecution history, and the prior art. The court concluded that, for the reasons discussed in its prior opinion, the claims failed to encompass the accused devices under the Doctrine of Equivalents.

The court then reviewed the ITC's findings of no literal infringement. While the CAFC agreed with the conclusion of the commission, it stated that the commission's methodology was flawed because "it analyzed each corresponding structure in the accused devices as if such structure were the only difference between the accused device and the claimed device."

Rather, the patentability of TI's combination of input, electronics, and display functions,

> depended on the *totality* of changes in the structures by which the functions were performed . . . it is the *totality* of means that achieved the claimed pocket-size calculator, as it is the *totality* of modified means that constitutes the accused calculators. Thus, the equivalency of each changed means is evaluated in the context of the accused device *as a whole.*

Commenting on the arguments of the *amici,* which suggested applying the Reverse Doctrine of Equivalents, the court stated that such an application would be inappropriate because, to be invoked, there must be a finding of literal infringement. Because the claims were not literally infringed, the Reverse Doctrine of Equivalents did not apply.

The test for equivalents under 35 USC 112 and the Doctrine of Equivalents is the tripartite test of the Supreme Court in *Graver Tank,* "if it performs substantially the same function in substantially the same way to obtain the same result." It should be emphasized at the outset, however, that while 112 focuses on those equivalents of those elements alone, the Doctrine of Equivalents focuses on the entire claim to determine equivalents of the claim as a whole. Equivalents under 112 are a question of fact.

The range of equivalents to which MPF language extends is therefore determined differently under 112 and the Doctrine of Equivalents. Equivalents under 112 take into consideration:

1. specification,
2. prosecution history,
3. other claims in the patent,
4. expert testimony, and
5. the language of the asserted claims.

The range of equivalents is not unlimited, even for pioneer inventions which are normally entitled to a broad range of equivalents. The CAFC in the 1986 *Texas Instruments* case viewed the claims as a whole and found no infringement, since, viewed as a whole, they were not entitled to the broad range of equivalents which would have been required to find literal infringement under 112. While it is still the rule that prosecution history estoppel does not apply in a literal infringement analysis, the prosecution history has a place in the analysis, and should never be ignored. In practice, the practitioner should disclose equivalent structures or devices in broad, general terms. Alternate structures which are not species of generic terms should be specifically disclosed in the specification to avoid even the necessity of an analysis as to whether the accused structure is the equivalent of the generic structure.

First, under the Doctrine of Equivalents the accused device/process is compared with the entire claim. While the equivalents of individual elements in the claim are sometimes important, they are not determinative in a Doctrine of Equivalents analysis. Second, under Section 112 the range is determined with special emphasis on the specification (as in the last paragraph), whereas, under the Doctrine of Equivalents, the range is determined without such weighted reference to the specification. In the case of devices and processes, the CAFC has outlined the procedure for making a Doctrine of Equivalents determination as follows:

In examining literal infringement of the means-plus-function clauses, the court determined that not just any means for performing a function is covered by a means-plus-function claim under Section 112, paragraph 6, but only equivalents that are shown in the specification of the *Pennwalt* patent. Hence, the court stated:

> [T]he statute means exactly what it says: to determine whether a claim limitation is meant literally, where expressed as a means for performing a stated function, the court must compare the accused device with a disclosed structure and must find equivalent structure as well as identity of claim function for that structure.

The court stated further that if the function of the means-plus-function clause is not carried out by the accused infringing device exactly, then Section 112, paragraph 6, "plays no role" in determining equivalency. Hence, in order to find literal infringement, a comparison must be made between the accused infringing device and the structure disclosed in the specification; and, equivalent structure, as well as identity of the claimed functions for the structure of the accused infringing device, must be found in the specification.

The most controversial portions of the *Pennwalt* decision were contained in the statement of the CAFC that the patent owner "must show the presence of every element or its substantial equivalent in the accused device . . . ," citing *Perkin-Elmer* and thereby ratifying the element-by-element comparison used by the District Court.

> It is clear from this that the district court correctly relied on an element-by-element comparison to conclude that there was no infringement under the doctrine of equivalents, because the accused devices did not perform substantially the same functions as the *Pennwalt* invention.

The dissent objected to element-by-element and relied upon the decision in *Hughes Aircraft v. U.S.* Judge Nies' "Additional Views" in the *Pennwalt* case distinguished the *Hughes Aircraft* decision.

> The *Hughes* analysis was directed to the confusing concept of equivalency under the doctrine and the different concept of equivalency under Section 112, paragraph 6. When we spoke of the doctrine applying to the "invention as a whole," it was not *by implication or sub silentio* rejecting the All Elements Rule. It was subsequently explained that the "statement dealt with *infringement* inquiry implicating an entire claim, as distinguished from a section 112, paragraph 6 inquiry implicating only a means plus function limitation of a claim." [See *Perkin-Elmer.*] As a careful reading of *Hughes* makes clear, the *elements* of the claim define

> the metes and bounds of protection, and an equivalent of each element was found in the accused device.

In support of the majority opinion, Judge Nies' additional views point out that the All Elements Rule is a well-known principle of patent law stating,

> [t]hus, when an element is entirely *missing,* that is, when the accused device does not contain either the exact element of the claim *or* its equivalent, there is no infringement. Conversely, an element is not "missing" if an equivalent has been substituted.

Judge Markey further defines a statement from the *Hughes* case with the following:

> That statement dealt with an infringement inquiry implicating an entire claim, as *distinguished from* a Section 112, Paragraph 6 inquiry implicating only a "means plus function" limitation of a claim. That statement was also a recognition that, in applying the doctrine of equivalents, each limitation must be viewed in the context of the entire claim. This statement should not be interpreted as sanctioning the treatment of claim limitations as insignificant or immaterial in determining infringement.

It would appear that while all limitations are important, some limitations, such as those that relate to the essence of the invention, are more important than others.

The meaning and application of 35 USC 112, 6th par., has been one of the most troublesome questions of infringement law. The distinction made in the *Texas Instruments* case, and by the panel in its denial of rehearing, is at best a fine line calling for the exercise of judgment. The accused calculators identically performed every function recited in the claim. Any one structure in the accused calculators could be held to be an equivalent of the structure performing the means described in the patent, if viewed in isolation. However, the cumulative effect of the changes in the accused calculators were so different from the calculator disclosed in the specification that the interactions of the various individual structures, each perhaps structurally equivalent to its corresponding means in the patent specification, were nevertheless not equivalent to those disclosed structures when viewed in the context of the entire device.

The Federal Circuit made clear in *Pennwalt* that literal infringement of means-plus-function claims require identity of function and then equivalent structure. In *RCA Corp. v. Data General Corp.* (D. Del. 1988), where the District Court merely found that both structure and function were equivalent, it technically found infringement by equivalents and not literal infringement of means-plus-function claims. While in general this might appear to be mere semantics, a finding of infringement under the Doctrine of Equivalents triggers the possibility of prosecution history estoppel that does not exist, or does not exist to the same extent, in assessing literal infringement.

Confusion in the Patent Bar. This Doctrine of Equivalents has led to considerable confusion, not only in the patent bar, but also in the lower courts, the Federal Circuit, and among a number of patent law commentators. It is probably not surprising that due to the countless number of products and processes in the world, some will be very close in appearance to others. Furthermore, in some instances, the problem is due to a basic misunderstanding of the very nature of our claiming system as compared with that of other countries.

Some commentators have gone so far as to say that the *Graver Tank* decision of the Supreme Court was overruled by the adoption of the Patent Act of 1952 due to the inclusion of the 6th paragraph of Section 112; that Congress intended only a restrictive, or narrow, application of the doctrine.

Nevertheless, as far back as the early 1800s, long before *Winans,* it was noted, "[mere] colourable differences, or slight improvements, cannot shake the right of the original inventor."

As recently as 1971, one commentator wrote, "[U]nder the modern U.S. Court decisions, the application of the doctrine of equivalents may render the claim either co-extensive with its terms or narrower. It never broadens the claim."

Another went on to say, "Under the *central definition system* the doctrine of equivalents broadens the claims—under the *peripheral system* the doctrine of equivalents narrows them." And again, "As anything 'which is not literally within the scope of the claim does not infringe', the doctrine of equivalents cannot extend the claim boundaries."

Our system of claiming is a peripheral system in that the claims define the "metes and bounds" of the invention, that is, as with real estate so that the public may know the precise limits of the patentee's rights. In other countries, the central system is used which defines the "core" or "gist" of the invention in the claims, leaving their courts to determine the precise limits of the patentee's rights. At least, those are the principles involved. However, the extreme central versus peripheral considerations are not supported under the U.S. case law in infringement cases.

The 1887 Supreme Court *Westinghouse* precedent, if anything, stands for the proposition that there is an exception to the Doctrine of Equivalents; that while the generally recognized Doctrine of Equivalents is used to broaden claims beyond their literal scope, it is recognized in the legal literature that as an exception claims may also be narrowed. This case is properly cited for the Reverse Doctrine of Equivalents.

In modern case law, there is seldom a word about the Doctrine of Equivalents as a doctrine for narrowing the scope of the claims of a patent. Rather, there are literally hundreds of examples where the issue considered has been whether the claims should be broadened beyond their literal scope to find infringement (versus whether the claims should be limited to their literal scope). In the real world of claim interpretation in the United States, the interplay between file wrapper estoppel and the Doctrine of Equivalents must also be confronted. This interplay would be meaningless if the Doctrine of Equivalents were a doctrine to narrow claims; there would be no reason for the Doctrine of File Wrapper Estoppel.

The Doctrine of Equivalents is an equitable doctrine created by the courts to do justice to the inventor so that one may not pirate another's invention by the mere substitution of "equivalents" which would be known to those skilled in the art. As has been said by courts many times, claim interpretation is not an exercise in mere literary skill. The Doctrine of Equivalents is relevant to the claim or the invention "as a whole."

Whereas, 35 USC 112, 6th par.,

> An element in a claim for a combination may be expressed as a means or step for performing a specified function without the recital of structure, material or acts in support thereof, and such *claim* shall be construed to cover the corresponding structure, material or acts described in the specification and *equivalents* thereof.

Perhaps, instead of saying "such claim shall be construed," it would have been clearer to have said "such *element* shall be construed."

In summary, the Doctrine of Equivalents has little to do with 35 USC 112, 6th par., which latter is restricted to the specification or equivalents thereof, whereas, the doctrine when used after having not found literal infringement has to do with the entire claim and the entire invention and the equities involved.

Corning. In *Corning Glass Works v. Sumitomo Elec. U.S.A. Inc.* (1989), the CAFC affirmed the District Court's (S.D.N.Y.) finding that Sumitomo's S-3 fiber infringed claims 1 and 3 of the '915 patent under the Doctrine of Equivalents by substituting an equivalent/interchangeable ingredient. The claimed invention was an optical waveguide wherein the index of refraction of the core was greater than the index of refraction of the cladding layer by means of adding dopant materials to each, *so that* "the index of refraction thereof is of a value greater than the index of refraction of said cladding layer."

In essence, the distinction between claim 1 of the '915 patent and the S-3 fiber was that the claim added a *positive* dopant material to the *core* to increase its index of refraction above that of the cladding layer, while the S-3 fiber added a *negative* dopant material to the *cladding* layer to lower its index of refraction below that of the core. It was undisputed that the S-3 fiber effected the same overall result as the claim, that is, a higher index of refraction in the core relative to the cladding layer. The dispute arose as to whether the S-3 fiber effected this result in "substantially the same way."

Sumitomo had argued that the S-3 fiber did not meet the *Pennwalt* standard because it lacked an element found in the claim, that is, a core having a dopant that made the index of refraction of the core greater than that of the cladding layer. However, the court disagreed with Sumitomo's characterization of what represented an element in the claim. The court reasoned that, under the All Elements Rule, an element is a claim limitation, whereas Sumitomo, according to the court, was arguing for an "equivalency of components." Furthermore, since a negative dopant in the cladding layer effected the same result as a positive dopant in the core, the All Elements Rule set down in *Pennwalt* was satisfied.

> Equivalency is a question of fact and must be resolved in each instance by analyzing the function of the elements or parts concerned [quoting *Tektronix, Inc. v. United States* (Ct. Cl. 1971)]. [I]t is appropriate for a court to consider in assessing equivalence whether the changed ingredient has the same purpose, quality, and function as the claimed ingredient [quoting *Atlas Powder Co. v. E. I. du Pont de Nemours & Co.* (Fed. Cir. 1984)].

The Federal Circuit, disagreeing that an element of the claim was entirely missing from the S-3 fibers, stated that Sumitomo's analysis illustrates the confusion from misunderstanding the term *element.* Element may be used to mean a single limitation, but it has also been used to mean a series of limitations which, taken together, make up a component of the claimed invention. In the All Elements Rule, element is used in the sense of a limitation of a claim.

Determining equivalency is not subject to such a rigid formula as expressed by Sumitomo that "it would require equivalency in components, that is, the substitution of something in the core for the absent dopant"; rather, the equivalent need only be present somewhere in the accused device, not necessarily in a corresponding component.

The Federal Circuit agreed with the District Court's finding that:

> [t]he use of fluorine as a [negative] dopant in the cladding thus performs substantially the same function in substantially the same way as the use of a [positive] dopant in the core to produce the same result of creating the refractive index differential between

the core and cladding of the fiber which is necessary for the fiber to function as an optical waveguide.

The Federal Circuit noted that its precedent does not set out a definitive formula for determining equivalency between a required limitation or a combination of limitations and what has been allegedly substituted therefor in the accused device. They found this to be a classic example of infringement under the Doctrine of Equivalents, stating that "[n]othing is taken from the 'public domain' when the issue of equivalency is directed to a limitation only, in contrast to the *entirety of the claimed invention.*"

In the *en banc* decision of *Pennwalt,* the CAFC adopted the All Elements Rule, that is, every claim element or its equivalent must be present in an accused device for that claim to read on the accused device. However, the seemingly clear answer given in *Pennwalt* was muddled in *Corning,* which further construed the "substantially the same way" part of the tripartite test for infringement under the Doctrine of Equivalents. *Corning* expansively defined a claim element under the All Elements Rule.

It should be noted that expressions such as "so that," as with the word "whereby," when properly used in a claim, introduce a clause describing the function or operation necessarily following from previously recited structure, whether a whole claim or an element thereof, that is, "it *necessarily* follows from the foregoing that." Such a "so that" clause is improper when it is used to imply structural or cooperational relationships which are not positively recited in the claim.

Second, *Corning* is significant because the decision of infringement was reached by focusing the equivalency inquiry on two limitations, not only what the element is (its structure), but also one of which was functional in character, that is, what the element does (that is, functional not in the sense of 35 USC 112, but functional in defining how the structural elements, components, or other limitations in the claim cooperate to produce a desired result of a particular part of the claim, invention, or of the entire invention). "Equivalence is not the prisoner of a formula. . . . Consideration must be given to the purpose for which an ingredient is used in a patent." [*Graver Tank*].

The court looked to *Graver Tank,* which advised that in determining equivalents an important factor is whether a person skilled in the art would have known of the interchangeability of an ingredient not contained in a patent with one that was. The court noted that those skilled in the art would have known of the interchangeability of fluorine as a negative dopant in the cladding for a positive dopant in the core.

Notably, neither *Corning* nor *Pennwalt* requires each element in the accused device to function in "substantially the same way" as a corresponding claimed element. The *Corning* opinion indicates that the District Court's "function/way/result" equivalency analysis with respect to a claim limitation (as opposed to an overall function/way/result of the entire claim) may be helpful in approaching the problem of equivalency. However, such is not a requirement.

In further support of its decision, the *Corning* court cited *Raytheon Co. v. Roper Corp.* (Fed. Cir. 1983), wherein claim 1 was held invalid because the "so that" functional clause in the claim rendered the claimed invention inoperative. This was the key to the determination of infringement. The key to the decision in *Corning* also appears to be the use of the "so that" functional clause. The functional clause defines the purpose of the dopant in the core, with respect to the dopant in the cladding, as providing an index of refraction in the core that was of a greater value than that of the index of refraction in the cladding layer. The "substantially in the same way" requirement of the Doctrine of Equivalents is met when the claimed "structural elements" are read in light of functional limitations and the limitations, taken together, are found at least equivalently in the accused device.

Practitioners rendering infringement opinions should be cautious of focusing their equivalency inquiry *only* on the "structural elements" without giving due consideration to functional limitations which, taken together, make up a "component" or part of the claimed invention. Likewise, practitioners drafting applications should consider utilizing at least a few claims having functional language which identifies the function and way in which the "structural elements" cooperate to produce the desired result. The use of functional language not only makes the claim more clearly defined and understandable but also may increase the chances that several of the "structural elements," if not all, will be taken together in determining equivalents at trial or on appeal. However, practitioners must be wary not to use functional language rendering the claimed subject matter inoperative.

The three-part test of *Graver Tank* is met only when *all* three parts of the test are met by the accused device. Quoting from another CAFC decision of 1987, the court said:

> The fact that the two devices achieved substantially the same results creates no presumption that they do so in substantially the same way.... The patentee has the burden of proof to show that the accused device infringes the patent claims, and to do so under the doctrine of equivalents requires a showing that all three components of the equivalency test are met.

A finding of equivalency is not supported, even though the same result was achieved, if it was not achieved in the same manner.

In conclusion, the *Corning* decision has extended the limits of the Doctrine of Equivalents by narrowing the All Elements Rule, even though a substitute element performs the "opposite" function of the claim element as long as the same result is obtained.

Corning has added to the uncertainty in the area of equivalence. In view of this uncertainty, industry will have difficulty predicting what would be considered a nonequivalent element for purposes of designing around a patent. Experience has shown that the Supreme Court formulation in *Graver Tank* is inadequate and has led to decisions which commentators have found ambiguous and confusing. Another commentator suggests that by analyzing the functional cooperation between combination claim limitations one can harmonize the opinions interpreting equivalents. Consideration of the doctrine to resolve an infringement issue assumes at least one difference between what is claimed and what is in an accused product.

There are many Federal Circuit decisions relying on equivalents in spite of differences in structure or structural cooperation between components of an accused product and analogous claim limitations. These cases demonstrate the futility of trying to predict equivalents based on structural variation alone. However, the differences in structure were of no significance to the functional cooperation of the claim limitations or accused elements taken in combination.

These cases illustrate the importance of designing a competing product that avoids the functional cooperation between claim limitations in order to avoid infringement. Avoiding claimed structure is insufficient.

Wilson. In *Wilson Sporting Goods Co. v. David Geoffrey & Assocs.* (1990), the Federal Circuit crafted a new analytical tool for resolving questions under the Doctrine of Equivalents: *hypothetical claim analysis.* Among the bar, this controversial case stimulated both oral and written discussion. Rather than refining the doctrine, the Federal Circuit added new and complex issues to the existing rules. Besides creating the hypothetical claim analytical tool, the court also held that an accused device could infringe a dependent claim under the doctrine without infringing the corresponding independent claim. This seemingly illogical holding generated substantial disbelief among the bar.

In applying the "Hypothetical Claim Doctrine," the court in *Wilson* creates hypothetical claims for the patent claims so that they read on the accused device, and if those "hypothetical" claims encompass the prior art, there is no infringement under the doctrine as in this case. Wilson's patent involved a golf ball having a certain configuration of dimples on the golf ball cover. In the District Court, the jury found that the accused balls of Dunlop infringed Wilson's patent under the Doctrine of Equivalents. Dunlop argued on appeal that allowing Wilson's "patent to reach Dunlop's balls under the doctrine of equivalents would improperly ensnare the prior art Uniroyal ball as well." Finding Dunlop's argument persuasive, the Federal Circuit reversed the finding of infringement.

The court first observed that the prior art necessarily must limit the range of a patented device's equivalents because "a patentee should not be able to obtain, under the doctrine of equivalents, coverage which he could not lawfully have obtained from the [Patent and Trademark Office] by literal claims."

The court then went on to say:

> [I]t may be helpful to conceptualize the limitation on the scope of equivalents by visualizing a *hypothetical* patent claim, sufficient in scope to *literally* cover the accused product. The pertinent question then becomes whether that hypothetical claim could have been allowed by the PTO over the prior art.

In other words, Wilson could not have written a claim that would literally cover the Dunlop ball, yet still be patentable over the prior art ball. The court's analysis did not end there, however; Judge Rich's opinion proceeded to examine whether Dunlop infringed any of Wilson's dependent claims.

Many practitioners have expressed doubt about a court's need to consider dependent claims after it has determined that an accused does not infringe an independent claim. After all, as the Federal Circuit has stated, "It is axiomatic that dependent claims cannot be found infringed unless the claims from which they depend have been found to have been infringed."

Before proceeding to investigate why the "axiom" can fail, a brief explanation of the nature of infringement may clarify the analysis. Much of the confusion caused by the apparent contradiction of the axiom and the analysis in *Wilson* results from the varied use of the term *infringement.* In one sense, infringement means that an accused device contains all of the claimed limitations or their substantial equivalents. When used in this manner, one might say that the accused device "factually infringes" the patent. In another sense, infringement means that a patent owner may obtain legal relief against an accused infringer under the patent laws. When such circumstances occur, one could say that the accused infringer "legally infringed" the patent. This difference should now be apparent: factual infringement is a necessary, but not a sufficient condition for legal infringement.

Because the axiom pertains only where the accused device does not factually infringe the independent claims, it does not apply in the *Wilson* factual setting. Indeed, the axiom may not hold true under the Doctrine of Equivalents. As noted, even if a patent owner establishes factual infringement under the doctrine, an accused infringer does not legally infringe a patent when either the prior art or prosecution history estoppel prevents such a finding. In *Wilson,* while Dunlop factually infringed the independent claim, it could not legally infringe it; such a holding would improperly ensnare the prior art Uniroyal ball.

The court then went on to hold that Dunlop did not legally infringe Wilson's patent because, although Dunlop's ball factually infringed some of the dependent claims, a holding of legal infringement of any dependent claims would improperly ensnare one or more prior art golf balls. The court's analysis demonstrates, however, that under different circumstances, an accused device could legally infringe a dependent claim without legally infringing an independent claim.

The principle results entirely from the prior art limitation to the range of equivalents. As Judge Rich observed, the prior art does not limit the range of equivalents in order to avoid a construction that would invalidate the claim. Rather, a court so limits the range of equivalents because a "patentee should not be able to obtain, under the doctrine of equivalents, coverage which he could not lawfully obtain from the PTO by literal claims."

Far from creating a new and bizarre principle of law in *Wilson,* the Federal Circuit merely expounded a principle that had long existed, yet remained undiscovered: a device can legally infringe a dependent claim of a patent under the Doctrine of Equivalents without legally infringing the corresponding independent claim where the device factually infringes the independent claim. This principle is independent of hypothetical claim analysis and only depends upon the legal rule that the prior art limits the permissible range of equivalents. Such a limitation has long existed in patent law.

On the other hand, some commentators say that the court has explicitly dictated an entirely new, and potentially exceedingly complex, test for determining whether or not a patent claim is infringed under the Doctrine of Equivalents. The rationale behind *Wilson* may very well transform infringement analysis into a near-impossible task and complicate the analytical process far beyond the Federal Circuit's original intent.

Nevertheless, *Graver Tank* and its discourse on the equities of the doctrine remains as the primary authority from the Supreme Court. Indeed, later decisions from the CAFC indicate a retreat from the element-by-element rule, or at least a continued split within that court as will be seen later. Thus, the prudent patentee will continue to offer evidence sufficient to prove its infringement case under both an element-by-element test and invention as a whole test.

Prior to *Wilson,* a determination of infringement, when taken to its fullest extent, involved resolving each of the following questions:

1. Has the patentee proven that the accused device or process literally fits within the asserted claims? If not,

2. How pioneering is the invention claimed in the asserted patent when examined in light of all the surrounding circumstances?
3. Has the patentee proven that the accused device or process performs substantially the same function in substantially the same way to achieve substantially the same result as the claimed invention? If yes,
4. Has the alleged infringer proven that the claimed invention is limited by the prosecution history so as not to cover the accused device or process? If not,
5. Has the alleged infringer proven that the asserted claim, if construed to cover the accused device or process, would be invalid in view of the prior art?

As extensive as this analysis appeared, it was, at least, manageable. *Wilson* has expanded question 5 to include not only an entire new series of issues, but has also shifted the burdens on those issues to different parties.

> Whether prior art restricts the range of equivalents of what is literally claimed can be a difficult question to answer. To simplify analysis and bring the issue onto familiar turf, *it may be helpful* to conceptualize the limitation on the scope of equivalence by visualizing *a hypothetical patent claim,* sufficient in scope to literally cover the accused product. The pertinent question then becomes whether that hypothetical claim could have been allowed by the PTO over the prior art. If not, then it would be improper to permit the patentee to obtain that coverage in an infringement suit under the doctrine of equivalents. If the hypothetical claim could have been allowed, then prior art is not a bar to infringement under the doctrine of equivalents.

While superficially the *Wilson* analysis seems easy enough to use, taken to its logical conclusion it will inject considerable confusion and complication into the presentation and consideration of evidence at trial. For example, the claim that the patentee is trying to prove "valid" is different than the claims that the defendant is trying to prove invalid.

It is well established that the burden of proving infringement is on the patentee and that an alleged infringer defending on the grounds of the invalidity of the asserted patent bears the burden of proving such invalidity. However, the patentee now has a burden of not only proving infringement, but also the subsidiary burden of proving the patentability of one or more hypothetical claims. Under the established law of infringement, it was axiomatic that a dependent claim could not be infringed unless the claim from which it depended was also infringed. This no longer holds true under *Wilson;* with respect to the hypothetical claim, no presumption of validity exists.

While it is too soon to tell, there is a distinct possibility that the end result of that decision will be a major expansion in the burdens imposed upon a patentee in pursuit of an infringement finding.

Current Trends. The first hint that the Federal Circuit was rethinking the doctrine as an *equitable* doctrine, and not one to be applied mechanically in every case came in *Slimfold Manufacturing Co. v. Kinkead Industries, Inc.* (1991). The court first noted that "application of the equitable doctrine of equivalents becomes desirable . . . only when the changes are so insubstantial as to result in a 'fraud on the patent.' " The court then set forth a preliminary test for when the doctrine should be applied:

> Thus, the *first question* which must be asked is *"has a substantial change been made?"* Only if the answer to that question is "no" should an accused infringer be liable for improperly trying to appropriate the claimed invention.

Because the court determined that the accused infringer's device did not operate in substantially the same way as the claimed invention, and therefore did not infringe under the doctrine, the court did not need to go beyond the tripartite test.

The opinion did, however, factor equitable considerations into its analysis. The court noted in particular that "the claimed invention is a mechanical combination in a crowded field" and was entitled only to a "narrow scope of equivalents." Thus, *Slimfold* revisits the idea that the Doctrine of Equivalents is an equitable doctrine, and that its application is "desirable" in only limited circumstances. It calls into question earlier statements to the effect that the doctrine comes into play whenever literal infringement is not found.

A fundamental weakness exists in determining the doctrine solely on the basis of the function-means-results test, as Judge Lourie has pointed out when asking the question, "Would ibuprofen infringe a patent on aspirin, since in a broad sense they appear to share the same function, means and result?"

Judge Rich stated that while "designing around patents" works to the advantage of the public, "It is only when the changes are so insubstantial as to result in 'a fraud on the patent' that application of the equitable doctrine of equivalents becomes desirable."

This brings us to the core question. Where is the law going in determining or applying the doctrine? The law appears to be going back to where it came from, to its roots in the Law of Equity.

Justice Jackson in *Graver Tank,* after inquiring as to whether it was known in the art to interchange the elements or whether it would be obvious to do so, observed, "And the record contains no evidence of any kind to show the Lincolnweld (the accused welding composition) was developed as the *result of independent research or experiments.*" This point about independent development has become an extremely important one.

The first case that attracted attention, however, was *London v. Carson Pirie Scott & Co.* In *London,* the Federal Circuit directly challenged the notion that the doctrine should be applied mechanically in every infringement case:

> Application of the doctrine of equivalents is *the exception, however, not the rule,* for if the public comes to believe (or fear) that the language of patent claims can never be relied on, and that the doctrine of equivalents is simply the second prong of every infringement charge, regularly available to extend protection beyond the scope of the claims, then claims will cease to serve their intended purpose. Competitors will never know whether their actions infringe a granted patent.

The opinion signifies a new focus on the equities and a return to the principles of *Graver Tank.*

London was a turning point in the doctrine. The public must be certain of the scope of the claims and the claim language. Dictum in *London* manifests a growing concern that application of the Doctrine of Equivalents has become a largely mechanistic application of the *Graver Tank* case. Concern has been raised in recent years that the pendulum between the rights of the patent owner and those of industry seeking to legitimately design around the claims of the patentee has skewed too far on the side of the patentee.

If there is one key element of the Doctrine of Equivalents that can be traced to its very origins it clearly is not the mechanistic function-means-result identity test. Rather, it is the element of *copying.* All of the earliest opinions from the members of the Supreme Court that form the basis of the doctrine were from circuit courts. Attention is given to the role of copying or piracy in the opinion of *London:*

> Although designing or inventing around patents to make new inventions is encouraged, piracy is not. Thus, where an infringer, instead of inventing around a patent by making a substantial change, merely makes an insubstantial change, essentially misappropriating or even "stealing" the patented invention, infringement may lie under the doctrine of equivalents.

While recognizing the element of copying, *London* breaks no new ground because it does not formulate a test of infringement that focuses on the equitable elements generally, or on copying or piracy specifically.

No equitable remedy such as the Doctrine of Equivalents should be straitjacketed into so inflexible a mode as the tripartite test of *Graver Tank.* If a universal, one-sentence formula is what is sought that is applicable to every situation, there will never be an answer, as equitable remedies cannot be crammed into a mechanistic, one-line formula or catch phrase. It should remain as *one* of the criteria for application of the doctrine. But where the *Graver Tank* test is met, however, this should not end the matter. Then, there should be more; then, the equitable nature of the doctrine should come into play.

In the end, the *London* case will be remembered as a correct holding of noninfringement within the parameters of the tripartite test of *Graver Tank,* but more importantly for the discussion of the equitable nature of the doctrine.

A commentator has noted that in the eighteen months ending in August 1993, Judge Lourie's dictum in *London* was cited with approval in ten decisions written by six different judges of the Federal Circuit. Thus, a majority on the Federal Circuit shares concerns that the equities should play a more conspicuous role in determining applicability of the doctrine.

The Doctrine of Equivalents is in a wind of change in two respects, separately identifiable but related. First, the Federal Circuit has voiced concerns that the doctrine in the past has been applied using the wrong analysis "overall" rather than "element-by-element." The consequence has been enlargement of patent scope and growing unpredictability in interpreting patents generally, to the detriment of the patent system and those who use it. Second, the Federal Circuit is finally revisiting *Graver Tank,* looking at its equitable origins. The court appears about to pronounce a necessary threshold proof of equity before a patent is infringed under the doctrine, even when the tripartite test is satisfied.

In *Insta-foam Products, Inc. v. Universal Foam Systems, Inc.* (1990), the court found no infringement using the tripartite test, and went on to say that simply because the accused's device contained an additional function, there was an insignificant difference between the patentee's and the accused's device.

In *Unique Concepts Inc. v. Brown,* decided in 1991, the Federal Circuit again found no infringement under the doctrine since the assembly functioned in a substantially different way from the corresponding element in the claims.

The shift to stricter patent interpretation appears in part motivated by a desire to reduce the fuzzy boundaries of patent claims. It also has produced a closer look at balancing the equities in applying the doctrine. Although the doctrine as expressed in *Graver Tank* was rooted in equity, it often has been applied when no equitable considerations were present or alleged.

In *Malta v. Schulmerich Carillons Inc.* (1991), once again the "way" leg of *Graver Tank* was pivotal and there was no infringement. The court specifically found that there was no evidence presented by the patentee as to "why" the function-means-result of the accused infringers device was the same as the patented device. The Federal Circuit did little to add some certainty to the troublesome issue of establishing infringement under the Doctrine of Equivalents. In *Malta,* Judge Rich stated that although the tripartite test set forth in *Graver Tank* is an acceptable way of showing that structure in an accused device is the substantial equivalent of a claim limitation according to *Pennwalt,* it is not the only way to do so. Judge Rich echoed the equitable principles set forth in *Graver Tank* and indicated that how equivalency to a required limitation is met varies from case to case depending upon many variables, and that there is no specific formula of general applicability for determining equivalency of a claim limitation.

More particularly, Judge Rich indicated that the Federal Circuit has never adopted the tripartite test set forth in *Graver Tank* to determine *equivalency of a limitation.* Furthermore, he said, *Pennwalt* did not set forth a test as to how one proves that an element in an accused device is the substantial equivalent of a claim limitation directed to a single element in dispute. This uncertainty is further compounded by the *Malta* panel's decision that the patentee must also explain why the overall function, way, and result of the accused device are substantially the same as those of the claimed device, and why the particular function in the accused device is the equivalent of the claimed limitation.

To establish infringement of a patent, every limitation set forth in a claim must be found in an accused product or process exactly (i.e., literal infringement) or by a substantial equivalent (i.e., infringement under the Doctrine of Equivalents). Correspondingly, the failure to meet a single limitation is sufficient to negate infringement of the claim. Thus, all claim elements are material and essential, and must be considered in order to determine whether a patent has been literally infringed. The less demanding standard under the Doctrine of Equivalents, as opposed to the exact similarity requirement of literal infringement, exists in order to hinder the "unscrupulous copyist" who could otherwise imitate a patented invention as long as he was careful not to copy every inconsequential detail of a claimed invention, or to make some "unimportant or insubstantial" change to the claimed invention.

Furthermore, because the test for equivalence derives from the principle that the public ought to be able to find out the precise limits of patent protection without recourse to a judicial ruling, application of the doctrine is the exception and not the rule. The doctrine is subject to two types of limitations which may prevent a finding of infringement: (1) estoppel based on the prosecution history of the patent; and (2) invalidity of the claims according to the proposed construction in view of the prior art.

Although the All Elements Rule of *Pennwalt* requiring an element-by-element analysis has been held to be the law of the Federal Circuit, this court has contravened this rule under certain factual circumstances. Specifically, in *Corning Glass,* the Federal Circuit stated that the term *element* was ambiguous and what the *Pennwalt* majority actually sought to promulgate was, in effect, an "All Limitations" rule. In other words, an equivalent must be found for every limitation of the claim somewhere in the accused device, but not necessarily in that corresponding element, although that is generally the case, there need not be one-to-one equivalency as to every component of the claimed invention.

Since *Pennwalt* was the last *en banc* decision by the Federal Circuit concerning the issue of infringement under the Doctrine of Equivalents, the element-by-element approach, as opposed to the "claim-as-a-whole" approach, set forth therein remains the controlling precedent in the Federal Circuit. In view of *Wilson,* a determination of infringement based on the doctrine cannot be made in a vacuum; the prior art must be examined to assure that the range of equivalents asserted by the patent holder does not encroach upon subject matter in the prior art.

As indicated above, a great deal of ambiguity remains concerning the establishment of infringement under the Doctrine of Equivalents. By adopting vague standards and then refusing to apply them uniformly, the Federal Circuit has done little to clarify this issue. Unfortunately, the Supreme Court is apparently unwilling to provide guidance in this area of patent law.

Explicit recognition of the equitable origins of the doctrine came in 1992 in *Charles Greiner & Co. v. Mari-Med Manufacturing, Inc.* There, the Federal Circuit traced the history of the doctrine from before *Winans* through *Graver Tank* and held that the doctrine was limited by equitable considerations:

> Whether in its earliest manifestations or its more recent rebirth, the doctrine retained its traditional equitable limits. It prevented "fraud on a patent." Specifically, it prevented a copyist from evading patent claims by what the court believed to be insubstantial changes.

Thus, in *Charles Greiner,* the court held the doctrine inapplicable in part because the accused infringer did more than simply "attempt to evade Greiner's patent by insubstantial changes."

The Federal Circuit is turning toward the equitable nature of the doctrine, that is, the doctrine is (1) an equitable doctrine to prevent fraud and is meant to prevent a copyist from committing a fraud on the patent and evading the claims of the patent, (2) with insubstantial changes; (3) the doctrine is the exception and not the rule. A number of unpublished decisions (nonprecedential opinions) further evidence the Federal Circuit's renewed emphasis on the equities in applying the doctrine. Although these opinions cannot be cited as precedent, they clearly indicate the trend in this area of the law.

In *Extrel FTMS, Inc. v. Bruker Instruments, Inc.* (1992), the court reversed a finding of infringement under the doctrine because the accused infringer's actions "did not involve 'insubstantial changes' by an 'unscrupulous copyist,'" and "the changes which avoided literal infringement were not merely 'colorable.'" The court reiterated that "application of the doctrine of equivalents is the exception, not the rule," as it "involves expansion of the scope of patent protection beyond the literal words of the claims for equitable reasons."

In *Shat-R-Shield, Inc. v. Trojan, Inc.* (1992), the court affirmed a finding of no infringement under the Doctrine of Equivalents where the accused process was "fundamentally different" from the claimed process even though the result was the same. The Federal Circuit found significant the District Court's finding that "[t]he concerns behind the doctrine of equivalents [are] not present in this case," although it did not identify those concerns specifically.

Similarly, in *Illinois Tool Works Inc. v. Rawplug Co.* (1992), the court upheld a summary judgment of no infringement, noting that the patentee "has also presented no evidence showing an equitable basis for invoking the doctrine of equivalents in this case." And in *American Home Products Corp. v. Johnson & Johnson* (1992), unpublished, the Federal Circuit vacated a preliminary injunction because the District Court had failed to take into account "a critical equitable aspect." The court first noted the equitable nature of the doctrine as follows:

> [T]he doctrine of equivalents is not an automatic second prong to every infringement charge. It is an equitable remedy available only upon a suitable showing. [The patentee] must put forth proof of the equities and the trial court must provide sufficient explication of its reasoning to support any finding of infringement under the doctrine of equivalents.

The Federal Circuit then remanded the case for the District Court to reweigh the equities, while highlighting some "important equitable aspects" for the trial court's consideration. First, the court noted that the record did not suggest that the accused infringer designed its product with knowledge of the patented method of use and "with the purpose of using such later technology to circumvent any claim language." Second, the patentee had not shown that the accused infringer's product was an "insubstantial change." And third, there was nothing to indicate that the patentee recognized the equivalency of the accused product at the time of filing of the patent application and that the accused infringer appropriated this knowledge.

The court vacated the preliminary injunction against the accused infringer (Johnson & Johnson). The court said that infringement by equivalents will also necessitate a fresh weighing of the equities: First, evidence of lack of *scienter,* that is, "knowingly"; second, a substantial change; and third, no evidence that J & J misappropriated the knowledge.

These cases signal a strong shift in the Federal Circuit away from the mechanical application of the function-means-result test to a balancing of the equities. Certainly if the *Graver Tank* test is not satisfied, then infringement under the Doctrine of Equivalents will not lie. But satisfying this test is not now enough. Equitable factors, such as lack of independent development, as well as the policy of preventing a "fraud" on the patent, must be considered. Otherwise, as the court held in *London,* claims will cease to serve the purpose of providing notice of the scope of the invention.

Decreasing the circumstances in which the Doctrine of Equivalents applies may promote certainty because the doctrine will be applied less often. But uncertainty may never be eliminated if the doctrine is to remain viable. In the *Perkin-Elmer* case, one judge in a dissent said that the Doctrine of Equivalents "necessarily dilutes the rigorous certainty that patent claims are intended to provide."

And in *Texas Instruments,* the court noted that "The determination of equivalency by its nature is inimical to the basic precept of patent law that the claims are the measure of the grant."

What about the person who makes a legitimate effort to design around a patent? In *Slimfold,* the Federal Circuit reversed a finding of infringement under the doctrine where the accused infringer had successfully designed around the patent because its product performed the same function as the claimed invention but in a different way.

But in *Read Corp. v. Portec, Inc.* (1992), the court upheld a jury verdict of infringement under the doctrine while expressly rejecting a finding that the infringer was guilty of "copying" the patented invention. The court held that the infringer had not copied, even though it had used the patented device as the starting point for its competing design, because it had also made specific changes in the design that were deemed adequate by counsel to avoid infringement. Thus, the infringement was not willful. The court noted that attempting to design around patents, however, while it is to be encouraged, can be a risky business because of the Doctrine of Equivalents:

> Of course, determining when a patented invention has been "designed around" enough to avoid infringement is a difficult determination to make. One cannot know for certain that changes are sufficient to avoid infringement until a judge or jury has made that determination. In the present case, the jury found that the changes made by Portec were not sufficient to avoid infringement. ... Portec is thus liable for damages caused by its miscalculation.

Most recently, in *Valmont Industries, Inc. v. Reinke Manufacturing Co.* (1993), the court clearly stated that unscrupulous conduct was necessary for the application of the Doctrine of Equivalents:

> An equivalent under the doctrine of equivalents results from an insubstantial change which, from the perspective of one of ordinary skill in the art, adds nothing of significance to the claimed invention.

Again, the court emphasized that "[t]he doctrine of equivalents *equitably* expands exclusive patent rights." The court reversed a finding of infringement because the accused device achieved the same result as the claimed invention but "in a very different way."

Furthermore, the court in *Valmont* distinguished the Doctrine of Equivalents from "equivalents" under 35 USC 112(6) as having different origins and purposes:

> A determination of section 112 equivalence does not involve the equitable tripartite test of the doctrine of equivalents. ... Section 112(6) limits the broad language of means-plus-function limitations in combination claims to equivalents of the structure, materials, or acts in the specification. The doctrine of equivalents equitably expands exclusive patent rights.

It should be noted that if application of the Doctrine of Equivalents is truly a matter of *equity,* a court may be able to decide the issue on its own without a jury. It should be further noted that the United States has recently been pursuing uniform application of the doctrine as one of the harmonization issues. The European Patent Convention's Protocol already provides for the consideration of equivalents in determining the extent of protection provided by a European patent. A recently proposed treaty by the World Intellectual Property Organization (WIPO) also addresses the issue. The proposed treaty also adopts the *Graver Tank* test as an additional way to determine equivalency. In the United States, the Doctrine of Equivalents is not found in any statute. It is purely a creation of the courts.

How far the Federal Circuit will carry this equitable approach to the doctrine remains to be seen. The question of when an infringer should be liable for patent infringement, even though technically avoiding the language of the claims, is not an easy one. But the Federal Circuit's recent emphasis on equitable considerations, rather than mechanical application of the test for equivalency, should lead to overall fairer and more predictable results under the doctrine. Until recently, a determination of equivalents in function-means-result appeared to be the only means to initiate invocation of the Doctrine of Equivalents. The tripartite test in itself appeared to constitute complete application of equity. However, the recent judicial remarks clearly indicate that proof of an additional equitable basis is required to invoke the doctrine.

In *Pall Corp. v. Micron Separations, Inc.* (D. Mass. 1992), which is on appeal for *en banc* review, the lower court based its decision strictly on function-means-result with no consideration of the equities.

In *Miles Laboratories, Inc. v. Shandon Inc.* (1993), the court held that the District Court did not err in determining that there was infringement under the doctrine, and although reciting the tripartite test, went on to state,

> [T]he doctrine of equivalents prevents pirating of the patentee's invention in the absence of literal infringement when liability is nevertheless warranted. . . . The doctrine of equivalents thus prevents the risk of injustice that may result from a limited focus on words alone.

Accordingly, the court would not allow the alleged infringer to escape infringement simply because the accused device performed additional functions than the patented device. The court stated that this "is the exact type of injustice the doctrine of equivalents prevents."

In *International Visual v. Crown Metal Mfg.* (1993), focusing on the issue of independent development, some judicial remarks have noted that the

> Supreme Court did not make it clear in *Graver Tank* whether the tripartite tests themselves constitute the application of equity or whether there is an equitable duty upon a court beyond the application of the tripartite tests.

This case was remanded to the District Court to determine infringement since the lower court erred in applying the "hypothetical" claim doctrine. However, Judge Lourie again provided a full commentary on *Graver Tank* and pointed out that while the court has over the years emphasized the equitable nature of the doctrine, nevertheless, the tripartite test has become a mechanistic test which has also been applied to accused infringers who are not unscrupulous copyists who have made more than insubstantial changes, under circumstances in which it may not have been equitable to do so. The doctrine has limits and although there is no set formula established for the determination of infringement under the doctrine, the placing of the accused device on the copying-independent development spectrum should also be a critical inquiry when evaluating the doctrine.

Judge Lourie's concurring opinion suggests that the courts should go beyond the tripartite test and consider (1) whether the accused device was copied or resulted from independent development, and (2) the degree of similarity of an accused invention to what is literally claimed, independent of the tripartite test. He observed that even if an accused product satisfied the function-means-result test, it still might not infringe as an equivalent "if independent research resulted in an invention or product significantly different from what is claimed." The objective set forth in *Graver Tank* was to prevent an injustice, to prevent misappropriation of the patentee's central idea or invention. Explicitly stated in Justice Jackson's opinion is that the test for determining the doctrine was not the prisoner of any formula. Nowhere does *Graver Tank* refer to function, means, and result as the decisive test, the *sine qua non* for determining the doctrine. The *Graver Tank* opinion, read in the context of the briefs before the court, is unmistakably clear in its focus on the potential inequities flowing from the misappropriation of the central idea of a patent by a change that leaves the accused infringer still in possession of that central idea, that is, piracy of the patented invention.

First, let us recall that the principal test for infringement is and remains whether the accused device or substance directly infringes (or is dominated by) the claims of the patent. Only if there is no direct infringement do the rules of equity come into play. A concurrent question is whether there is still room for the functions, means, and result test as part of the larger equity issue. Just what standards do we have to look for when we are looking to measure infringement within the principles of the Law of Equity?

Justice Jackson said: *One may not practice a fraud on the patent.* There are a number of elements that we would consider in a determination of fraud on a patent including, for example, whether there is any evidence of an intent to deceive. The inquiry starts with the proper scope of the patent, that is, is there a pioneer invention. From there we look to whether there is any evidence of independent research on the part of the accused infringer. This last question depends not only on whether the accused infringer actually engaged in independent creative work but also whether such work was necessary. It is not suggested that independent work alone would excuse infringement but that independent work is evidence of lack of misappropriation. In particular, where there is concurrent evidence that independent research was necessary because of the lack of predictability in the art, evidence of such independent creation is inconsistent with misappropriation.

Some commentators seem to be arguing that use of the doctrine requires the application of the formal procedures of equity. Such an argument may be discerned from the following, as an example.

In *American Home Products,* the Federal Circuit seems to recognize that an equitable determination of fraud involves the element of *scienter* (knowledge), that is, whether the accused infringer intentionally made changes within the skill of the art as part of a deliberate effort to circumvent the claim language while still making use of the patented invention, without the benefit of independent creative work. These recent cases such as *London, International,* and *American Home* require a continuing inquiry into the elements commonly associated with fraud and misappropriation as common law torts.

If the issue is in the Law of Equity, then the criteria for determining that issue must be equitable. Thus the element of *scienter* is meaningless in the determination of direct infringement, a statutory prohibition which presumes knowledge. But *scienter* is, or should be, central to the determination of equitable infringement, because it is central to the concepts of fair play and fraud.

If an accused product is to be an equitable equivalent then it is only fair to ask that the patent enable that specific product without undue experimentation, so that it is obvious and readily achieved without independent research. The doctrine was never intended to close the marketplace to products of independent effort and invention, but rather to prevent the copier, or the pirate. Once more, it is essential that we recognize that the independently created product, derived from independent research, is not, by definition, a copy of another's property. Regardless of whether there are substantial similarities in function, means, and result, an independently created product, with meaningful differences in activity or properties, is not born of a misappropriation or piracy, and cannot be said to infringe, as a matter of equity, under the doctrine. The standards for determining "inequitable" equivalence under the doctrine, therefore, must ultimately rest on the criteria, in equity, for determining fraud and misappropriation.

This kind of argument has appeared in a number of places where the proponent seems to have represented an accused infringer who did not copy, who conducted independent research, and whose invention purportedly showed meaningful differences in activity or properties, yet was declared to have infringed. As can be seen from the above, the very recent case law and some commentators, in trying to get around the mechanistic formula for applying the function-means-result test, may end up using a mechanistic formula for applying equitable considerations which is not the purpose of equity at all.

Certainly copying and thereby producing a product or process with relatively minor differences from the patented invention is to be abhorred. In *Graver Tank,* the court said,

> The essence of the doctrine is that one may not practice a fraud on a patent . . . it has been consistently applied by this Court and the lower federal courts, and continues today ready and available for utilization *when the proper circumstances for its application arise.*

Furthermore, Lincolnweld was designed as the result of copying. The court noted, "the record contains no evidence of any kind to show that Lincolnweld was developed as a result of independent research or experiments." Thus, this copying by the infringer constituted "the proper circumstances" for application of the doctrine in the *Graver Tank* case.

So too, in the leading case in 1853, *Winans,* the key element there was also copying. Thus, it is clear beyond doubt that the courts created the doctrine, using their equitable powers, to protect the patent owner from the rigorous limitations of literal infringement in cases where the accused infringer had copied the patented product, or derived a product which differed from the patented product in only one or more minor and insignificant ways. Accordingly, it would seem that the doctrine could be invoked only in cases where the evidence clearly showed the existence of copying. But of course this is not the case at all. At the present time, and for many, many years, our courts have routinely considered application of the doctrine in cases where literal infringement was not present, irrespective of whether copying had been proven.

A glaring example of consideration of the doctrine without regard to whether the accused infringer actually copied is *Pennwalt.* In this *en banc* decision, not a single word in any one of these opinions is devoted to whether or not Durand-Wayland, the accused infringer, copied or otherwise derived its fruit sorting machine from the patented machine. It seems clear from *Pennwalt* that a showing of copying or substantial derivation is not a prerequisite for invoking the doctrine.

In *Coleco Industries, Inc. v. U. S. ITC* (1978), Judge Rich wrote,

> As to applying the doctrine of equivalents in this case, no basis has been laid for its application by showing, for example, that appellant's invention has made a great advance in the art or that appellees have appropriated the essence of the invention. The doctrine is an exception to the rule that patentees are limited to what they claim and is not applied in every case. I would point out that in *Graver Tank* . . . the Court said at 608 that the doctrine of equivalents *may* be applied "when the proper circumstances

> for its application arise." *One such circumstance is appropriating the invention while avoiding claim limitations through use of equivalents therefor.*

In *Slimfold*, Judge Rich wrote,

> Inherent in our claim-based patent system is also the principle that the protected invention is what the claims say it is, and thus that infringement can be avoided by avoiding the language of the claims. It is only when the changes are so insubstantial as to result in "a fraud on the patent" that application of the equitable doctrine of equivalents becomes *desirable.* Thus, *the first question which must be asked is "has a substantial change been made?"* Only if the answer to that question is "no" should an accused infringer be liable for improperly trying to appropriate the claimed invention. This is where the *Graver Tank* tripartite test comes into play.

In *Valmont,* the court considered whether Reinke infringed under the doctrine; however, the opinion is silent as to whether or not Reinke was a copyist.

In *International Visual,* Judge Lourie wrote,

> Unfortunately, however, the tripartite test has become a mechanical formula which can often be applied to accused infringers who are not unscrupulous copyists and who have made more than insubstantial changes, under circumstances in which it may not be equitable to do so.
>
> If there is no prosecution history estoppel, if application of the doctrine would not encompass the prior art, and if the tripartite tests are met, I believe that a court should make a separate equitable determination . . . in order to find infringement under the doctrine of equivalents.

Application of the doctrine and a consequential finding of infringement can work an injustice on party who designed its product without knowledge of the patent owner's product or patent. A finding of infringement by equivalents can also result in hardship on an accused infringer who made substantial changes in a good faith effort to avoid the patent claims. In situations such as these, the equities may be more with the accused infringer than with the patent owner. It appears that the Federal Circuit and the lower courts may have lost sight of the reasons which gave rise to the doctrine.

A revolution against patentees has been consummated largely outside the view of most patent practitioners. It is now about as difficult to get a patent claim held infringed on passage through the CAFC as it was to have one held valid under Section 103 more than ten years ago when the regional U.S. Courts of Appeal reviewed patent cases. The court and its panels have been issuing opinions and decisions in conflict with its own clear precedent, to the dismay and massive economic loss of parties appearing before it. Doctrinal stability, so sought at the inception of the CAFC, is a stranger in many areas of patent law; this is especially true with respect to the application of the Doctrine of Equivalents.

Moreover, extraordinary philosophical hostility to the doctrine has been announced in sheer dictum by the recently appointed Judge Lourie. Not only has he stated that infringement by equivalents is not to be examined in every infringement suit, but further, by requiring the patentee *to prove* the infringer to be a conscious copier before infringement by equivalence may be permissibly evaluated by the trial court. Thus, an infringing copier may be enjoined but an innocent infringer may, at the same time, infringe with impunity.

The landmark published precedential opinions which narrowed the Doctrine of Equivalents to a largely empty shell for patent enforcement purposes are well-known, for example, *Pennwalt, Slimfold,* and *London.* Not well-known is the fact that an avalanche of unpublished, nonprecedential opinions has descended unseen and unnoticed by most, wherein the cases, in a 6 (or more)-to-1 ratio, have held claims not infringed under the doctrine, almost always in affirmance of summary judgment. And erosion of the doctrine is proceeding headlong. Dicta in some recent cases has suggested that only "copiers" or other inequitable entities may be held to be infringers under the doctrine. Does this mean that there may be two entities who infringe but only the one who copied is culpable? Does the noncopying infringer whose accused device is identical to that of the copying infringer get a free ride?

Patent practitioners, as required by the PTO canons of ethics and disciplinary rules, are obliged to zealously represent their clients. Today, practitioners representing potential infringers can counsel competitive product design under the guidance of CAFC cases, which will be viewed as mere "designing around" by judge or jury 95 percent of the time; but which would have been held infringements by equivalents prior to *Pennwalt* and its progeny.

Hilton-Davis. This and other equitable issues are likely to be addressed when the Federal Circuit decides, *en banc, Hilton-Davis Chemical Co. v. Warner-Jenkinson Co., Inc.,* Appeal No. 93–1088. The issues to be addressed in *amicus curiae* briefs requested by the court are:

1. Does a finding of patent infringement under the Doctrine of Equivalents require anything in addition to proof of the facts

that there are the same or substantially the same (a) function, (b) way, and (c) result, the so-called triple identity test of *Graver Tank,* and cases relied thereon? If yes, what? This question asks whether a patentee has a right to have infringement under the Doctrine of Equivalents determined solely by satisfaction of the tripartite, function-way-result test?

2. Is application of the Doctrine of Equivalents by the trial court to find infringement of the patentee's right to exclude, when there is no literal infringement of a claim, discretionary in accordance with the circumstances of the case? The second question asks whether a patentee, upon demand, always has a right to a determination of infringement under the Doctrine of Equivalents.

3. Is the issue of infringement under the Doctrine of Equivalents an equitable remedy to be decided by the court, or is it, like literal infringement, an issue of fact to be submitted to the jury in a jury case? (*en banc* order of December 3, 1993.) This last question raises a substantial constitutional issue: Does the Seventh Amendment give a patentee, upon timely demand, the right to a jury trial of the factual determination of equivalents, or is the Doctrine of Equivalents an entirely equitable issue, like laches and inequitable conduct, whereby the factual determination of equivalents can be determined solely by the court?

Since *Hilton-Davis* is likely to be one of the most significant Federal Circuit cases in recent years, this *en banc* hearing may well fix the court's direction in this area for many years to come. Accordingly, the AIPLA filed a brief on January 7, 1994. The summary of argument follows:

> Amicus AIPLA suggests that this Court should articulate a procedural framework by which the Doctrine of Equivalents can be used by the public and applied by the courts as objectively as possible, along the following lines:
>
> Applications of the equitable Doctrine of Equivalents should involve each of the following inquiries:
>
> (1) Determining whether the accused device, composition or process is a *de facto* equivalent of the patented invention, by applying the tripartite factual *Graver Tank* test;
>
> (2) determining any objective limitations on any *de facto* equivalent arising from (a) any limiting prior art, and (b) any prosecution history estoppels; and
>
> (3) determining whether, in all the circumstances of the case,

> the equities favor or disfavor a judgment of infringement via the doctrine of equivalents in the particular case.
>
> While the ultimate decision to render a judgment of infringement via the doctrine of equivalents is an application of a court's equitable powers, as indicated in the aforestated procedural framework, and therefore a trial court would ultimately be exercising such powers in concluding whether or not equities require a finding of infringement, trial courts should *not* be given discretion concerning whether or not to make the inquiries articulated above.
>
> Finally, it has long been the rule that there is no Seventh Amendment right to a trial by jury of an equitable claim, and therefore the question of infringement via the doctrine of equivalents is susceptible to trial entirely by a court, sitting without a jury.

Finally, a word to patent practitioners. This doctrine is *the* topic in most of the cases that come up in the district courts and in the Federal Circuit. "The Federal Circuit has provided less than crystal clear guidance as to how equivalency in claim interpretation is to be established." This is a very difficult issue, and to win a case based on the doctrine one must (1) have a very good case; and (2) win below, since the CAFC has usually deferred to a trial court's decision. The overriding theme is that one must know the history of the doctrine and why it has developed to its present state.

An interesting aspect of the *Graver Tank* case in 1950, which had to do with a dramatic improvement in the field of automatic welding, relates to the two major reasons why the claims were found infringed:

1. The invention grew up from a joint research project of which the defendant was aware; and
2. this invention was of great importance during wartime. "[T]his country owes a debt of gratitude. . . ."

In substance one had substantially the same thing, functioning in the same way to produce the same results with no change in principle.

With respect to the All Elements Rule and the Invention-as-a-Whole, perhaps it does not make any significant difference; plaintiff or defendant may be able to win on either basis. One can argue the factual part of the case and use either argument. If you are to win a case, have someone available to argue as a legal expert as well as a technical expert. Be prepared not just to argue, but have witnesses argue, have exhibits, and over-try the case. If you are to win as a plaintiff, you must have the *why* and the *how*.

Nearly every case on appeal involves the doctrine. In the last few years, up until about 1992, the patentee, out of 28 cases, has won 7 and lost 21—only a 25 percent success rate. Three times out of four, the claims are insufficient.

1. The problem will remain the same in the future (unless *Hilton-Davis* is handled well);
2. there is no precise definition of the test; and
3. the CAFC prefers to find a claim valid and not infringed rather than invalid.

Although the Doctrine of Equivalents only comes into play when there is no literal infringement, nevertheless, it may be advisable to sell the trial court on any and all theories of infringement. If the patentee, in a jury trial, fails to argue equivalence, choosing instead to concentrate only on direct or literal infringement, and there could, on the facts, exist infringement under the Doctrine of Equivalents, the patentee may forfeit the right to have the jury instructed on the doctrine.

Equivalence to the invention's structure, function, or operation should be emphasized or sold by the patentee. The patent owner almost invariably should talk in terms of his invention and/or its contribution to the public, and of the general similarities of the accused device or practice, composition or device, to the teachings of the patent.

Conversely, the alleged infringer should emphasize nonequivalence to the claims using element-by-element analysis as set forth in *Pennwalt.* The alleged infringer should attempt to break down the claims into their separate elements; then, every arguably nonequivalent element should be emphasized in the presentation of the defense. The greater the number of elements or structures the more likely it is that some element or structure will be found nonequivalent in terms of structure and/or function. Expert testimony is particularly useful. When complicated technology is involved, the expert for the alleged infringer should emphasize and enumerate the differences between the invention and the accused device even though minute.

In arguing the Doctrine of Equivalents to triers of fact unversed in patent law, the best way to start may be by way of example. The case of *Kolene Corp. v. Motor City Metal Treating* (6th Circuit, 1971), is illustrative. The patent in suit concerned a metal-treating process utilizing an alkali metal salt comprising 25 to 40 percent cyanate. The defendant used a bath containing 46 to 50 percent cyanate, selected on advice of counsel specifically to avoid infringement. No improvement in the process resulted from defendant's chosen composition. The 6th Circuit found literal infringement under the Doctrine of Equivalents since the accused process required the same steps, operated in the same manner and achieved the same result as the patented process.

In *S. C. Johnson & Son v. Carter-Wallace* (S.D.N.Y. 1985 . . . affirmed Fed. Cir. 1986), plaintiff's patent for shaving cream claimed that a water-soluble gelling agent should be present in the amount of "about 0.01–5% by weight." The total amount of gelling agent present in defendant's product was 6.532% by weight. The court noted that 0.01–5% is a broad range but that "it was nowhere indicated to be a critical one." The court thus found 6.532% to be literally "about 5%" and equivalent to 5%, entering a judgment of infringement. These examples are intended to show how the Doctrine of Equivalents has even been applied to instances where numerical specifications have been used to circumscribe the outer limit of claims.

Although the Federal Circuit was created to bring uniformity and consistency to patent law, it plainly appears that there exist many and deep divisions among the members of that court on the issues, *inter alia,* discussed above. Practitioners should make careful note of such differences and adopt, prove, and sell a case of infringement (or noninfringement) depending on what facts they have at hand, consistent with the point of view of either the majority or minority where alternate views have been espoused, as, for example, in the *Pennwalt* situation.

If a minority view can be sold to the District Court within the context of the facts of a particular case, it is unlikely that the Federal Circuit will reverse on appeal. In a survey until February 1988, for example, 30 decisions had been issued by the CAFC holding patents not infringed, and of these only two represented reversals of District Court decisions.

Doctrine of File Wrapper Estoppel (Prosecution History Estoppel)

The word *estoppel* signifies a *bar.* The Doctrine of File Wrapper Estoppel bars or precludes one from asserting a fact or truth where (1) he had previously taken a position inconsistent with his present position; and (2) another has acted in reliance upon his earlier representation.

Applied to patent claims, the Doctrine of File Wrapper Estoppel precludes a patent owner from recapturing in patent litigation the breadth which was given up in the PTO to secure allowance of the application. In other words, the essence of the Doctrine of File Wrapper Estoppel is that an applicant who has limited or modified a claim in order to avoid its rejection by the PTO may not thereafter expand the claim by including subject matter thus excluded or any equivalent thereof, or by omitting limitations he thus has been caused to add. "When the doctrine is invoked, a close examination must be made as to, not only what was surrendered, but also the reason for such a surrender."

The Federal Circuit has held that in assessing the prosecution history estoppel, one must look to what the applicant actually gave up in order to secure a patent and to the actual substance of his arguments in prosecution. In other words, if the applicant withdrew several features of the invention in order to gain allowance of the application, he may not then try to recapture those features which he relinquished.

In another case, the CAFC concluded:

> When an accused device is the same as a disclosed embodiment, and claims covering the disclosed embodiment were rejected on appeal and cancelled, the yielded claim scope cannot be recovered in order to encompass the accused device through the doctrine of equivalents. . . .

The file wrapper connotes the official record of the case within the PTO, and includes the amendments and the arguments submitted by the applicant. A continuation or a division of an earlier application includes the file history of such earlier application. Some lower courts have carried the doctrine so far as to have found the mere arguments of an applicant or his attorney constitute file wrapper estoppel. A still further extension of the concept has been denominated file wrapper estoppel *by admission* where, after rejection, the applicant clarifies the meaning of a claim without rewriting it. The Doctrine of File Wrapper Estoppel has no applicability to a claim that has been literally infringed.

The CAFC, in *Hughes Aircraft v. U.S.* (1983) has said,

> The Doctrine of Prosecution History Estoppel precludes a patent owner from obtaining a claim construction that would resurrect subject matter surrendered during prosecution of the patent application. The estoppel applies to claim amendments to overcome rejections based on prior art . . . and to arguments submitted to obtain the patent.
>
> The Doctrine of Equivalents is unnecessary when literal infringement is present.
>
> [A]mendment of claims is a common practice in prosecution . . . no reason . . . exists . . . for limiting application of the Doctrine of Equivalents to those comparatively few claims allowed exactly as originally filed and never amended. . . . It is not fatal to an application of the doctrine itself.

Since 1984, the CAFC appears to be moving away from the strict constructionist view (e.g., a patentee who amended a claim to overcome a prior art rejection, was not able to recapture that which was explicitly given up during the prosecution of the patent), and considering the specific reasons for the submission of a particular amendment or for making a particular representation. In a 1986 case, the court noted that an estoppel is not necessarily created by an amendment designed only to remove an indefiniteness rejection.

Under clear Federal Circuit precedent, file wrapper estoppel, where it exists, properly applies not only to amendments, but also to arguments and representations made before the PTO to obtain the patent. Consequently, the alleged infringer should carefully and repeatedly examine all statements, amendments, representations, affidavits, and so on, made or filed by the patentee in the file wrapper, and attempt to show that the patentee made the amendments, argued as it did, and so on, only in order to gain allowance in view of the prior art. The alleged infringer should also use such statements in aid of interpretation of the claims.

The patentee must argue the alternative reasons for making a particular argument or amendment, and must make it appear that such argument was made for some reason totally unrelated to the avoidance of prior art, and that the statements have no effect on the scope of the claims. The case law in this, like other areas of the law, has evolved to the point where it can be used to lend support to either position.

The Federal Circuit, in *du Pont v. Phillips Petroleum* (1988), emphasized that when interpreting claims, courts must remember that the claims define the invention. The interpretive aids, such as the specification or prosecution history, can only be used to interpret terms included in the claims. They cannot be used to rewrite the claims or to add limitations not included by the applicant. Thus, in *du Pont* the Federal Circuit rejected an interpretation by the District Court that the claimed invention included two features described in the specification but not recited in the claims.

A District Court has noted:

> Where infringement is asserted under the doctrine of equivalents, prosecution history estoppel prevents the asserted claims from being expanded to cover what was disclaimed by argument or amendment in the Patent Office during prosecution. Where literal infringement is asserted, the prosecution history is used along with the specification to interpret the claim language.

In *du Pont,* the Federal Circuit also noted:

> [U]sing the prosecution history in that manner [to interpret the claims] is different from prosecution history estoppel, which is applied as a limitation upon the doctrine of equivalents after the claims have been properly interpreted.

The Doctrine of Equivalents is designed to do *equity;* it is not designed to permit a patent to expand the scope of its claims. "Improper claim construction, i.e., an improper determination of the scope of the claims can distort the entire infringement analysis." The practitioner must precisely consider the grammatical implications of what has been written.

In *Diversitech Corp. v. Century Steps, Inc.* (1988), the CAFC held that where a patentee, during prosecution, cancelled a claim that had been earlier rejected on appeal, which claim covered a disclosed embodiment, the patentee is estopped from later asserting infringement under the Doctrine of Equivalents against a device which is the same as the disclosed embodiment.

In *LaBounty Manufacturing, Inc. v. U.S. International Trade Commission* (1989), the Federal Circuit held that an analysis of the prior art is necessary to determine whether prosecution history estoppel prevents the assertion of equivalency. There is no mechanical rule for determining prosecution history estoppel's effect on the range of equivalents. Even though claims are narrowed during prosecution, prosecution history estoppel does not necessarily completely prohibit a patentee from recapturing some of what was originally claimed.

The Doctrine of Prosecution History Estoppel will only reduce or preclude applicability of the Doctrine of Equivalents when the nature and the purpose of the limitation added by amendment requires application of the doctrine. At least, where claims are rewritten, the substance of the cancelled claims and the amended claims must be examined in judging whether or not prosecution history estoppel will limit the scope of amended claims during litigation.

In conclusion, in determining the range of equivalents to be afforded an invention under the Doctrine of Equivalents, the practitioner should consider the specification, whether those skilled in the pioneer/nonpioneer status art would have known of the prior art interchangeability, and the totality of change.

In determining whether the Doctrine of Prosecution History Estoppel applies, a practitioner should consider: the manner in which claims were narrowed by amendment; the reasons why the claims were narrowed; the extent to which the claims were narrowed; equitable and public policy principles underlying the doctrines involved; and the facts of the particular case. The law is not settled and should be an active area for the CAFC in coming terms.

Reverse (Inverse) Doctrine of Equivalents

The Reverse Doctrine of Equivalents or *negative* Doctrine of Equivalents had its genesis in 1897 when the Supreme Court, in *Westinghouse v. Boyden Power Brake Company* stated:

> We have repeatedly held that a charge of infringement is sometimes made out, though the letter of the claims be avoided. The converse is equally true. The patentee may bring the defendant within the letter of his claims, but if the latter has so far changed the principle of the device that the claims of the patent, literally construed, have ceased to represent his actual invention, he is as little subject to be adjudged an infringer as one who has violated the letter of a statute has to be convicted, when he has done nothing in conflict with its spirit and intent.

In *Graver Tank* (1950), the Supreme Court also said,

> The wholesome realism of this doctrine is not always applied in favor of a patentee but is sometimes used against him. Thus, where a device is so far changed in principle from a patented article that it performs the same or a similar function *in a substantially different way,* but nevertheless falls within the literal words of the claim, the doctrine of equivalents may be used to restrict the claim and defeat the patentee's action for infringement.

The Federal Circuit, more recently, outlined the procedural pattern for the application of a Reverse Doctrine of Equivalents defense in the seminal case of *SRI International v. Matsushita Electric Corp.* (1985). First, the patentee bears the burden of proving infringement by a preponderance of the evidence. Initially that burden is carried when literal infringement has been established. Significantly, at this juncture of its discussion, the court noted in a footnote that

> [b]ecause products on which patent claims are readable word for word often are in fact the same, perform the same function in the same way, and achieve the same result, as the claimed invention, a defense based on the Reverse Doctrine of Equivalents is rarely offered.

Second, nevertheless, when a patentee has proved literal infringement, the accused infringer may undertake the burden of going forward to establish the fact of noninfringement under the Reverse Doctrine of Equivalents. The fact that it has been part of the experience of the law is evidence that it has been undertaken. Finally, should the accused infringer make out a *prima facie* case, then the patentee, who retains the burden of persuasion on infringement, must rebut that *prima facie* case.

In *Leesona Corp. v. United States* [Court of Claims (1976), a court whose decisions are looked to as precedent by the CAFC], the court held that under the Reverse Doctrine of Equivalents the plaintiff's patent on a certain electrode structure for a battery was not infringed by the defendant's battery. Each of the claims at issue called for a "porous self-sustaining metal layer of uniform and controlled porosity." However, the court found

> [w]hile [defendant's battery] is porous and self-sustaining and, in a very loose sense, could be said to have a uniform and controlled porosity, it is clear that it is neither intended to perform the function of the micro-porous metal layer disclosed, nor in fact does so.

While the patent disclosed a means for controlling bubble pressure, the court found that any effect the accused product had on bubble pressure was incidental and insignificant.

The Federal Circuit, hopefully referring to the posing of the question, remarked in *SRI* that "[t]he fact question is simple and direct: . . . Is the accused product so far changed in principle that it performs the function of the claimed invention in a substantially different way?"

None of these words are clearly subject to rigorous definition. Accordingly, the ultimate answer to the question of infringement depends on the facts in each case. Facts cited by the Supreme Court by way of example include whether the accused product resulted from independent research and whether the interchangeability of the elements or means would have been known to one skilled in the art.

Notably, the Reverse Doctrine of Equivalents defense has been held either inapplicable or insufficient to overcome the patentee's *prima facie* case in every Federal Circuit case in which it has been asserted. However, cases in the CAFC's predecessor court, the U.S. Court of Claims, and in a number of U.S. Circuit Courts of Appeal and U.S. District Courts have not resulted in so uniform or seemingly inevitable decisions on the doctrine.

In cases where the Reverse Doctrine of Equivalents has been successfully asserted as a defense to charges of infringement, the courts have weighed the following factors in the balance:

1. Whether the accused product resulted from independent research;
2. whether interchangeability of elements or means of the accused device was known;
3. differing function or use of the accused device;
4. same result but accomplished by significantly different means;
5. significant improvement embodying inventive insight: not included in patent in suit; and

6. patent teaches away from the concept embodied in the accused product.

The Reverse Doctrine of Equivalents in essence stands for the proposition that the patentee has claimed more than the invention he has made, and the scope of protection will be restricted to what was actually invented. It is nothing more than a necessary corollary to the rule which holds that functional expressions are interpreted to extend only to the equivalent of that which is disclosed in the patent.

Thus, even though the claim language reads on all things which perform the function, those which are not within the range of equivalents to be afforded the disclosed structure are excluded from the scope of the claim. Since function is a relative concept, and broad claims can be overbroad whether functional or not, the Reverse Doctrine of Equivalents can be applied to all types of claims, and not just MPF language. In the *Texas Instruments* case, the court implicitly found that the accused devices were so far changed in principle, and operated in such a substantially different way, that they did not capture the essence of the invention; and, therefore, did not infringe, even if there was literal infringement.

The Reverse Doctrine of Equivalents breathes life into the platitude that "an infringer appropriates an invention, not words." The negative or reverse application of the doctrine provides that no matter what the words of the claims provide when seen in a vacuum, infringement cannot be made out unless the accused process performs substantially the same function, in substantially the same way, to obtain the same result. Both infringement under the Doctrine of Equivalents, and noninfringement under the Reverse Doctrine of Equivalents, are questions of fact. The question of substantive infringement must always be determined if raised.

When a patentee establishes literal infringement, the accused infringer has the burden of going forward to establish noninfringement under the Reverse Doctrine of Equivalents. By analogy to the Doctrine of Equivalents, the Reverse Doctrine of Equivalents also raises a fact question (which is simple and direct) as to whether a product has been so far changed in principle that it performs the same or similar function in a substantially different way. Thus, this fact question is not normally susceptible to a summary judgment. A court's election to ignore the claims and substitute a gist drawn from the operation of a disclosed embodiment cannot convert the factual question raised by the Reverse Doctrine of Equivalents into a legal question of claim construction.

The Reverse Doctrine of Equivalents says, in effect, that an incidental infringement is no infringement at all. The Doctrine of Equivalents is thus a two-edged sword. Where a device is so far changed in principle from a patented article that it performs the same or similar function in a substantially different way, but nevertheless, "falls within the literal words of the claim," the Doctrine of Equivalents may be used to restrict the claim and defeat the patent owner's action for infringement.

Infringement is not a mere matter of words; otherwise, patent law would reward literary skill and not mechanical creativity. Even though claims of a patent read to some extent upon the accused device, a court will look beyond the claims and consider the function and operation of devices themselves if there is infringement. Claims are construed by the PTO so as to give them the broadest reasonable interpretation; while a more liberal interpretation may be accorded them in infringement litigation.

In denying rehearing, the CAFC held that the Reverse Doctrine of Equivalents could not come into consideration in the *Texas Instruments* case because the claims were not literally infringed.

> The "reverse doctrine" is explained in *Graver Tank & Mfg. Co. v. Linde Air Products Co.* (1950) as the "wholesome realism . . . where a device is so far changed in principle from the patented article but nevertheless falls within the literal words of the claims . . . the doctrine may be used to restrict the claim," thereby avoiding infringement. Indeed, it might better be called a doctrine of non-equivalence. Its invocation requires both that (1) there must be apparent literal infringement of the words of the claim; and (2) the accused device must be sufficiently different from that which is patented that despite the apparent literal infringement, the claims are interpreted to negate infringement.

The District Court, in *Ethyl Molded Products Co. v. Betts Package, Inc.* (1988), made the interesting assertion that

> [t]he reverse doctrine of equivalents, although argued by infringers, has never been applied by the Federal Circuit. In cases far more compelling than [defendant's], the court has consistently held that infringer's attempts to escape liability under the equitable doctrine were unavailing.

In *Moleculon Research v. CBS, Inc.* (CAFC 1989), the court noted that, to escape literal infringement of a patent method claim under the Reverse Doctrine of Equivalents, the accused infringer must

> prove that its different method [using a mechanism that was different from and superior to that illustrated in the patent] . . . was a method step "so far changed in principle . . . that it performs the same or a similar function in a substantially different way."

Because reverse equivalents applies only when there is literal infringement, the improvement at issue has to be very significant to qualify for infringement immunity under the Reverse Doctrine of Equivalents.

APPLICATION TO ACCUSED DEVICE

Where an accused device does not literally infringe an independent claim, it cannot literally infringe an associated dependent claim even if it has all the elements added by that particular dependent claim. "Dependent claims are not infringed unless the accused device infringes the independent claim upon which they are based." The patentee must prove by a preponderance of the evidence that the claims, as properly interpreted, encompass the accused device. The Federal Circuit reviews such a determination under the clearly erroneous standard.

1988 saw the first cases citing the *en banc Pennwalt* decision of 1987. Judge Nies succinctly expressed her views of the changes wrought by *Pennwalt* when she wrote in her dissent from the Federal Circuit's denial of rehearing *en banc* of the *Texas Instruments* case:

> It is now settled law that each element of a claim is material and essential and, in order to find infringement, the patent owner must show the presence of every element or its substantial equivalent in the accused device. . . . The *Pennwalt* court rejected the view of a minority of the court that only literal infringement required an element-by-element analysis and that infringement under the doctrine of equivalents could be found under an "invention as a whole" standard, even though an element of a claim was not present, at least by an equivalent, in the accused device or process. That debate has ended.

The great difficulty that the Federal Circuit has had in dealing with the Doctrine of Equivalents is nothing new for courts examining the issue. The first Doctrine of Equivalents case, *Winans,* was decided by a vote of 5 to 4 and included a dissent. The modern classic Doctrine of Equivalents, *Graver Tank* (1950) was also a split decision and included two vigorous dissents. In one recent case the CAFC said, "the doctrine recognizes a fact of the real business world: words are not misappropriated; claimed inventions are." Under *Pennwalt,* once it is determined that the accused device lacks a corresponding element or function there can be no infringement as a matter of law.

In *Spectra Corp. v. Lutz* (1988), the thrust is a reaffirmance of *Pennwalt* and a conclusion that summary judgment of noninfringement is proper when a single function described in the specification for an element in a composition cannot be found in the accused device.

In *Ethyl v. Betts* above, the evidence showed that the patentee's and infringer's bottle closures were being run by the same bottlers on the same lines using the same equipment and processes and achieving the same results. The District Court found clear interchangeability and thus equivalent in function, result, and operation.

The District Court, in *Sun Products Group, Inc. v. B & E Sales Co.* (1988), erroneously stated that infringement under the Doctrine of Equivalents can be properly determined by a comparison of the accused device and the patentee's commercial embodiment, rather than the words of the patent claim.

CONDUCT NOT CONSTITUTING INFRINGEMENT

The following do NOT constitute infringement:

1. mere *solicitation of orders*
2. mere *advertising*
3. mere *display*
4. mere *managerial activities*
5. a *contract* to manufacture which *would* infringe
6. *partial delivery*
7. *conspiracy to infringe* does not violate any federal statute
8. *selling* exclusively *to the patent owner*
9. *invalid patent*
10. a dependent claim unless the independent claim is infringed
11. use solely for reporting requirements of federal drug laws
12. a structure possessing *anything less* than the entire combination as claimed.

The performance of any one of the activities of making, using, or selling, expressed in disjunctive language in 35 USC 271, constitutes patent infringement, and that a patentee need not have any evidence of damage or lost sales to bring an infringement action. [*Roche v. Bolar,* getting a head start by sampling the FDA to sell a generic version of a drug before the patent expired. This case has been effectively overruled by 35 USC 271 (e)(1) of the "Drug Price Competition and Patent Term Restoration Act of 1984."]

The so-called *experimental use defense,* an experiment for the sole purpose of gratifying a philosophical taste or for curiosity amusement, was not an infringement: *any* commercial reason is not allowed. Further, where significant unpatented assemblies of elements are tested during the patent's term, enabling the infringer to deliver the patented combination to a buyer without testing the entire combination, testing the assemblies can be held to be infringement of the patented combination.

UNITED STATES CODE ANNOTATED

Factors Determining Infringement Generally

Issue of infringement is tested solely by consideration of accused device and invention claimed in patent alleged to be infringed and, if a claim of such patent defines accused device, it is infringed. Three separate elements must be established before there can be a finding of infringement: (1) the invention be made, used or sold (2) during the term of the patent (3) by one without authority to do so.

The four basic issues in normal patent litigation are:

1. state of prior art,
2. the improvements, if any, which patented article makes over prior art,
3. whether these improvements, considered in light of prior art, are sufficiently novel to meet statutory tests of inventiveness, and
4. whether the accused device infringes on the patent device.

The determination of patent infringement is a two-step process: First, the meaning of claims in issue must be determined by study of all relevant patent documents, and second, claims must be read on accused structures.

Patent infringement claims are normally tried in two parts and, if patent validity is established in first trial, a trial on issue of claimed infringement must follow.

In applying a general test of infringement, courts follow a two-step analysis: (1) whether accused device, process, or composition of matter literally infringe patent in question and, if not, (2) whether the Doctrine of Equivalents nevertheless leads to a finding of infringement. In determining whether the accused device constitutes an infringement, the court must first look into the art to find what the real merit of the invention is and whether it has advanced the art substantially, and, if it has done so, then the court should be liberal in construing the patent and in finding infringement in the use of equivalents to the end that the inventor may secure the reward which he deserves.

The fact that device may be operated in noninfringing manner does not resolve issue of infringement if it can be found that device also operates in an infringing manner.

In considering question of patent infringement, accused product or device must be compared with teaching of patent, as disclosed by specification and claims, rather than with patentee's commercial device.

Where extrinsic evidence is not needed in patent infringement suit to explain terms of art involved and court is able, from mere comparison, to comprehend what the invention is, and, from a mere comparison of structures, to determine whether one device infringes on another, question of infringement is one of law.

Past infringement of a patent that has subsequently expired is as much an injury to the property of the patentee as a present infringement.

Where defendants manufactured a device capable of an infringing use, they infringe a patent, even though they instruct that it shall be used in a noninfringing way.

If manufacture of infringing article is accidental, and is not in substantial number, damages are not recoverable.

Infringement is measured by results, not intent.

Infringement may be entirely inadvertent and unintentional and without knowledge of patent.

A machine that was adapted to infringe constituted infringement.

More is necessary to support finding of willful patent infringement than that infringement acts were not inadvertent; court must determine that infringer acted in disregard of patent, that is, that infringer had no reasonable basis for believing it had right to do acts at issue.

Failure of patentee to make or sell patented device does not affect right to exclude competitors.

Proof of the single sale of infringing composition may be sufficient to establish infringement.

Infringement is not avoided merely because all objectives of patent are not achieved.

An infringement may be found and equivalents may be recognized, even though infringing device utilizes only part of a patent in suit or otherwise utilizes it imperfectly.

Though patent laws of the United States do not have extraterritorial effect, active inducement may be found in events outside the United States if they result in direct infringement in the United States.

Even though alleged acts of defendant were all performed prior to issue of patent to plaintiff, if they were performed by defendant with intent to infringe the patent when issued, or intent that infringing conduct continue after patent was issued, they would constitute infringement.

Only on claims found to infringe is it necessary to reach decision on validity.

In patent infringement suit it is better practice for court to first inquire fully into validity of patent.

Though it was found that patent had not been infringed, court had power to adjudge patent invalid.

In general, infringement issues will not be decided until the validity and scope of the patents in suit are determined.

If a base claim can be extended by the Doctrine of Equivalents, the dependent claim may, depending on the circumstances, also be extended in comparable respects.

Dependent patent claim can be infringed only if independent claim, which is incorporated by reference therein, is infringed.

Not only result, but elements combined, manner of combination and functions of each, must be same.

A feature of a *design* which is wholly functional cannot be relied upon to prove infringement.

The test of infringement, so far as method claim is concerned, is whether or not any apparatus, no matter how different the apparatus may be, will, in its normal use, perform the acts recited in the claim.

A pioneer or generic patent which opens a new path is entitled to broader protection than a patent which merely improves upon that which is already known.

Infringement of one patent constitutes infringement of broader claims of another patent which is generic to and comprehensive of infringed patent.

When accused process does not embrace those steps which distinguish the patented one from the prior art, it does not infringe it.

Test of process infringement is not similarity of apparatus, but whether process is utilized.

Infringement may not be established by a mere showing that words of claim of patent are literally readable upon accused process, but it must appear that accused process consists of steps that are equivalent of steps of the patented method in that they accomplish substantially the same effect in substantially the same way.

Identity Between Accused Device and Patented Invention

Machine or device which performs same function or accomplishes same result by substantially different means or by substantially different principle or mode of operation or in substantially different way does not infringe patented invention.

Infringement is not avoided by the addition of other steps or embellishments to the patented process or by an imperfect practice of the patented invention.

Even where patented invention must be restricted, in view of prior art, to form shown and described by patentee, and cannot be extended to embrace new form which is substantial departure, a merely colorable departure constitutes infringement.

One does not escape infringement by providing a single element which fully responds to a plurality of elements in the patent.

The substitution of two steps for one to accomplish the same end does not avoid infringement.

Infringement cannot be avoided by mere fact that accused device is more or less efficient or performs additional functions.

Two patents may both be valid where second is improvement on first, in which event, if second includes first, neither of two patents can lawfully use other's invention without other's consent.

In considering literal infringement, patent's claims must be read in connection with patent's specification and its file history, and claims of patent cannot be given construction broader than teachings expressed in patent.

Patentee cannot rely on the Doctrine of Equivalents to recapture the broad claims that he has surrendered by amendments adopted to induce the grant of a patent.

When the claims in suit read literally on the accused activity, there is no need to resort to the Doctrine of Equivalents or to file wrapper estoppel.

Infringement is not avoided by an equivalent that was not known at time of invention.

Because the Doctrine of Equivalents rests on equitable considerations, principle has developed that an inventor, with respect to his patent, is entitled to a range of equivalents commensurate with scope of his invention.

The invoking of the Doctrine of Equivalents is application of equity principles, and it permits expansion of scope of written claims of patent if equity demands it to prevent fraud on patentee by too narrow a construction of an invention, or to prevent fraud on alleged infringer by too broad a construction.

Combination patents are to be narrowly construed, and there will be infringement only if same steps or their precise equivalents are followed by infringer.

Patents on simple combinations are not easily infringed for, while in principle the Doctrine of Equivalents is applicable to them, it is only when most narrowly circumscribed.

Where the patent is a pioneer, the patentee is allowed to claim a wide range of equivalents, but where the patent represents only a small but significant advance because the art is crowded, the Doctrine of Equivalents is given a corresponding narrow range.

In determining question of infringement, devices involved are to be examined in light of function they perform and how they perform such function.

Accused device which performed same function and obtained same result as patented device, but which did not operate in same manner or utilize same principle as patent claim, was not equivalent of patented device and did not infringe.

Only means protected by patent are means described in specifications and their equivalent, and other means of entirely different character, though they bring about same result, do not infringe.

Infringement of a method patent is not dependent upon form of apparatus used.

Where an essential element of claim of patent was not present in any accused device, infringement by the accused devices was precluded, despite argument that function of accused devices was impaired to evade infringement.

Subtraction of unnecessary element of invented device could not avoid infringement where accused device otherwise adopted basic features of patent claims.

As a combination, all elements disclosed are deemed to be material; the omission of a single element voids infringement unless that which remains does all the former combination did.

The grant of a later patent is evidence only that a patentable difference exists between the device shown and that of a prior patent, and not that it does not infringe the earlier patent.

Manufacture of article which as a result of wear becomes identical with patented article does not necessarily constitute infringement.

Words of the Claim

A plaintiff fails to show infringement when he is obliged to read his patent claims so broadly that they entirely cease to represent the invention.

Patent owner may not apply narrow construction to a claim to avoid prior art and then apply broad construction of same claim when infringement is alleged.

Patent claim cannot be read one way to avoid anticipation and another way to find infringement.

Where patent involved in an infringement suit was a paper patent in a crowded field, claims were required to be rather narrowly construed in light of specification.

In order to establish double patenting, it is necessary that claims of patent cross-read, that is, that not only must practice of first patent be an infringement of second, but practice of second must be an infringement of first.

Issue of patent infringement can seldom be determined on the literal words of the claim.

Limitation in patent claim may not be disregarded by court in determining infringement.

In order for infringement of a claim to occur, the device under consideration must satisfy the claim, element for element, and limitation for limitation.

Test of infringement is not whether claim of alleged infringing process literally reads upon claim of another process but whether the accused matter falls clearly within the claim.

In determining scope of a patent, courts consider such things as state of the art into which the patent came, language of the patent, and proceedings in the Patent Office.

5

DEFENSES

Defenses to allegations of patent infringement fall into two broad groups, statutory defenses and equitable defenses.

In statutory defenses, proof of such allegation will result in invalidity of the patent because it does not meet the requirement of the statute to obtaining a patent or that the patent is not infringed. These defenses include the public use and on sale defenses of 35 USC 102; or the defense of obviousness under 35 USC 103; or the defense of enablement and best mode under 35 USC 112.

The other broad class of defenses, equitable defenses, result in the unenforceability of the patent due to fraud and inequitable conduct, or misuse or delay in filing suit resulting in laches or estoppel. Laches, in general, refers to the conduct of a party which has placed the other party in a position where his rights will be imperiled and his defenses embarrassed. Usually, it is based on delay, attended by or inducing a change of condition or relation. An estoppel arises when one is concluded and forbidden by law to speak against his own act or conduct. Estoppel by laches is a failure to do something which should be done or to claim or enforce a right at a proper time.

Generally speaking, a defendant will respond to a complaint by alleging through the answer or counterclaim every defense possible for fear that failure to allege a defense will be later prohibited, and at the time of filing the answer, the defendant will not have had sufficient time for adequate discovery on many of the defenses.

Enforcement of a patent against otherwise infringing conduct may be precluded by three major defenses:

1. *Invalidity* is the first major defense, and liability may be escaped if the alleged infringer can establish that the invention failed to meet the requirements of patentability. Because of the importance to the public interest, a court should inquire into validity even if it finds no infringement.
2. *Inequitable conduct* or so-called fraudulent procurement will render a patent unenforceable.
3. Finally, extending the patent beyond its lawful scope or using it in a manner which results in antitrust law violations may result in *patent misuse,* which may render the patent unenforceable at least until the misuse actions are purged.

35 USC 282: Presumption of Validity; Defenses

A patent shall be presumed valid. Each claim of a patent (whether in independent, dependent, or multiple dependent form) shall be presumed valid independent of the validity of other claims; dependent or multiple dependent claims shall be presumed valid even though dependent upon an invalid claim. The burden of establishing invalidity of a patent or any claim thereof shall rest on the party asserting such invalidity.

The following shall be defenses in any action involving the validity or infringement of a patent and shall be pleaded:

(1) Noninfringement, absence of liability for infringement, or unenforceability;

(2) invalidity of the patent or any claim in suit on any ground specified in part II of this title as a condition for patentability;

(3) invalidity of the patent or any claim in suit for failure to comply with any requirement of Sections 112 or 251 of this title;

(4) any other fact or act made a defense by this title.

35 USC 282: PRESUMPTION OF VALIDITY

Prior to the inception of the CAFC, the circuit courts gave varying effect to the presumption of validity statute. Each started with a clear and convincing standard of proof.

3rd Circuit—presumption is weakened or overcome when relevant prior art had not been considered by the PTO.

7th Circuit—same as above, but that this subjects the patent to grave scrutiny in the court's validity review.

9th Circuit—as with the 7th, holding that pertinent prior art references not cited to the examiner destroyed the presumption.

10th Circuit—presumption diminished or dissipated altogether.

The Federal Circuit has firmly established an interpretation of 35 USC 282 which holds that the presumption of validity is a procedural device and the patent validity challenger always has the burden of overcoming it by clear and convincing evidence, and this applies to each element of the alleged infringer's proofs.

The introduction of more pertinent prior art does not weaken or destroy the presumption, nor does it shift the basic burden of persuasion. However, the introduction of more pertinent prior art can facilitate carrying that burden. In stating that the presumption of validity is a clear statutory procedural device, the Federal Circuit has said further that this presumption is not augmented by an earlier adjudication of patent validity, that is, *stare decisis.* A patent is not held valid for all purposes but, rather, is held *not invalid* on the record before the court. This presumption of validity does not apply to reexamination proceedings because it does not meet the statutory purpose of the presumption of administrative correctness to apply it to a procedure whose purpose is the remedy of administrative error.

A very high proportion of litigated patents are held invalid for lack of compliance with one or more of the statutory requirements. Due to the nature of the examination, the PTO is ordinarily incapable of detecting much of the possible prior art. Moreover, it has no facilities for testing, but must rely on representations made by applicants and their counsel. The presumption is of validity, not of infallibility. There is a presumption that earlier pertinent prior art was not considered by the PTO when the file wrapper did not contain any reference to it; when it was considered, the presumption has been deemed to have been strengthened. To overcome the presumption, more than a mere preponderance of the evidence is required, "strong, clear, cogent and convincing evidence" is usually necessary; occasionally, evidence "beyond a reasonable doubt" was required to invalidate a patent.

The CAFC has held that the presumption is *never* annihilated, destroyed, or even weakened, regardless of what facts are of record. Rather, the presumption is merely a statutory procedural device which assigns to the party asserting invalidity the "burden" of proving invalidity. Furthermore, the burden of proof never shifts. The only question to be decided is whether the attacker is successful. The statutory presumption of validity attaches to each claim independent of other claims.

INVALIDITY

Invalidity or Infringement: Which Issue First?

Introduction. Perhaps no axiom of patent law has seemed to be so indisputable and has been proven to be as durable as "that which infringes, if later, would anticipate, if earlier." This axiom, which has been referred to as the classic test [*Chenault v. Nebraska Farm Products* (D. Neb. 1956)], broadly stands for the proposition that patentability is precluded if the prior art contains an item that would be found to infringe the patent being sought or enforced.

Nevertheless, the CAFC, in *Lewmar Marine, Inc. v. Barient, Inc.* (1987, cert. denied, 1988), pointed out that the classic test had to be narrowed to more accurately reflect the current state of the law. In doing so, the court raised an interesting question as to the relationship between aspects of patent invalidity (specifically, *obviousness*) and patent infringement (specifically, the Doctrine of Equivalents). The *Lewmar* court did not pursue this issue.

Patent Invalidity. In any action involving the validity or infringement of a patent, the patentee's adversary must plead and prove, *inter alia,* the invalidity of the patent (or any claim at issue) on any ground specified as a condition of patentability [35 USC 282(2)]. Thus, unpatentability may be at issue before a patent is issued (and, indeed, may preclude such issue) and unpatentability may be a basis for invalidating a previously issued patent. Both circumstances will be considered under the umbrella of invalidity or unpatentability. It should be noted, however, that there are differences between the two circumstances.

For example, claims of a pending patent application are given their broadest reasonable construction consistent with the specification. This rule is considered appropriate because an applicant is at liberty to narrow his claims to avoid the prior art. This rule also applies during reexamination of an issued patent within the PTO. On the other hand, in a court proceeding, claims are normally construed to uphold their validity. Thus, claims of a pending patent application might be construed broadly to read on a given prior art reference and thus preclude patentability. The same claims, as part of an issued patent, might conceivably be read narrowly to avoid the same prior art reference.

Given the strictness of the test for anticipation (or lack of novelty), it was apparent that a further requirement was needed to prevent patents from being issued for trivial improvements that technically avoided anticipation by a prior art reference. In *Hotchkiss v. Greenwood* (1851), the Supreme Court embarked on a chain of decisions that imposed a requirement of *invention* to sustain the validity of a patent. In 1952, the requirement of invention was codified at 35 USC 103 (Obviousness). As with anticipation, the requirement of nonobviousness is partially rooted in the notion that patents should not withdraw from the public that which was previously available.

Patent Infringement. Patent infringement is typically approached in two steps: First, it must be determined whether there is literal infringement of the patent, which requires that the accused device embody every element of the claim. Second, if literal infringement is not present, then it must be determined if the Doctrine of Equivalents applies.

In its 1987 decision in *Lewmar Marine, Inc. v. Barient, Inc.,* the Federal Circuit decided that the classic axiom, "that which will infringe, if later, will anticipate, if earlier" had outlived its usefulness and had become less than totally accurate. The court stated that

> [w]hile "the classic test of anticipation" was indeed as stated, under the current statute "anticipation" does not carry the same meaning as before, and the "classic test" must be modified to: That which would literally infringe if later in time anticipates if earlier than the date of invention.

The court noted that, prior to the Patent Act of 1952, the term *anticipation* was used in a broader sense than it is today. Prior to 1952, anticipation meant either that the subject matter of the claims was not novel (i.e., that it would be deemed invalid under today's 35 USC 102) or that it was not inventive (the predecessor of the nonobviousness standard now embodied in 35 USC 103). The court observed that anticipation has become "a restricted term of art in patent law meaning that the claimed invention lacked novelty, or was unpatentable under 35 USC 102."

The relationship between anticipation and obviousness is not altogether different. The novelty requirement, which precludes patentability where a single, prior art reference completely anticipates the claimed invention, prevents an applicant withdrawing from the public domain the exact device or process that existed previously and which the public had a right to believe was freely available. The requirement of nonobviousness, like the Doctrine of Equivalents, is a more subtle concept. It also prevents a patent applicant from withdrawing subject matter from the public domain, even though that subject matter does not exist in any one reference, but is nonetheless available to the general public.

Stated in other terms, the nonobviousness requirement prevents a patentee from withdrawing from the public domain that which differs only slightly and unimportantly from a prior art reference that would otherwise anticipate it. In a similar manner, the Doctrine of Equivalents prevents an infringer from misappropriating from the patentee that which differs only slightly and unimportantly from the patentee's invention as expressly claimed.

There is a strong relationship between the two concepts of invalidity and infringement given the similar objectives that the doctrines are designed to achieve. As Justice Jackson noted in the majority opinion in *Graver Tank:*

> Consideration must be given to the purpose for which an ingredient is used in a patent, the qualities it has when combined with other ingredients, and the function which it is intended to perform. An important factor is *whether persons reasonably skilled in the art would have known* of the interchangeability of an ingredient not contained in the patent with one that was.

Two additional judicial doctrines of patent law that stand for similar propositions have coexisted for many years. Under both doctrines, a device or process that fits squarely within the literal language of a patent claim is excused, disregarded, or otherwise dismissed. In the case of an accidental anticipation, the disputed patent is not invalidated because the patentee has not withdrawn anything from the public domain in any real sense. On the contrary, in such instances the public never truly had the benefit of the purported anticipation. This is also true with regard to the Reverse Doctrine of Equivalents. Here, infringement is avoided because the accused infringer has not appropriated the patentee's invention in any real sense, even though the accused item falls within the scope of a claim.

As early as *Tilghman v. Proctor* (1881), the Supreme Court held that if certain products

> were accidentally and unwittingly produced, whilst the operators were in pursuit of other and different results, without exciting attention and without it even being known what was done or how it had been done, it would be absurd to say that this was an anticipation.

And, of course, the Reverse Doctrine of Equivalents continues to be the law today, though rarely effectively applied.

To determine both, very similar three-step inquiries must be conducted.

INVALIDITY	**INFRINGEMENT**
1. Is there a single prior art reference that precisely comes within the metes and bounds of a claim?	1. Does the accused item come within the literal scope of a claim?

2. If so, then an apparent anticipation is established and one may then consider whether such anticipation should be disregarded because it is accidental or unappreciated.	2. If so, there is an apparent literal infringement and one may go on to determine whether to disregard it based on the reverse doctrine.
3. If no, one must then consider whether the patent claim is still invalid because of the obviousness of the invention in view of the prior art as a whole.	3. If not, then one must determine whether there is infringement under the Doctrine of Equivalents.

The attitude of the Supreme Court has fluctuated over time, during some periods being very flexible, during others being quite rigid. While patent claims are sometimes described as though in terms of metes and bounds (a very exact set of measurements), it is unrealistic to suggest that something as inherently difficult of description as an invention can be so precisely measured. Claims are merely required to particularly point out and distinctly claim the subject matter which the applicant regards as his invention.

The reason for the above similarities is apparent. The source of Congress' authority to create a patent system lies in the constitutional provision. The Constitution did not authorize Congress to first issue patents and then provide for remedies. It expressly states that the exclusive rights should be given to inventors for their respective discoveries.

A patent system in which the legal tools for ensnaring an infringer are more restrictive than the tools for invalidating a patent has the potential to cheat the inventor. By the same token, a system in which expansive rules capture infringers, but only narrow rules invalidate a patent, is a system in which the public may not be treated fairly and fair competition may be thwarted. There is a significant problem in the courts as to which issue, that of infringement or invalidity, should be resolved first. In most litigation, the plaintiff patentee is charging the accused infringer while the latter is pleading invalidity as one of his defenses.

Judge Hand, in 1950, noted,

> A decision resting upon non-infringement is generally much more secure than one on invalidity, at least when the question is whether there is a patentable invention. The issue is as fugitive, impalpable, wayward, and vague a phantom as exists in the whole paraphernalia of legal concepts.

Judge Frank, in 1942, stated,

> [I]f we must here choose between deciding that the patent is not valid or is not infringed—a choice I think we are not required to make—our choice should be the former. By such a choice, we will do no harm to the patent system. It is under fire today, and may not survive attack unless its major abuses are removed. Among such abuses is the persistence of cancerous "spurious" patents.... Their attacks on the public interest bring the patent system into disrepute.

On the other hand, Judge Frank, in 1951, stated,

> For a finding that a patent is valid, when it is held uninfringed, involves three vices: (1) It is a decision of a hypothetical case, and, as such, is improper, and perhaps unconstitutional... (2) It may, in future litigation, unfairly prejudice the successful defendant... (3) It gives the patent owner, gratuitously, a highly persuasive precedent for use in litigation, or threatened litigation, with other prospective defendants, thereby hurting the public interest.

The Supreme Court, in 1939, indicated that a finding of validity of a patent absent a finding of infringement is "immaterial" and should be omitted from a judgment, whereas, in 1945, it characterized inquiry into validity as the "better practice" ever in a case that could be disposed of on grounds of noninfringement.

Some Consequences of Invalidity

Res Judicata and Collateral Estoppel. In Anglo-American jurisprudence, civil litigation is generally a private affair between the parties thereto. The opinion of the court is usually entitled to deference as precedent on the principle of *stare decisis,* nevertheless, the judgment rendered binds only the parties to that suit and their successors in interest.

When the judgment relied upon and the instant suit are based upon the "same cause of action," such prior judgment is said to be *res judicata,* being conclusive not only as to issues that were actually determined in the earlier suit, but also to all issues that might have been raised there, the legal theory being that the cause of action has become "merged" in the final judgment. The objective is to bring an end to litigation of the cause of action between the parties. Where the judgment relied upon was based upon a cause of action different from the instant one, such prior judgment is said to constitute collateral estoppel barring relitigation of those issues—but only those issues—actually litigated in the earlier suit.

Since 35 USC 282 provides that each claim of a patent shall be presumed valid, a question arises with respect to claims which have not been adjudicated. In 1974, the 6th Circuit held,

> *collateral estoppel* is available as a defense when unadjudicated claims present questions of fact identical to the questions presented in the adjudicated claims; when each unadjudicated claim merely restates, without significant difference, an adjudicated claim; and when none of the unadjudicated claims defines an invention separate and apart from the invention defined in the adjudicated claims.

With respect to prior holdings of validity or invalidity, the CAFC in 1983 has held,

> [T]he prior holding of validity is not necessarily inconsistent with the subsequent of invalidity. In one action, the defendants did not overcome the statutory presumption of validity; in the other they did. The difference in result could be attributable to many neutral facts: e.g., different prior art references or different records. It cannot be said that of two "inconsistent" determinations, one is correct, and one is incorrect. Thus, we do not believe that the existence of a seemingly inconsistent prior holding on "validity" should change the inquiry from a full and fair opportunity to litigate to one of correctness; rather, it should serve only as a "red flag warning" to the court to apply the full and fair criteria more carefully.

While a judgment of invalidity binds the patent owner and his successors because he is a party to the suit and has the opportunity to contest, a judgment of validity cannot bind persons who are neither parties nor in privity with parties to the suit.

In either a *res judicata* or collateral estoppel situation, the party seeking the benefit of the prior judgment must have been a party to the earlier suit. For many years a majority of courts adhered to the view that there could be no estoppel by judgment unless the estoppel was mutual, that is, the party invoking the benefit of a prior judgment as conclusive would have to be bound by the determination had it been adverse to him. Such, the courts said, was a requirement of due process.

Because of the absence of mutuality, it was possible for a patentee, though his patent had been declared invalid by one or more courts, to sue another, relitigating the validity of his patent. Nevertheless, the Supreme Court has held that mutuality is not an absolute requirement and that, where a patentee has had a "full and fair opportunity" to litigate the validity of his patent, a resulting judgment of invalidity may be interposed as a bar even by one not a party to the earlier suit. What constitutes a "full and fair opportunity" is not completely clear; consider invalidity based upon a summary judgment, for example.

Even a simple stipulation of *Dismissal With Prejudice* can be accorded *res judicata* effect in an infringement suit. Like a consent decree, it is an agreement recorded and acknowledged in court, and it is, therefore, generally entitled to *res judicata* effect on all matters over which it extends; it is considered an adverse judgment on the claims so dismissed.

Collateral estoppel does not apply to a mere holding of noninfringement; there must have been a determination of invalidity in the earlier litigation. A prior holding of validity, while it enhances the presumption of validity, is not conclusive and the presumption may still be rebutted in subsequent litigation. A federal court is not bound by findings of validity by federal district and appeals courts in other circuits. The Court of Claims did not deem itself precluded from enforcing a patent, although a U.S. District Court had held the patent invalid, where the Court of Claims had rejected, as being without merit, the very basis on which the District Court held the patent invalid. One accused of infringing a patent previously held invalid may apply to the CAFC for a *writ of mandamus* ordering the District Court to dismiss the suit, thus precluding the District Court from proceeding with relitigation of the patent.

Comity, the principle in accordance with which the courts of one jurisdiction will give effect to the judicial decisions of another, is not a rule of law, but one of practice, convenience, and expediency. It declares not how a case shall be decided, but how it may with propriety be decided. The Supreme Court has said, "Comity, however, has no application to questions not considered by the prior court, or, in patent cases, to alleged anticipated devices which were not laid before that court."

Licensee and Licensor Estoppel. The doctrines of *res judicata* and collateral estoppel in the above situations have been used against a patentee whose patent has once been declared invalid. Until recently, another application of estoppel accrued to the benefit of the patentee. For many years it was the law that a licensee was estopped from challenging the validity of any patents under which he was licensed, the theory being that the licensee, by taking out a license, admitted, in effect, the validity of the licensed patents. It was considered inequitable to allow the licensee to sue since he himself was immune from a suit for infringement.

In 1969, the Supreme Court in *Lear, Inc. v. Adkins* abolished as inconsistent with federal patent and antitrust policy the doctrine that a licensee was estopped from contesting the validity of a patent. A patent, in the last analysis, simply represents the legal conclusion reached by the PTO. Moreover, this legal conclusion is predicated on factors as to which reasonable men can disagree. Therefore, the public interest in ferreting out invalid patents overrides the general principles of contract law. *Lear* apparently extends to assignees as well as to licensees. Even one charged with inducing breach of a patent license contract may defend by challenging the validity of the patent. Furthermore, a licensee may file an action for declaratory judgment of invalidity without exercising a right to terminate given in the patent license. As the law now stands, an inventor may challenge the validity of a patent that he himself has assigned. A licensee's covenant not to contest the validity of his licensor's patent is void and unenforceable and does not bar raising the issue of validity, either affirmatively or as a defense.

It should be noted that the Doctrine of Licensor Estoppel is still viable. This doctrine holds that a licensor is estopped from asserting his nonownership of a patent at the time he granted a license, where the license purported to cover a patent which, in fact, was not acquired by the licensor until after the license was granted.

Furthermore, the Supreme Court observed that licensees may avoid further royalty payments, regardless of the provisions of their license, once a third party proves that the patent is invalid. It has been held that a licensee under a patent which has been declared invalid is not entitled to recoup royalties which he has already paid, a judgment of invalidity, in this regard, operating only prospectively and not retrospectively. Where, however, a patent has been cancelled, it is void *ab initio,* so that the patentee would be liable to his licensees for whatever consideration they paid.

INEQUITABLE CONDUCT

A breach of the Duty of Candor to the PTO constitutes *Fraud on the Patent Office,* now known as *Inequitable Conduct. Common law fraud* is much more difficult to prove and when proven would result in *invalidation* of the patent; inequitable conduct, on the other hand, results in unenforceability.

Fraud or inequitable conduct can lead to:

1. striking of an application from the files of the PTO;
2. invalidity or unenforceability;
3. a government suit for cancellation of the patent;
4. an award of attorney fees and punitive damages in an infringement suit; or
5. liability under the
    (a) antitrust laws,
    (b) Federal Trade Commission Act, or
    (c) securities laws.

The primary areas of concern during the course of prosecution of an application for patent are:

1. Prior public use not disclosed in the inventor's oath;
2. failure to cite known prior art;
3. False Rule 131 affidavits relating to the Date of Invention;
4. False Rule 132 affidavits as they relate to test results, so-called secondary considerations or unexpected superior properties in an effort to overcome an obviousness rejection.

The concepts of materiality, *scienter,* and burden of proof have been considered elsewhere. Inequitable conduct in essence is related to the equity Doctrine of Unclean Hands, although technical differences with common law fraud are basically disappearing as a result of recent CAFC decisions.

PATENT MISUSE

A patent owner may not extend his patent beyond its lawful scope nor may he use the patent in violation of the antitrust laws. If such misuse is found, the courts will withhold any remedy for infringement or breach of a license agreement. The rights of the patent owner will be restored if and when the misuse is purged.

In early lower court decisions, improper use of a patent by the plaintiff was no defense to a defendant otherwise guilty of infringement.

1892 "Even a gambler, or the keeper of a brothel, cannot be deprived of his property because he is an obnoxious person or a criminal; and it is no defense to the trespass upon it . . . that it was used in carrying on the unlawful occupation."

1903 "It is difficult to understand how or why a violation of the Sherman antitrust law by this complainant, if there has been such a violation, confers any right on the defendant to infringe this patent."

This view continued to prevail even after a 1931 Supreme Court decision which a lower court interpreted to mean,

> one who supplies unpatented materials to a licensee to be used in disregard of an unlawful condition is not liable to the patentee as a contributory infringer. . . . [It had] no bearing upon the right of an owner of a patent to sue for its infringement.

The Supreme Court made it clear in *Morton Salt Co. v. G. S. Suppiger Co.* (1942), where the Court held,

> the use of a [patent] to suppress competition in the sale of an unpatented article may deprive the patentee of the aid of a court of equity to restrain an alleged infringement by one who is a competitor. . . .
>
> Equity may rightly withhold its assistance from such a use of the patent by declining to entertain a suit for infringement, and should do so at least until it is made to appear that the improper practice has been abandoned and that the consequences of the misuse of the patent have been dissipated.

In another case, the Supreme Court noted that misuse may be made out even though the challenged practice does not actually violate the antitrust laws.

The relationship between the misuse doctrine and the federal antitrust laws is complex. However, conduct may still constitute misuse even though it may fall short of an antitrust violation. On the other hand, if a practice does rise to the level of an antitrust violation, it will also constitute misuse. Both involve a common inquiry: Is the practice an appropriate exercise of the patentee's statutory patent rights? If the answer is yes, then the practice is not an improper extension within the meaning of the patent misuse doctrine and should enjoy an immunity from antitrust liability even though, but for the patent, the practice would violate the antitrust laws. From these decisions, it is clear that the courts lack a clear and general theory for resolving that inquiry.

The three classic acts of misuse are: (1) requiring the purchase of unpatented goods for use with patented apparatus or processes, (2) prohibiting production or sale of competing goods, and (3) conditioning the granting of a license under one patent upon the acceptance of another and different license. There are, however, a number of other practices which have been studied. Acts of misuse will probably shift with antitrust policy as they have in the past.

1. Tying arrangements; royalties on unpatented components: Misuse.
2. Covenant not to deal in competing goods: Misuse.
3. Package licensing: It is normally not unlawful to confer rights under more than one patent. However, mandatory or coercive package licensing wherein the patent owner refuses to license patents separately has been treated as a species of tying.

4. Post-expiration royalties and restraints: Unenforceable since the patent right is exhausted after the patent expires.
5. Royalty based on total sales: Misuse since an improper extension of the patent grant. However, the parties may agree to such an arrangement.
6. Refusal to license; excessive or discriminatory royalties: Generally, the patent owner has discretion whether and to whom he will issue a license. Furthermore, he can set a price at whatever level he feels will maximize the return. Whether a patent owner commits misuse by discriminating in royalties charged or offered to different persons is a more difficult issue. A District Court, in 1973, held,

In order to sustain a finding of patent misuse or a Sherman Act violation based on discriminatory licensing, at least the following must be present: (a) the plaintiff took a license; (b) the royalty rate charged plaintiff and that charged a competitor were unequal; (c) in all particulars relevant to equality of rates plaintiff and its licensed competitor were similarly situated; and (4) royalties were an important expense factor in the production costs and the discriminatory rate caused substantial impairment of competition in the relevant market.

7. Since price-fixing constitutes a *per se* violation of the antitrust laws, a patent owner commits misuse if he practices it in connection with a patent. Control over price after the first sale by the patent owner or by a licensee is not authorized by the patent laws. On the other hand, there is case law allowing the patentee to fix the price of sale of a licensee who also has the right to make and use, so that he may protect his own right to secure adequate pecuniary reward on the product which he makes. In other words, if he did not, the licensee could undercut the patentee's selling price and prevent him from a normal recovery for his patent right.
8. Territorial restrictions; resale restraints: It is generally assumed that a patent owner may assign or license the right to practice the invention on a territorially restricted basis. However, attempts to restrict the disposition of a patented product after the first sale exceeds the scope of the patent monopoly. This right to impose territorial limitations is based in part on 35 USC 261, "to the whole or *any specified part of the United States.*"

It is a fundamental rule of patent law that the owner of a patent may license another and prescribe territorial limitations.... Exclusive territorial licenses granted under patents are old in the law. Unless they run afoul of the antitrust laws for other reasons, and based on additional facts . . . they are legal.

9. Field-of-use and customer limitations: A patented product or process may be useful in more than one field-of-use. The Supreme Court has held that use-restricted licenses were not illegal and violation of such restrictions could be enforced through suits for infringement. However, as in the case of price-fixing and territorial restrictions, attempts to restrain use or disposition of a patented product after the first authorized sale exceed the scope of the patent monopoly. Unprotected by patent law, such attempts may constitute patent misuse.
10. Grant-back clauses: The Supreme Court has held that such clauses were not illegal *per se* but warned that under some circumstances "the device could be employed with the purpose or effect of violating the anti-trust laws."
11. Restraints on the patentee; covenants not to license: While most covenants are for the protection of the patentee-licensor, occasionally, the patentee may covenant not to grant further licenses or not to grant licenses without the consent of the licensee. There is a difference of opinion and some recent lower court decisions question the validity of covenants not to license.
12. Suppression; compulsory licensing: Generally, a patentee owner may refuse either to issue licenses or to make or sell the claimed invention. Such suppression does not constitute misuse; however, compulsory licensing may be provided for by statute (Atomic Energy; Clean Air; etc.) for a particular category of inventions or as a remedy for past violation of the antitrust laws.

It should be emphasized that the individual defendant raising a misuse defense need not show that he was personally harmed by the abusive practice. Patent misuse is an affirmative defense that must be pleaded and proved.

PATENT ANTITRUST

Many of the difficulties encountered with the antitrust laws by patent holders relate to restrictions in how the patent is exploited through licensing arrangements. The improper actions of a patent licensor may lead to misuse and some patent misuses lead to violation of the antitrust laws despite the fact that the purposes of both laws are to promote competition.

While a patentee by definition adds his invention to the public storehouse of knowledge, he must not be allowed to use the patent grant for the invention to restrict the free use of anything else already known or available to the public. It is at this point where antitrust questions come into being, and it is for the courts, on a case-by-case basis, to decide whether given subject matter is within or without the public domain and whether antitrust violations have occurred. Because the underlying goal of the antitrust laws is to increase competition, the patent and antitrust laws are complementary, and federal laws seek to maintain a balance between these two socially desirable objectives. Congress, in its statutory enactments, has consistently adhered to the principle that free competition, subject to limited regulation, is the best means of securing a prosperous and stable economic environment in the United States.

The thrust of antitrust laws cannot be avoided merely by claiming that the otherwise illegal conduct is compelled by contractual obligations. Such obligations cannot supersede statutory imperatives. The antitrust laws do not require a patent holder to forfeit the exclusionary power inherent in the patent the instant the monopoly affords power over a relevant product market. The tests of illegality under the Clayton and Sherman Acts are complementary.

The Sherman Act is violated when patent owners unlawfully conspire to exclude competition. A course of dealings including cross-licenses and an interference settlement designed to limit the competitive position of outsiders evidences such a conspiracy. However, the courts have continually emphasized that a prosecution under the Sherman Act cannot be based merely on the possession of a lawfully issued patent.

After the Supreme Court decision in *Henry v. A. B. Dick Co.* (1912), upholding a so-called tying agreement restricting the use of a patented device to certain unpatented articles to be furnished by the patentee, Congress enacted the Clayton Act of 1914 prohibiting the making of such tying agreements involving patented or unpatented articles.

In 1922, the Supreme Court held,

> the franchise secured by a patent consists only in the right to exclude others from making, using, or vending the thing patented without the permission of the patentee . . . but the right to make regulation, in the public interest, under the police power of the states, or in the exertion of the authority of Congress over matters within its constitutional power, is controlled by general principles of law, and the patent right confers no privilege to make contracts in themselves illegal, and certainly not to make those directly violative valid statutes of the United States . . . the rights secured by a patent do not protect the making of contracts in restraint of

trade, or those which tend to monopolize trade or commerce in violation of the Sherman Act.

Where a patent misuse involves an antitrust violation, the remedy may include, in addition to normal antitrust remedies, compulsory licensing at reasonable royalty rates, including the licensing of know-how and of future patents in some cases. Such extreme results are proposed only when necessary to restore and maintain normal market conditions free from the effect of the antitrust violation.

DELAY IN FILING SUIT: LACHES AND ESTOPPEL

35 USC 286 is a Statute of Limitations which bars recovery of damages for any infringement committed more than six years prior to the filing of the complaint or counterclaim for infringement in the action. This Statute of Limitations applies only to Remedies at Law, namely, Damages; the Doctrine of Laches applying to the equitable remedy of injunctive relief. Estoppel, on the other hand, acts as a total bar to the enforcement of a patent. Equitable estoppel requires proof of four elements:

1. an unreasonable and unexcused delay;
2. prejudice to the defendant;
3. affirmative conduct by the patent owner inducing the belief that he had abandoned his claims; and
4. detrimental reliance by the infringer.

The hallmark of estoppel is an infringement notice threatening prompt and vigorous enforcement of the patent which is followed by a period of unreasonable and unexcused delay. Laches and estoppel are equitable doctrines enforced in patent cases because the federal patent statutes prescribe no specific period of limitation for a patentee's initiation of an infringement suit. Laches, being an equitable doctrine, would not be available to willful infringers or to an accused infringer found to have committed egregious conduct. The Doctrine of Laches precludes equitable relief where there has been: (1) an inexcusable delay in instituting suit seeking enforcement of patent rights; and (2) such delay has prejudiced the accused.

It has been held that the laches period begins to run when a patent owner first discovers facts that give rise to a cause of action for infringement, not when the owner first receives an opinion from an attorney that the patent has been infringed.

The ancient equitable defense of laches bars recovery for prefiling infringements when the owner unreasonably delays suit to the prejudice of the accused infringer. Laches alone does not bar recovery for postfiling infringements.

The defense of estoppel bars *all* recovery for infringement when the owner represents in some way that he will not enforce his patent against the infringer and the infringer reasonably relies on that representation. A threat to enforce a patent followed by a long period of inaction may constitute an estoppel.

The first major element of the laches defense is that the patent owner delay filing suit for an unreasonable period of time, which depends upon the circumstances of the particular case. The courts apply a six-year presumption by analogy to the damage limitation statute 35 USC 286.

1. "For purposes of laches the relevant time period begins to run when a patentee has either actual or constructive *knowledge* of the alleged infringement."
2. "[P]laintiff is chargeable with the sum total of the laches of itself and of its predecessor."
3. "[U]nexplained delay is presumed to have injured a defendant, unless the contrary can be shown by a plaintiff, after *six years*—the period of time specified in 35 USC 286, which in its application to patent suits for damages is the equivalent of the statute of limitations in actions at law, frequently adopted by courts of equity in determining whether laches existed."

The patent owner may avoid the consequences of otherwise unreasonable delay by establishing a legally adequate *excuse.*

1. "Where the plaintiff is engaged in *other litigation* involving the patent to escape a defense of laches he must at least inform the potential infringer of his intent to pursue his rights under the patent."
2. "[D]uring this entire period, plaintiff was honestly endeavoring to effect an *amicable settlement* of the dispute and avoid litigation. Certainly, such activity is not incompatible with proper diligence to protect one's patent interests."
3. "[P]arty's *poverty* or pecuniary embarrassment [or *illness*] was not a sufficient excuse for postponing the assertion of his rights."
4. "With respect to laches, we find that *post-war conditions* must be taken into account and that, because of them, a more liberal application of the doctrine of laches is justified than might otherwise be the case."

5. "There was no laches, for the bringing of a lawsuit prior to the instant action was unwarranted due to the *poor financial condition* of Defendant with consequent non-likelihood of recovery of damages for infringement, if proven."
6. "Whether General Electric might have been influenced by the fact that Sciaky was making substantial purchases of electrical supplies from it is not material [Desire to Maintain *Infringer's Goodwill*]."
7. "To bring a patent infringement action one must have title or grant to title. . . . Since *Title to the Patents* . . . was in issue until 1964 any inaction on the part of Fish during that period of time was excusable."
8. "[I]t cannot be maintained that it is the duty of an assignee in *Bankruptcy* to institute suits for infringement of a patent owned by the bankrupt, and that his failure to do so is negligence."

The second major element of the laches defense is that the patent owner's delay cause material prejudice to the infringer. This prejudice can take the form of the loss of evidence (death of witnesses; loss of documents; etc.) preventing the defendant from adequately proving his case, or prejudice due to the defendant's having invested considerable funds during the delay period. This latter is a more controversial matter.

Laches is an equitable defense, hence the fairness and reasonableness of the infringer's conduct is as much an issue as that of the patent owner. The court, for example, may reject the defense "[if the infringer] has engaged in particularly egregious conduct which would change the equities significantly in plaintiff's favor."

While estoppel is closely related to laches, and infringers often raise both defenses, the courts recognize a clear distinction:

1. Laches arises from unreasonable delay by the patent owner coupled with material prejudice to the infringer. Laches precludes recovery of damages for infringements occurring prior to the filing of suit but not an injunction or damages as to post-filing infringements.
2. Estoppel arises from misrepresentation and reliance and bars prospective as well as retrospective relief. Silence alone will generally not create an estoppel.

NONINFRINGEMENT

Where there are a number of infringers, a plaintiff can pick his target, but is under no obligation to notify the others that they are in range. To establish a *prima facie* case of patent infringement, the plaintiff need only introduce into evidence: (1) Letters Patent; (2) evidence to his title to such patent; and (3) evidence that the defendant has engaged in *any* of the activities proscribed by 35 USC 271.

After the plaintiff has presented his case, the defendant may attempt to avoid liability for infringement by offering evidence in rebuttal, including evidence tending to establish any of the defenses enumerated in 35 USC 282 and/or evidence of a defect in the plaintiff's title to the patent or patents in suit. To avoid liability for infringement, one need only establish any one of the above defenses or defects.

In this regard the conditions for patentability should be reviewed: (1) statutory subject matter; (2) novelty; (3) utility; (4) nonobviousness; (5) no statutory bars; (6) an adequate disclosure; and (7) proper inventorship.

The two key issues in every patent infringement suit are: (1) the *validity* of the patent or patents alleged to have been infringed; and (2) whether the defendant *did infringe* the claims of the patent in suit. The plaintiff has the burden of proving the affirmative of the ultimate issue by a fair "preponderance of the credible evidence."

Infringement is a question of fact; its resolution being therefore the province of the trier of fact, and a most difficult and technical issue it is. 35 USC 271 defines patent infringement as the unauthorized making, using, or selling of any patented invention. Accordingly, it is necessary to determine just what constitutes the patented invention. One can infringe a patent only by infringing one or more of its claims.

SUMMARY OF DEFENSES

1. Noninfringement under 35 USC 271

   Absence of liability for infringement

   (a) License under the Patent

   (b) Intervening Rights [Sections 251 and 252 (Reissue)]

   Unenforceability

   (a) Fraud/Inequitable Conduct

   (b) Misuse

   (c) Laches

   (d) Estoppel

   (e) Statute of Limitations

   (f) Expired Patent

   (g) *Res judicata*

2. Invalidity—Conditions for Patentability

(a) [Section 101]
   (1) Nonstatutory Subject Matter
   (2) Double Patenting
   (3) No Utility
   (4) Inoperable Invention
(b) [Section 102]
   (1) Anticipation . . . (a), (b), (d), (e) and (g)
   (2) Abandonment . . . (c)
   (3) Improper Inventorship . . . (f)
(c) [Section 103]: Obviousness

3. Invalidity—Failure to Comply with . . .
   (a) [Section 112]: Description/Enablement/Best Mode, Definiteness
   (b) [Section 251]: Reissue
4. Any Other Fact or Act Made a Defense by This Title
   (a) Improper Scope of Claims
   (b) No Title in the Patent
   (c) [Section 271(e)(1) and (2)] . . . Federal Drug Law Requirements
   (d) Antitrust Law Violations
   (e) Jurisdiction
   (f) Bankruptcy

UNITED STATES CODE ANNOTATED

35 USC 282: Presumption of Validity; Defenses

A patent shall be presumed valid.

The following shall be defenses in any action involving the validity or infringement of a patent and shall be pleaded:

(1) noninfringement, absence of liability for infringement or unenforceability,

(2) invalidity of the patent or any claim in suit on any ground specified in Part II of this title as a condition for patentability,

(3) invalidity of the patent or any claim in suit for failure to comply with any requirement of Sections 112 or 251 of this title,

(4) any other fact or act made a defense by this title.

It is no answer to a claim of damages that defendant made no profits by his infringement.

In view of no actual sales of instrument similar to patented device and in view of unsuccessful experimentation therewith and abandonment of use thereof by patent assignee's competitor, the *de minimus* doctrine was applicable [i.e., "The law does not concern itself with trifles"].

Absent proof of total incapacity, defense of nonoperativeness, or nonutility is not available in suit for infringement of patent.

Private parties may challenge patent validity in two situations: as defense to patent infringement and in suits to enforce antitrust laws.

Invalidity of patent, noninfringement of patent, and unenforceability of patent because of misuse are defenses which can be raised in a patent infringement action; such defenses can also be litigated by way of action for declaration of invalidity, noninfringement, and unenforceability.

Anticipation is a narrow technical defense which requires showing of virtual identity between patent in question and specific prior art device; by comparison, *obviousness* is intended to be a demanding standard where court looks at the whole of the prior art, in considering it together for all that was disclosed therein.

Mismarking is not a defense to patent infringement.

Defense of *estoppel* to infringement exists where there is: (1) proven infringement, (2) knowledge by the patent owner of the infringement, (3) conduct of the patent owner which misleads the infringer into believing that the patent owner has abandoned his patent or acquiesced in the infringement, and (4) reliance by the infringer on such conduct.

Defense of misuse of a patent in suit for infringement is outgrowth of equitable principle of *Unclean Hands.*

Misuse is an equitable defense and serves only to bar enforceability of patent.

Improper use does not invalidate a patent, but courts will not assist an offending patent owner against persons who infringe the patent while such improper practices continue, and improper use does not vest an infringer with a license for the life of the patent, since if a patent owner *purges* himself of improper business practices he may then enforce his patent and recover damages for infringement occurring thereafter.

Injury to defendant by patent misuse is unnecessary to successful assertion of the defense of patent misuse.

Patentee who utilizes so-called tying arrangement will be denied all relief against infringement of his patent.

Misuse of patent in no way affects validity of patent itself, and once patentee has purged himself he may again enforce his patent by infringement suits.

Notwithstanding former Equity Rule 30, this section is still in force as to the *Necessity for Pleading each Defense* relied on.

Laches need not be pleaded.

Defense that complainant's articles were not marked with the date of his patent must be raised by the answer.

Strong public policy underlying misuse doctrine allows alleged to interpose the defense without allegation or proof that it was the victim of any misuse.

In patent infringement action, unclean defense that plaintiff is using patent unlawfully to extend purported monopoly *need not be pleaded* but may be taken up without affirmative claim therefor.

In a suit in equity, insufficiency of the specification must be set up in the answer.

The denial [of infringement] should not be a mere denial of infringement generally, which is a conclusion of the pleader, but the facts from which such conclusion is drawn should be alleged.

The charge of infringement must be answered by the defendant *fully, distinctly and unevasively.*

The defendant, who sets up matters of anticipation or the like, must state the precise nature of the right asserted by him, but not reasons for his attitude.

Where a party attacks the validity of invention on the grounds of anticipation, identification of alleged prior publications, public sale, and public use must be furnished by that party, regardless of whether such party nominally occupies the status of plaintiff or defendant.

An answer pleading prior publications must certainly identify the publications, or a copy must be filed, but where prior patents are relied on, it is sufficient to give their number and date and name of the patentee.

In patent infringement suit *alternative and inconsistent defenses* may be pleaded.

Defendant sued for infringement, though claiming license, may also set up invalidity and noninfringement.

Inconsistent pleas are available to defendant.

In patent infringement case, where *counterclaim* attacked validity of patent, public aspect of question required a decision on counterclaim notwithstanding dismissal of bill.

Patent is presumed valid, based on acknowledged *experience and expertise of the PTO* and recognition that patent approval is a species of administrative determination supported by evidence.

Presumption of validity of patent relieves patent holder of burden of establishing validity as a requisite for successful maintenance of infringement action and places burden of establishing invalidity on alleged infringer who asserts it; presumption requires that reasonable doubt on question of validity be resolved in favor of patent holder.

Presumption that a patent is valid can not relieve court of duty of inquiring into validity of patent in patent infringement suit.

Proof of inoperativeness or nonutility must be strong as every reasonable doubt is resolved in favor of a patentee.

Patents are *prima facie* evidence of their validity, since they are not issued as a matter of course, but after consideration of underlying questions, such as the state of the art, as it bears on the question of novelty, discovery, invention, and the like.

The grant of letters patent is *prima facie* evidence that patentee is first inventor of device described in letters patent, and of novelty thereof.

The issuance of patent is *prima facie* evidence of both novelty and utility, and when one attacks a patent he must make good his attack with reasonable clearness and he has the burden of proof, and every reasonable doubt will be resolved against him.

A patent carries with it not only a presumption of validity but a further presumption of the absence of interference.

Inventors named in an issued patent are presumed to be correct.

Issuance of patent creates presumption that it is workable.

Although granting of patent carries with it presumption that invention claimed is patentable, there is no presumption that such invention does not infringe on earlier issued patent.

Every patent comes into court clothed with presumption of validity, and party challenging validity of patent bears heavy burden of demonstrating by clear and convincing proof of prior use or sale of patented invention or patent's deficiency in some other respect.

6

REMEDIES

35 USC 281: Remedy for Infringement of Patent

A patentee shall have remedy by civil action for infringement of his patent.

35 USC 283: Injunction

The several courts having jurisdiction of cases under this title may grant injunctions in accordance with the principles of equity to prevent the violation of any right secured by patent, on such terms as the court deems reasonable.

35 USC 284: Damages

[D]amages adequate to compensate for the infringement but in no event less than a reasonable royalty for the use made of the invention by the infringer, together with interest and costs as fixed by the court.

When the damages are not found by a jury, the court shall assess them. In either event the court may increase the damages up to *three times* the amount found or assessed.

35 USC 285: Attorney Fees

The court in exceptional cases may award reasonable attorney fees to the prevailing party.

35 USC 286: Time Limitation on Damages

Except as otherwise provided by law, no recovery shall be had for any infringement committed more than *six years* prior to the filing of the complaint or counterclaim for infringement in the action.

35 USC 287: Limitation on Damages; Marking and Notice

In the event of *failure* so *to mark,* no damages shall be recovered by the patentee in any action for infringement, except on proof that the infringer was notified of the infringement and continued to infringe thereafter, in which event damages may be recovered only for infringement occurring after such *notice.*

35 USC 289: Additional Remedy for Infringement of Design Patent

[S]hall be liable to the owner to the extent of his *total profit,* but not less than $250 . . ."

35 USC 284: DAMAGES

The three traditional modes of measuring compensatory damages are (1) lost profits, (2) established royalty, and (3) reasonable royalty. The statutes also allow for (1) prejudgment interest, (2) increased damages, and (3) attorney fees, these last especially in the case of willful infringement (which see).

Prior to the creation of the Federal Circuit there were many differences between the various circuits in the interpretations of provisions relating to damages, interest, and injunctive relief:

—effect of an established royalty on a reasonable royalty rate

—concept of noninfringing alternative

—interpretation of the entire market rule

—standards of proof for validity and infringement in determining whether to grant preliminary injunctions.

Difficulties in measuring damages and profits dominated the period from about 1870 to 1946. With damages, the difficulty was in finding an appropriate measure when a patent owner could prove neither lost profits nor an established royalty rate. The courts finally resolved the difficulty by recognizing the reasonable royalty measure, which was thereafter codified in the 1922 and 1946 acts. With profits, the difficulty was in finding a basis for apportionment of the infringer's profits when such profits were clearly not all attributable to the patented invention. The courts never succeeded in developing a fully satisfactory approach to the apportionment difficulty.

Early Supreme Court decisions stressed the compensatory nature of the monetary damages recoverable in an action at law for patent infringement: The plaintiff was to recover what he would have made *but for* the defendant's infringing activity. Damages were a matter to be proved, not presumed. The Court viewed a license royalty rate established by the patent owner in actual transactions as the best and primary measure of damages. In the absence of such a rate, the Court allowed a patent owner to prove damages by way of lost sales or diminished revenues caused by the defendant's illicit price competition. In such cases, however, the Court required substantial proof of causation; that is, that the defendant's sales would have inured to the benefit of the plaintiff or that the plaintiff's price reduction was not due to other causes.

In 1922, Congress amended the patent equitable remedy statute to authorize the award of a "reasonable sum as profits or general damages," in cases where it appeared that the defendant realized profits or the complainant suffered damages but that such profits or damages were "not susceptible of calculation and determination with reasonable certainty." The language of the statute, unfortunately, was less than satisfactory. It failed to refer to the reasonable royalty recognized previously, and added the reasonable sum concept only to the equitable remedy provision, leaving unchanged the legal damage provision.

Where the defendant's infringement consisted of the use of the plaintiff's patented machine or process, the Supreme Court established a comparative measure of profits: What profit increment did the infringer realize over what he would have realized had he used other means "open to the public?" Where the defendant's infringement consisted of the sale of a device covered by the plaintiff's patent, the Supreme Court established an apportionment rule.

Professor Robinson, in his classic, *The Law of Patents for Useful Inventions,* published in 1890, had this to say:

> two great classes: (1) Those in which the infringement consists in the unlawful use, or making and use, of the patented invention; (2) Those in which the infringement consists in the unlawful sale, or manufacture and sale of the patented invention....
>
> The cost of using the invention may present little difficulty, but the benefit derived from its employment rarely assumes the form of a specific sum of money... may manifest itself either in the increase of direct pecuniary receipts, or in the decrease of expenses... the data for computation are less capable of definite ascertainment.

Robinson went on to distinguish between where the article sold is the exact patented invention (for which the whole profit is awarded), and where the article embraces more than the patented invention (in which case apportionment is required).

A most important decision on the burden of proof was handed down by the Supreme Court in *Westinghouse Elec. v. Wagner Elec.* in 1912, wherein the Court began its opinion by noting that the question "as to who has the burden of proof, in cases like this, is one of great practical importance and constantly arises in patent cases." It found "controversy on the subject" and "conflict in the decisions."

> It will be sufficient for the present purposes to say that
>
> (a) Where the infringer has sold or used a patented article, the plaintiff is entitled to recover all of the profits.
>
> (b) Where a patent, though using old elements, gives the entire value to the combination, the plaintiff is entitled to recover all the profits. [*Hurlburt v. Schillinger,* 130 US 456, 472].
>
> (c) Where profits are made by the use of an article patented as an entirety, the infringer is liable for all the profits "unless he can show—and the burden is on him to show—that a portion of them is the result of some other thing used by him." [*Elizabeth v. Pavement Co.,* 97 US 126].
>
> (d) But there are many cases in which the plaintiff's patent is only a part of the machine and creates only a part of the profits. . . . In such case, if plaintiff's patent only created a part of the profits, he is only entitled to recover that part of the net gains.

The Court noted that strict application of a rule placing the burden of proof on apportionment on the plaintiff would allow nullification of the statutory right to monetary compensation "by those infringers who had ingenuity enough to smother the patent with improvements belonging to themselves or to third persons."

In 1946, Congress made a substantial change in the statute on monetary recovery for patent infringement by dropping any reference to the infringer's profits. Although Congress' exact intent in making the change is unclear, subsequent court decisions construe the change as eliminating the patent owner's traditional equitable remedy of an accounting of the infringer's profits. While the infringer's profits may be considered as evidence tending to establish what constitutes a reasonable royalty or the amount of damages, they may not be recovered as such.

Most of the Report of the House and Senate Patent Committees on the bill which became the 1946 Act is consistent with an intent to eliminate profits recovery entirely. It stresses the intricate and insolvable problem of apportionment and the expense and delay of complex and technical accounting procedures before masters. However, the last paragraph of the report states that the bill "would not preclude the recovery of profits as an element of general damages." Since prior law clearly distinguished between damages and profits, and since Congress expressly retained infringer's profits as a measure of recovery in the design patent statute, such makes the omission of the word "profits" from the 1946 Act more conspicuous.

The basic theory of damages is to make the patent owner whole for losses caused by the infringer's illicit activity, to be restored financially to the position he would have occupied *but for* the infringement. The term *profits,* when used without further qualification, refers to what an infringer makes; *damages* signifies what a patent owner loses. The determination of a damage award is hardly an exact science. While a patent owner is not entitled to an infringer's profits *per se,* such profits can be used to reckon the patent owner's damages.

Lost Profits

A patent owner may recover as a measure of damages the lost profits caused by the illicit competition of an infringer. The owner must establish a factual basis for causation, that is, that but for the infringer's improper acts, he would have made greater sales, charged higher prices, or incurred lower expenses. Causation need be proved only as a reasonable probability. An inference that the patent owner lost sales equal in quantity to the infringing sales may arise if the patent owner establishes (1) demand for the patented product, (2) an absence of acceptable noninfringing alternatives, and (3) his own capacity to have met that demand.

The problem of apportionment—how to compute monetary recovery for infringement when the patent in question is for a "mere improvement" or small part of the commercial device sold or used by the patent owner or infringer—remains a most persistent problem. Courts may grant a mixed or split award, using lost profits as a measure for some infringing sales or uses, and lost royalties (established or reasonable) as a measure for other such sales or uses. Such an award is appropriate when the infringer's acts of infringement occur under market conditions which vary in terms of customer type, product type, time period, or geographic area to such an extent as to alter the extent and provability of the damages of the patent owner.

In *Lam v. Johns-Manville* (1983), three types of damages were affirmed:

1. profits based on plaintiff's potential sales lost to defendant's actual sales (lost profits);

2. profits lost because plaintiff reduced its prices to meet defendant's prices (reduced profits); and
3. profits from projected lost sales as a result of defendant's infringement (projected lost profits).

The trial court also awarded prejudgment interest on the lost profits and reduced profits figures.

The Federal Circuit reversed the award of prejudgment interest on the punitive portions of the damage award. The proper question is "had the infringer not infringed, what would the patent holder . . . have made?" In a two-supplier market as here, a court may properly infer the existence of the *but for* causation. Where damages cannot be ascertained with precision, doubts are resolved against the infringer.

The *Panduit* four-part test for awarding lost profits [this is one test, not necessarily the only test]: (1) demand for product during the period in question; (2) absence of acceptable noninfringing substitutes; (3) manufacturing/marketing ability to meet demand; and (4) profits which would have been made (detailed computation).

The infringer's failure to have made a profit is irrelevant in measuring damages because the emphasis in awarding damages is on placing the patentee in the position he would have been absent infringement. Jury damage awards, unless the product of passion and prejudice, are not easily overturned or modified on appeal. 35 USC 284 does not instruct what method is to be used to compute damages; the size of the award is left to the trial court's discretion.

Under the lost profits test, the patent owner must establish that *but for* the infringement he would have made the sales. Use of an incremental income method for computing lost profits has been affirmed, even though approximate, as the product of a just and reasonable inference, not mere speculation or guess. The Court has affirmed application of the lost profits royalty rate to the value of the entire combination rather than to the value of only the patented element of the combination. Affirmed, where an exclusive licensee sued the patentee/licensor for infringement of its own patent by marketing a redesigned product in competition with the licensee.

In *Hartness v. Simplimatic* (May 1987), the CAFC affirmed an award of lost profits. The court observed that, while the District Court's opinion referred both to lost profits and to reasonable royalty, "it should be recognized that these terms are usually used to describe two analytically different approaches to the determination of damages in patent infringement cases." In fact, a reasonable royalty was not involved.

Established Royalty Rate

An established royalty rate is a uniform one freely negotiated and paid by a sufficient number of licensees. Rates agreed to under threat of suitor in settlement of litigation are not conclusive. A patent owner may recover as a measure of damages the royalty rate established by prior actual licenses for acts comparable to those engaged in by the infringer without authority. While existence of an established royalty normally sets the minimum recovery by a patent owner for infringement, it does not necessarily set the maximum recovery. A number of decisions state that a reasonable royalty may be higher than an established royalty when the established royalty was depressed because the patent had not yet gained public recognition or acceptance or because of widespread infringing activity.

Reasonable Royalty

The courts developed the reasonable royalty measure as a means of providing a just recovery to a patent owner who could not, for evidentiary or other reasons, prove lost profits or an established royalty. 35 USC 284 now expressly provides that the court shall award the successful patent claimant "in no event less than a reasonable royalty." Courts frequently define a reasonable royalty as that which would have resulted from a hypothetical negotiation between a willing patent owner and a willing potential user. It is of "little relevance" that a patentee may have eventually agreed to a lower royalty, for this would in effect permit infringers to impose a compulsory license on patent owners. The financial negotiation is as of a date when infringement by the defendant began and is based on the assumption that the patent was valid. This definition rarely provides guidance to a trier of fact faced with the task of setting the measure of recovery for patent infringement. Consequently, the courts focus on a number of factors as probative of what rate would have been set in such a supposititious license. Courts give weight to:

1. Actual prior and existing licenses under the patent in suit even though such licenses fail to meet the standards for an established royalty.
2. The licensing customs in the industry and actual licenses on comparable patents in determining both the royalty rate and the base for the reasonable royalty.
3. The licensing policy of the patent owner with respect to the patent in suit and to the relationship between the parties.
4. The anticipated profits or cost savings that the infringer would derive from use of the patented product or process.
5. The comparative utility of the patented invention and in particular to the existence of noninfringing alternatives open to the infringer.
6. The collateral benefits, including sales of parts, supplies, acces-

sories, and related products that flow or would be expected to flow to the infringer from the right to manufacture, use, or sell the patented invention.

7. The relation to the feature claimed in the patent and the infringer's commercial product or process.
8. Actual state of development and commercialization of the product or process covered by the patent.
9. The duration of the patent, that is, the portion of the seventeen-year term that remained when infringement began.

The courts have stressed that the determination of reasonable royalty should be based on evidence, not conjecture. The testimony of expert witnesses is a primary means by which the parties may introduce evidence on what constitutes a reasonable royalty. Because of the difficulty of recreating a negotiation in such a hypothetical manner, the courts admit evidence of subsequent events as a basis for inferring what the preinfringement negotiated value would have been.

The use of a reasonable royalty as a measure of damages for patent infringement has been criticized as a "handy means for competitors to impose a compulsory license upon every patent owner." The concept of a reasonable royalty represents the minimum of damages provided by 35 USC 284, which allows "trebling" of damages where the infringer has knowingly, deliberately, intentionally, willfully, or wantonly infringed the patent. Award of enhanced damages is punitive in nature, therefore, deliberate wrongdoing or bad faith.

Under 35 USC 284, a patentee may recover damages, not an infringer's profits, which it defined as "compensation for the pecuniary loss he [the patent holder] suffered from the infringement, without regard to the question whether the defendant gained or lost by his unlawful acts." The purpose of a damage award is to place the patentee in at least as good a position as he would have been had he and the infringer entered into a reasonable royalty agreement.

The use of hypothetical licensing negotiations is proper where lost profits are speculative and there is no established royalty rate. However, industry practices (food processing) of granting lump-sum rather than use-based royalties, for example, should best be followed. It is also within the District Court's discretion to award damages greater than a reasonable royalty as a deterrence to infringers.

A damage award may be based on actual lost profits caused by the infringement or if actual damages are not ascertainable, a reasonable royalty defined as a "hypothetical royalty resulting from arm's length negotiations between a willing licensor and a willing licensee." An actual established royalty rate is generally the best measure of reasonable damages. "A single licensing agreement does not generally demonstrate uniformity nor acquiescence in the reasonableness of the royalty rate."

For a royalty to be "established," it "must be paid by such a number of persons as to indicate a general acquiescence in its reasonableness by those who have occasion to use the invention." The reasonable royalty should be based on what reasonable parties to hypothetical negotiations would have contemplated at the time of the negotiations, rather than what one of the parties said they would have actually agreed upon.

Under the entire market value rule, recovery of damages is allowed based on the value of an entire apparatus containing several features (inclusion of unpatented parts, e.g.) when the patented feature constitutes the basis for customer demand.

In *Hughes Tool v. Dresser Industries* (April 1987), the Federal Circuit vacated and remanded the District Court's computation for a royalty for patent infringement of 25 percent of defendant's dollar sales amount. The reasonable royalty rate selected by the lower court, based on a clearly erroneous finding of projected profits of 60 percent as a percentage of sales, "was *ipso facto* arbitrary and must be set aside."

Prejudgment Interest/Increased Damages

The court in an infringement suit may award, in addition to compensatory damages, collateral assessments in the form of prejudgment interest, increased damages, and attorney fees.

In 1983, the Supreme Court resolved divergent views of the lower courts by holding that "prejudgment interest should ordinarily be awarded where necessary to afford the plaintiff full compensation for infringement." This amount represents the interest that would have accrued had the infringer made annual royalty payments under a license where the court bases damages on a royalty rate determined by the court.

In *General Motors v. Devex* (1983), the Supreme Court held that prejudgment interest *should* be awarded under 35 USC 284 absent some unusual justification for withholding interest. The purpose of prejudgment interest is to place the patent owner in as good a position as he would have been had the infringer entered into a reasonable royalty agreement at the time of the infringement. The interest is awarded to compensate for the delay in payment of damages, not to punish the infringer. Where the damages are increased to punish for willful infringement, prejudgment interest cannot be assessed on the increased or punitive portion of the damage award. The Court has also upheld an award of interest at or above the prime rate, that is, where the plaintiff had demonstrated that he had borrowed money at or above the prime rate in order to remain in business following defendant's infringement.

For infringement occurring after the final judgment of a District Court, the Federal Circuit decided that the rate of interest applicable to those damages would be awarded at the coupon issue yield of U.S. Treasury bills (according to 28 USC 1961). Prejudgment interest should ordinarily be awarded for both lost profit and reasonable royalty recovery. A District Court has substantial discretion in determining the rate of prejudgment interest, even a simple, state-statutory rate was affirmed. There is no conflict in awarding both increased damages and prejudgment interest. Prejudgment interest may be denied under certain circumstances. The normal procedure is to award interest from the date of infringement. The merits of the infringer's challenge to the patent is immaterial in determining the amount of prejudgment interest.

The patent remedy statute authorizes the court to "increase damages up to *three times* the amount found or assessed" [35 USC 284]. The decision to increase damages is discretionary with the trial court but should normally be exercised only in cases of willful and wanton infringement or bad faith litigation. An increase is inappropriate when the infringer mounted a good faith and substantial challenge to the validity of the patent or the existence of infringement.

Contempt

The sale of component parts having no substantial noninfringing use, and individuals operating devices that directly infringe a patent after this action was enjoined are subject to contempt proceedings.

Amstar v. Envirotech (1987): In denying Amstar's motion for contempt, the District Court said it was not "essentially obvious" that Envirotech had violated the permanent injunction. In affirming, the CAFC observed that, in a civil contempt proceeding, the movant must prove a violation by clear and convincing evidence. Here, Amstar's expert compared the accused device with the adjudicated infringing devices, saying the respective devices "were equivalents." Citing *KSM Fastening v. H. A. Jones* (1985), the Federal Circuit said the correct comparison should have been with the patent claims. Amstar's expert (who used a device/device comparison) therefore failed to submit evidence capable of establishing that the redesigned units fell within the adjudicated scope of the patent claims.

Failure to seek the opinion of patent counsel militates considerably in favor of a finding that the infringement was willful. In assessing damages for infringement, courts have said that they owe no duty to exercise meticulous care to avoid hardship on an infringer. Absent an award of enhanced damages, a patentee's potential monetary recovery is, at least, purely compensatory and not punitive or exemplary.

Use of a "Master" to Determine Damages

After an interlocutory decree has been entered holding the patent in suit valid and infringed, the court may appoint a "master" to determine damages, and it is up to the complainant to take the initiative to introduce evidence before the master to prove the amount of damages. This practice is sanctioned by FRCP Rule 53: "Masters" (the FRCP are the Federal Rules of Civil Procedure). As used in these rules the word "master" includes a referee, an auditor, an examiner, and an assessor. A reference to a master shall be the exception and not the rule. In actions to be tried by a jury, a reference shall be made only when the issues are complicated; in actions to be tried without a jury, save in matters of account and of difficult computation of damages, a reference shall be made only upon a showing that some exceptional condition requires it. In an action to be tried without a jury the court shall accept the master's findings of fact unless clearly erroneous.

The Order of Reference to the master may specify or limit his powers and may direct him to report only upon particular issues or to do or perform particular acts or to receive and report evidence only, and may fix the time and place for beginning and closing the hearings and for the filing of the master's report. The practice of using a master has been established for many years. The labors of a judge in a court of equity are often materially lightened by referring the consideration of matters of fact to a Master in Chancery, who is directed by it to investigate the same and report his opinion thereon to the court.

35 USC 285: ATTORNEY FEES (AND COSTS)

The patent statute authorizes the court "in exceptional cases" to award "reasonable attorney fees to the prevailing party." The award of such fees is discretionary with the trial court. Exceptional circumstances might be when the infringer is guilty of willful and deliberate infringement, or when the patent owner has engaged in inequitable conduct in obtaining the patent or in pursuing litigation.

Attorney fees in patent cases may be awarded either by the trial court or by the Federal Circuit on appeal under 35 USC 285, which provides that "the court in exceptional cases may award reasonable attorney fees to the prevailing party." Attorney fees may also be awarded under FRCP 38 and FRCP 37(c) as well as sanctions under FRCP 11. The CAFC initially decided the issue of attorney fees on a case-by-case basis, occasionally citing and discussing a circuit court decision. Presently, the court is citing its own precedents almost exclusively. The most common way to obtain an award of attorney fees is to first show that the patent infringement is willful and then to show that the degree of willfulness is of such magnitude as to make the case exceptional under 35 USC 285. Proof must be clear and convincing. The District Court must make factual findings and articulate the legal principles applied.

In reviewing trial awards under 35 USC 285 there are two standards:

	Reviewed on the Basis of:
(1) court decides *not* to award because case is *not* exceptional	(1) "clearly erroneous" standard
(2) court decides exceptional and awards attorney fees	(2) "abuse of discretion" standard

Establishing that a patent was procured by fraud or with such egregious conduct as to render it unenforceable requires clear, unequivocal, and convincing evidence of an intentional misrepresentation or withholding of a material fact from the PTO. Simple negligence, oversight, or erroneous judgment made in good faith are not enough to establish fraud. Absent unfairness, bad faith, inequitable conduct, vexatious litigation, or similar circumstances, the granting of attorney fees is an abuse of discretion. In determining the reasonableness of the award, there must be some evidence to support the reasonableness, *inter alia,* the billing rate charged and the number of hours expended. (For example, "where the appeal is *frivolous* and an *abuse* of the court system. . . .")

A case under 35 USC 285 may be exceptional for some other reasons than inequitable conduct during prosecution. Award of attorney fees is discretionary; the award may be proper where: (1) the infringer failed to obtain competent legal advice before initiating possible infringing activities, and (2) the infringer had no reasonable basis for believing it had a right to do what it did.

Rohm & Haas v. Crystal Chemical (1984) was a case of first impression that addressed the issue of whether 35 USC 285 authorized the CAFC to award attorney fees for an appeal. The court held that neither 35 USC 285 nor its legislative history distinguishes between awarding attorney fees in the District Court and in the appellate court. "[A] frivolous appeal filed or proceeded while in this court, will result in imposition of damages and costs upon appellant *and counsel* in accordance with Rule 38." Having failed to prevail on the issue of willful infringement, there was no basis for an award of attorney fees.

Double costs on appeal (1986) were awarded where "flagrant misrepresentations"; "gross violations" of the high standards expected; "no possible excuse" for "distorting the record." Attorney fees are not to be "routinely assessed" against a losing party for defending a lawsuit but are to be awarded to avoid a "gross injustice." Any bad faith does not rise to the level of inequitable conduct.

The Federal Circuit has seemingly increased the number of areas where an award of attorney fees is recognized. Thus, exceptional circumstances, allowing for an award of attorney fees, may be present:

1. where there is willful and deliberate infringement; or
2. in the prolongation of litigation in bad faith; or
3. fraud or inequitable conduct; or
4. bad faith defenses; or
5. misconduct during litigation; or
6. some equal element of unfairness or bad faith.

The court has also granted attorney fees on appeals, which was not done by its predecessors. Without specifically enumerating the case citations, there have been a number of "attorney fee" cases before the Federal Circuit. An appeal was held frivolous because of the lack of any coherent legal theory under which the District Court could be reversed and the agreement set aside. The absence or presence of an opinion of counsel is not amenable to the development of a rigorous rule and the totality of circumstances must be considered. The failure to disclose highly material information through gross negligence does not prove bad faith or an intentional misleading of the PTO.

A decision on a motion for attorney fees under 35 USC 285 involves a two-step process [*J. P. Stevens v. Lex Tex*, June 1987]:

1. is the case "exceptional";
2. is an award within the court's discretion. . . . According to the court, an abuse of discretion may reside in either:
   (a) an error of law,
   (b) a clear error of judgment, or
   (c) in the exercise of discretion in making findings which were clearly erroneous.

The Federal Circuit found no abuse of discretion. The small amount of damages involved ($285.75), the spurious and specious arguments presented, and the distortion and disregard of the record and opposing authorities on appeal led to an award of attorney fees. The Federal Circuit found that the conduct of counsel for the parties on appeal had been unprofessional (*Ballard v. Wright,* June 1987) including improper insertions in the appendix, carelessly made charges, lack of candor, intemperate language, and reciprocal finger-pointing by counsel. "[M]anipulation and suppression of evidence . . . ; counsel's assertions . . . were absurd, disappointing and outside the bounds of legitimate advocacy."

Frivolous Appeals

Federal Rules of Appellate Procedure: Rule 38

> If a court of appeals shall determine that an appeal is frivolous, it may award just damages and single or double costs to the appellee.

It is settled that damages may include attorney fees as well as damages caused by delay imposed by the appeal.

In the 9th Circuit

> an appeal is considered frivolous in this circuit when the result is obvious, or the appellant's arguments of error are wholly without merit . . . ; regrettable lack of candor due this court . . . , therefore frivolous.

The court refrained from holding appellate counsel jointly and severally liable with his client because of the fact that a favorable jury verdict had been obtained in the District Court. The court declined to award attorney fees, however, because it felt that other factors besides frivolity, for example, excessive advocacy and inexperience, were the reason for this appeal.

In another case, since no more than rumors were presented to support infringement, the court found the appeal frivolous and held the defendant and its counsel jointly and severally liable for plaintiff's costs and attorney fees on appeal. "[I]t is difficult to hold an appeal frivolous when it is partially successful."

The Federal Circuit restated the proposition that "a frivolous appeal filed or proceeded within this court will result in imposition of damages and costs upon appellant and counsel in accordance with Rule 38"; may include attorney fees but do not necessarily. The court emphasized that an appeal is not a second chance to try the case. An appeal was not deemed frivolous, however, because it raised two issues of first impression in the Federal Circuit.

In one case, the court dismissed an appeal holding that appellant's arguments fell "just within the ragged edge of the penumbra surrounding legitimate advocacy"; did not award attorney fees, but appellant was entitled to costs.

—ignoring *cited* legal authorities;

—arguments contrary to settled law or the facts;

—"cropping" quotes from cases to leave out damaging portions; will all likely lead to sanctions.

Winning a portion of the appeal may be enough to avoid frivolousness.

The Federal Circuit, led by numerous opinions of Chief Judge Markey, has been aggressively imposing sanctions when it believes a party has been misleading or disingenuous with its arguments or when an appeal has absolutely no merit. The "appeal brief" is the court's primary focus in determining whether an appeal is frivolous. Sanctions may often be avoided if the brief confronts the authorities contrary to the asserted position and makes arguments in good faith. It also may be noted that a finding that an appeal is frivolous may be avoided by winning a portion of the appeal. The win need not be on a major issue.

In conclusion, the Federal Circuit decisions are proceeding within established principles of law. It seemingly has increased the number of areas where an award of attorney fees is recognized.

INCREASED DAMAGES FOR WILLFUL INFRINGEMENT

While the CAFC has not actually formulated a specific definition, and is unlikely to, it has at least set out a basic guideline which reflects its overall policy on the subject:

> "The court must determine that the infringer acted in disregard of the patent, that is, that the infringer had no reasonable basis for believing it had the right to do the acts."
>
> "Where, as here, a potential infringer has actual notice of another's patent rights, he has an affirmative duty to exercise due care to determine whether or not his is infringing."
>
> "Such an affirmative duty includes, *inter alia,* the duty to seek and obtain competent legal advice from counsel before the initiation of any possible infringing activity."
>
> (1) The timing of the opinion is critical. The sooner the infringer has its opinion after notice of the patent, the better the infringer can defend a charge of willful infringement.
>
> (2) If a legal opinion does exist, another important qualification is that it must be "competent." This means that the opinion itself must be an authoritative opinion of invalidity or noninfringement. As such, a conclusionary letter without supporting reasons is insufficient.

(3) There appears to be very little likelihood of avoiding willful infringement if the infringer did not actually rely on the legal opinion it received.

Other factors may avoid infringement if the affirmative duty is not met. At the very least, however, it may require evidence which indicates the infringer's respect for the patent (e.g., design-around work or modification to avoid infringement).

In conclusion, it is apparent that a major focus of the willful infringement inquiry is almost always on the infringer's actions once it learned of the patent in suit. In this regard, three questions are of critical importance:

1. Once the infringer learned of the patent, did the infringer immediately seek and get proper legal advice, which indicated it could continue to do the activities later proved infringing?
2. If so, did the infringer actually (and immediately) rely on the advice?
3. If there was no opinion, did the infringer take some other concrete steps which show respect for the patent (e.g., design-around work or other modifications to avoid infringement)?

A negative answer to questions one or two places the potential infringer in considerable jeopardy. If the answer to the third question is also no, the potential infringer had best hope that the patent is found invalid or not infringed.

35 USC 289: ADDITIONAL REMEDY FOR INFRINGEMENT OF DESIGN PATENT

The monetary remedies provided for by 35 USC 284 and 285 for patent infringement apply equally to design patents. 35 USC 289 provides, as an additional remedy for infringement of a design patent, that the infringer "be liable to the owner to the extent of his total profit, but not less than $250." Thus, the design patent owner, unlike the utility model patent owner, may recover infringer profits as a measure of damages.

The last sentence of Section 289 states that the design patent owner "shall not twice recover the profit made from the infringement." This is interpreted to mean that the patent owner may not recover both the infringer's profits and some measure of damages. These profits recoverable do not constitute damages that may be increased three times under Section 284.

Congress enacted the design patent law in 1842 and rarely, if ever, could such an owner show that the article sold by the infringer derived its "entire value" from the illicit use of the owner's design. As a result of some unjust court decisions, Congress responded in the Act of 1887 with a provision which has been unchanged to this day.

Test for determining the infringement of a design patent:

> [I]f, in the eye of an ordinary observer, giving such attention as a purchaser usually gives, two designs are substantially the same, and if the resemblance is such so as to deceive such an observer, inducing him to purchase one supposing it to be the other, the first one patented is infringed by the other.

Likelihood as to the source of goods was neither a necessary nor appropriate factor for determining infringement of a design patent, since the holder of a valid design patent need not have progressed to the manufacture and distribution of a "purchasable" product for its design patent to be infringed by another's product. There is a clear line which exists between the test for infringement of a design patent and the "likelihood of confusion" test for infringement of a trademark. In determining infringement, the design must be analyzed as a whole (ornamental). The Federal Circuit has adopted an activist approach in addressing infringement issues.

UNAUTHORIZED MANUFACTURE OR USE BY THE U.S. GOVERNMENT

In the case of unauthorized manufacture or use of a patented invention by or for the U.S. government, the patent owner's exclusive remedy is a suit for monetary relief in the U.S. Claims Court (formerly the Court of Claims). The statutory measure of recovery is "reasonable and entire compensation." As with suits against other infringers, an established royalty is the best measure of damages. There is some doubt as to whether lost profits is a permissible basis for recovery against the United States.

A patent owner may recover prejudgment interest but may not recover attorney fees or increased damages. These latter remedies, while appropriate for deliberate or willful patent infringement, a species of tort, are inappropriate for the eminent domain taking of a license which 28 USC 1498(a) entails. One ground often relied upon to justify an award under Section 285 against private parties, willful infringement, will normally not apply to the United States since Section 1498 gives it the right to take a license under the patent by eminent domain. Note that 28 USC 2412(d) provides for a mandatory award of attorney fees against the United States in certain limited circumstances. The opposing party must be either an individual with limited net worth or the sole owner of a small business.

In procurement cases, the Court of Claims has normally adopted the total cost of procurement as the compensation base. This may include closely related items not covered by the patent but may not include spare parts or additional supplies.

28 USC 2501 of the Judicial Code dealing with Court of Claims procedure generally, provides an express six-year Statute of Limitations. Whereas 35 USC 286 bars recovery for any infringement committed more than six years prior to the filing of the complaint, this is a time limit on damages, not a statute of limitations.

LIMITATIONS ON THE PATENT OWNER'S RIGHT TO RECOVER MONETARY DAMAGES

Various statutory rules and judicially developed doctrines provide for limitations on the patent owner's right to recover monetary damages for infringement: time, amount, notice.

35 USC 286: Time Limitation on Damages

35 USC 286 operates as a time limitation on the recovery of damages rather than as a true statute of limitations.

> A patentee has a right to sue for infringement of his patent for seventeen years.... But the patentee may only recover for the infringements which occurred within six years of filing the action. ... The action itself is barred only by laches as no statute of limitations covers a suit for enforcement of a patent.

Multiple Recoveries

Since the Patent Law confers separate rights to make, use, and sell, a patentee may have multiple recoveries by separate suits against those who perform any of these acts without authority. Furthermore, liability is also imposed upon persons who contribute to or induce direct infringement by others, and these may be individually sued, they are all joint tort-feasors. However, under certain circumstances, recovery on a judgment or even a settlement will constitute full compensation to the patent owner for related acts of infringement and will bar further relief.

Unfortunately, the Supreme Court fails to provide clear guidance on this issue. In 1884, its landmark decision in *Birdsell v. Shaliol* suggested that (1) recovery against one person who makes or sells an infringing item confers no privilege on another to continue use or escape liability, *but* (2) recovery against one person of "full compensation" for an infringement would in fact exempt others from liability. Most decisions after *Birdsell* recognize the patent owner's right to recover separately the provable profits of manufacturer, reseller, and user. The cases split on whether recovery of damages in lieu of or in addition to the profits of the manufacturer would preclude the recovery of profits from users or resellers.

In considering a patent owner's remedies against manufacturers, resellers, and users, it is important to distinguish between the issue of liability and that of monetary recovery. As to recovery, entry of judgment alone against one infringer will not relieve other related infringers from liability. While the basic idea of full compensation is sound, that is, a patent owner ought not recover twice for the same injury, confusion remains in determining what constitutes full compensation when an infringing product passes through several hands. This confusion is even more complicated when considering the inducer or contributor to infringement. Amounts paid under a settlement agreement may diminish the liability of other infringers and may trigger the full compensation rule.

35 USC 287: Limitation on Damages; Marking and Notice

The Patent Act imposes a duty to mark on patent owners. If the patent owner or his licensees fail to mark as required, the patent owner may only recover damages for acts occurring after the infringer received notice charging infringement. The filing of suit for infringement constitutes notice. The patent owner must police compliance by his licensees. The persons under the duty to mark must so mark *all* patented articles made and sold. Omissions from any substantial number constitutes noncompliance.

As to the content of the marking, Section 287 now requires "the word *'patent'* or the abbreviation *'pat.', together with the number of the patent.*" This section also provides that "in the event of *Failure so to mark* as specified," no damages may be recovered against an infringer "except on proof that the infringer was notified of the infringement and continued to infringe thereafter."

In applying the notice provision, the cases generally require that the patent owner give specific and actual notice to the accused infringer charging infringement of the patent in question. It is not normally sufficient that the infringer had actual knowledge of the patent. On the other hand, the notice need not contain a detailed statement or an explanation of the patent owner's theory concerning infringement. It is sufficient to give the information that would be contained in a proper marking under Section 287 (i.e., the patent number) together with a general charge of infringement.

A plaintiff who seeks to recover the damages for acts prior to the filing of suit bears the burden of pleading and proving compliance with either the marking requirement or with the specific notice requirement. Section 287 is only a limitation on the patent owner's recoverable damages. A patent owner who fails to mark may still obtain an injunction against further infringement. The patent owner may also recover monetary relief for infringements occurring after the giving of specific notice, even though he failed previously to mark or notify. 35 USC 287 does not require plaintiff to mark products made by the patented *process* in order to recover for infringements occurring before plaintiff notified defendant of its claim.

35 USC 292: FALSE MARKING

35 USC 292 prohibits three types of false markings:

1. counterfeit marking (i.e., use of a patent mark without permission of the patent owner);
2. false patent marking (i.e., the use of a patent mark on an unpatented article); and
3. false patent pending marking (i.e., the use of *"patent applied for"* or *"patent pending"* when no patent application covering the article is in fact pending).

The statute specifies a fine of "$500 for every such offense." It authorizes "any person," no injury need be shown, to sue for the penalty and keep one-half of the sum collected. A claim for false marking will fail if there is absence of "the intent of deceiving the public." The purpose of the statute is to protect the public. False marking discourages competition and research and development, it creates an impression that the product may be technologically superior and is a form of unfair competition.

Determining what is a single offense is a difficult matter.

> It can hardly have been the intent of Congress that penalties should accumulate as fast as a printing press or stamping machine might operate.... It follows that a plaintiff, in order to recover more than a single penalty, must go further than to prove the marking of a number of unpatented articles. The proof must be sufficiently specific as to time and circumstances to show a number of distinct offenses, and to negative the possibility that the marking of the different articles was in the course of a single and continuous act.
>
> In colloquy below Brose replied to the Judge's inquiry on the number of "offenses"... that "there are at least" 70,000 "of the Sears kits involved." His share adds up to a tidy 17½ million dollars although on one basis or another—limiting it to each day or week or month—a Court would find a way to prevent such a result.

In one case, inclusion of a false patent statement in two publications constituted two offenses; reproduction in a catalog constituted a third offense.

35 USC 283: INJUNCTION

Protection of the patentee's right to exclude has been provided in part through 35 USC 283, which expressly permits the courts to: "grant *injunctions* in accordance with the principles of equity to prevent the violation of any right secured by patent, on such terms as the court deems reasonable."

Relief is discretionary, governed by the traditional and historic principles that govern all extraordinary relief; as such, the grant or denial of an injunction is reviewed for abuse of discretion. Since the establishment of the Federal Circuit, permanent injunctions have been routinely granted, and preliminary injunctions may be more readily granted.

The injunction is an "extraordinary" form of relief. It was developed under equity jurisprudence in England. The historical origin of this type of remedy can be traced back to Roman law under the Interdicts. They were generally used in exceptional circumstances including situations where it was necessary to prevent wrongs, to restore violated possessions, to restrain somebody from undue exercise of rights, and to secure the permanent enjoyment of the rights of property.

Mr. Justice Story stated that,

> A writ of injunction may be described to be a judicial process whereby a party is required to do a particular thing or refrain from doing a particular thing according to the exigency of the writ.

In 1983, the CAFC held:

> Without the injunctive power of the courts, the right to exclude granted by the patent would be diminished, and the express purpose of the Constitution and Congress, to promote the progress of the useful arts, would be seriously undermined.

A preliminary injunction is one which is granted after the filing of a complaint and before a case is ready to be decided in respect of its prayer for a permanent injunction or for damages. The function of preliminary injunctive relief is to preserve the *status quo* pending a determination of the action on the merits (e.g., before infringement).

FRCP Rule 65(a)(1) provides that "No preliminary injunction shall be issued without notice to the adverse party."

A Temporary Restraining Order (TRO) may be made by the court where there clearly appears to be danger of irreparable harm because of delay. It may be given "without notice" where: (1) it clearly appears from specific facts shown by an affidavit or by a verified complaint that immediate and irreparable injury will result before the adverse party or his attorney can be heard in opposition, and (2) the complainant's attorney has certified to the court, in writing, the efforts, if any, which have been made to give notice and the reasons supporting his claim that notice should not be required.

Any TRO given without notice should expire within a limited period of time, not to exceed ten days, unless good cause for continuing it is shown or the adverse party consents to a longer period. Security must be required as a condition for granting a TRO or a preliminary injunction in such sum to cover costs and damages to the party being wrongfully enjoined or restrained. All proceedings concerning injunctions must be in accordance with the current FRCP. Rule 65 relates to injunctions and should be consulted as well as decisions relating thereto.

The courts have been clear in stating the requirements for a preliminary injunction, saying: "a patent holder can make a sufficient showing of patent validity in three ways: a prior adjudication of the validity of the patent, [long] public acquiescence to its validity, or direct technical evidence proving its validity." The requirement for security from the complainant is contained in FRCP Rule 65(c). A motion to dissolve a preliminary injunction may be made at any time, upon reasonable notice.

A consent decree is one which is entered by the consent of both parties when the defendant is not in default and before the judge has decided the case on its merits. A consent decree providing for perpetual injunction against violation of a patent has the same effect as a judgment rendered on a contest of the issue. One may be subject to contempt for violating the terms of a consent decree. Violations of injunctions, colloquially known as *Contempt,* have been considered by courts for a long time. "Contempt of Court" has been defined by one author as:

> Conduct tending to bring the authority and administration of the law into disrespect or disregard, interfering with or prejudicing parties or their witnesses during the litigation, or otherwise tending to impede, embarrass, or obstruct the court in the discharge of its duties. *Civil contempt* is a severe remedy and should not be resorted to where there is a fair ground of doubt as to the wrongfulness of the defendant's conduct.

35 USC 283 empowers the courts to "grant Injunctions in accordance with the principles of equity to prevent the violation of any right secured by patent, on such terms as the court deems reasonable." Injunctions are of two types: (1) Preliminary injunctions, also referred to as "interlocu-

tory" injunctions or injunctions *pendente lite* (during the course of the suit), and (2) permanent injunctions. The former will not be granted except upon a strong showing of: (1) probable success on the merits, (2) irreparable injury, and (3) an imbalance in the relative hardships.

The latter are issued after the patent owner prevails on the merits and will normally be granted unless the public interest otherwise dictates. A permanent injunction normally follows a decision in favor of the complainant on the interlocutory hearing of a patent case unless some special reason exists for its being refused or being postponed till after the master's report or being suspended pending an appeal. It may also be granted in certain special circumstances, for example, bankruptcy, after a declaratory judgment, and so on.

In patent cases, the courts require an especially strong showing of probable success before granting a preliminary injunction, many decisions requiring that the plaintiff establish the elements of validity and infringement "beyond question." Reluctance to issue preliminary injunctions in patent cases sprang initially from the division between law and equity in the common law court system. As a general practice, the equity court hesitated to grant relief if plaintiff's substantive claim involved disputed issues of fact, more appropriate for initial determination by law to a jury. In a patent case, disputed issues of fact often existed as to validity and infringement of a patent that had not previously been the subject of an action at law for damages. Yet the courts would grant preliminary injunctions as to previously unadjudicated patents if the owner had enjoyed a long period of unchallenged dominion over the patented invention, in a way, giving some support to validity.

In 1927, Judge Hand stated: "We have often said that an injunction *pendente lite* should not go except when the patent is beyond question valid and infringed."

To obtain a preliminary injunction in a patent infringement suit, the plaintiff must establish "clear title" to the patent, normally a routine matter. He must also make a strong showing that the patent will likely be upheld as valid and enforceable, a far-from-routine matter. Many decisions require the patent owner to show validity "beyond question," which rests upon (1) a prior adjudication of the patent's validity in a suit against another party, or (2) a long period of acquiescence by the industry in the patent owner's rights.

As in the case of validity, prior adjudication may lay a basis for probable infringement. The plaintiff must establish that he will suffer irreparable injury during the litigation if such an injunction is denied. This requirement is merely a specific application of the general doctrine that equitable relief cannot be granted unless plaintiff shows that the remedy at law is inadequate. There are four common situations in which the courts usually find the legal remedy of damages inadequate:

1. Defendant is depriving plaintiff of a unique and needed item of property;
2. defendant acts so as to require plaintiff to bring more than one suit to effectuate his legal remedy;
3. defendant is insolvent and unable to pay any judgment for money damages; and
4. the damages being caused by defendant are speculative and difficult to measure.

Once the patent owner establishes the critical elements of probable validity and infringement and irreparable injury, the trial court has considerable discretion whether to grant or deny a preliminary injunction. That discretion is to be exercised through a "balancing of the relative conveniences and inconveniences." The court considers not only the comparative hardship to the parties of granting or withholding a preliminary injunction but also implications for the public interest.

Rule 65(c) of the Federal Rules of Civil Procedure provides that "no restraining order or preliminary injunction shall issue except upon the giving of security by the applicant, in such sum as the court deems proper, for the payment of such costs and damages as may be incurred or suffered by any party who is found to have been wrongfully enjoined or restrained."

Courts have declined to issue injunctions where:

1. An injunction would have meant that the infringer would have been out of business and the patentee would get no future royalties because he was not himself engaged in the exploitation of the invention.
2. Where a license had been refused by the patentee "solely because of a personal feud between plaintiffs and defendants." "One who elects to build a business on a product found to infringe cannot be heard to complain if an injunction against continuing infringement destroys the business . . . ; patent rights do not peter out as the end of the patent term, usually 17 years, is approached."

When there has been a prior adjudication of the patent, the outcome of the litigation is given substantial weight as to validity or nonvalidity. It is not a question of *res judicata* but rather it is evidence on the question of the likelihood of success in the subsequent proceedings. The

> grant of a preliminary injunction does not require that infringement be proved beyond all question, or that there be no evidence supporting . . . "non-infringement; rather, the grant turns on" . . . the likelihood that the patentee will meet its burden at trial of proving infringement.

The movant is required to demonstrate in a patent case that he will suffer irreparable harm if the injunction is not granted. In addition to the potential damage to business and marketing opportunities which are irreparable, there are several other reasons why the position that being solvent and having adequate funds is considered to be unsound:

> First, the option of compulsory licensing was considered by Congress and rejected;
>
> second, inventions are personal property, there are more than economic rights involved; the inventor is allowed to exclude others even if he is not himself making full use, or any use at all, of the invention;
>
> third, another factor to be considered is the balance of hardships; and
>
> fourth, and not least, is the impact of the injunction on the public interest.

The best known "public interest" case is *City of Milwaukee v. Activated Sludge* (1934):

> [I]f, however, the injunction . . . is made permanent, it would close the sewage plant, leaving the entire community without any means for the disposal of raw sewage other than running into Lake Michigan, thereby polluting its waters and endangering the lives of that and other adjoining communities.

The grant or denial of a motion for an injunction is a matter of discretion. Where validity and continuing infringement have been clearly established, immediate and irreparable harm is presumed, and an injunction may issue. More than a "reasonable" showing of irreparable injury is required, "but a strong showing indeed," to justify the issuance of a preliminary injunction. Without injunctions, infringers could become compulsory licensees for as long as the litigation lasts. The court has also held that "things equal to each other may not be equal to the same thing," saying an accused device that was an "equivalent" of an infringing device did not therefore necessarily infringe the patent claim.

Joy Manufacturing v. National Mine Service (January 1987): In 1984,

National agreed, *inter alia,* not to contest validity of the patent in any suit in any U.S. court, and the parties stipulated to dismissal of the lawsuit without prejudice. The Federal Circuit affirmed the District Court's denial of a motion by plaintiff/patentee Joy to enjoin defendant National's post-judgment request for reexamination, on two grounds: (1) the settlement agreement did not, by its literal terms, proscribe National's filing of a reexamination request, and (2) the requested injunction could have no practical effect because National had no future role to play in the commissioner's nonreviewable decision to reexamine the patent.

In *T. J. Smith v. Consolidated Medical Equipment* (June 1987), the Federal Circuit affirmed denial of a motion for preliminary injunction:

1. Smith had not shown a substantial likelihood of success on infringement;
2. the presumption of validity on which Smith rested was procedural, not substantive;
3. Smith waited fifteen months before seeking a preliminary injunction;
4. Consolidated had presented evidence of invalidity; and
5. Smith had long licensed its patent to two licensees.

> An actual recovery of a full royalty for making, and selling to others to be used, operates as an implied license to any purchaser of the thing thus made and sold, to use it to the same extent he could lawfully have done if the maker had been licensed to make and sell it.
>
> [T]he relative size of multiple infringers should not alone serve as a basis for enjoining continued infringement by some and not by others.

Because successors and assigns may be instrumentalities through which a defendant seeks to evade an injunction, they may be brought within the scope of that injunction.

UNITED STATES CODE ANNOTATED

35 USC 281: Remedy for Infringement of Patent

> A patentee shall have remedy by civil action for infringement of his patent.

In private litigation, such as a patent infringement action, it is primarily the function of law officers of the United States serving as *amici curiae,* such as the attorney general, to protect the public interest by rendering impartial assistance to the courts in uncovering and punishing frauds upon the courts, and it is a function of a party in such cases to raise and prosecute such accusations primarily in his own interest and only secondarily in interest of the public.

Manufacturer suing for patent infringement and unfair competition may report facts involved in pending litigation and disclose them to its dealers or to dealers generally but such reporting must be reasonable and not calculated to unduly alarm recipients by way of threats or rash conclusions.

No cause of action for patent infringement exists until the infringement has occurred.

In general, the right to sue under the patent laws on a patent, as distinguished from the right to sue for breach of contract concerning a patent, depends upon the patent laws.

In a patent infringement action, equitable principles are applied.

Right to maintain bill for infringement of patent rests upon this section and not upon equitable principles.

Infringement, whether direct or contributory, is essentially *tort,* and implies invasion of some right of patentee.

A suit with issues affecting the legality or infringement of a patent is a *patent suit* falling within jurisdiction of federal district court.

Patent case is within exclusive federal jurisdiction when it seeks to enforce patent against alleged infringer, even though complaint may show, in anticipation of defense, existence of agreement between parties relating to patent.

In patent infringement suit, where infringement issue was the only federal question involved, upon disposal of infringement issue, federal court, in nondiversity case, was without jurisdiction to decide non-federal issue.

Redress to injury to patent holder's business must be sought in Courts of State where cause of action arose.

When patented article rightfully passes from patentee to purchaser, the article is no longer within the limits of the monopoly, or under the protection of the patent act, and redress for injury, in such a case, must be sought in the state courts.

The federal district court had jurisdiction of causes of action seeking declaration of rights of parties with respect to defendant's patents.

Where patent infringement and unfair competition are based on substantially the same facts, if the first fails, the court may proceed to adjudicate the second.

The courts of one circuit are not controlled by the views taken with regard to a patent by the courts of another, nor absolved from an independent examination of the questions involved; such decisions being simply entitled to proper deference, as those of courts of equal standing and authority.

Inasmuch as applicant for patent could have no right of action in federal court against patent holder for damages by virtue of his application for patent until patent was issued and no damage could accrue to him prior to issuance of patent, applicant did not have potential claim upon which he could sue patent holder in federal court and no controversy was presented under patent laws.

A cause of action for the infringement of a patent survives, upon the death of the patentee, to his representatives.

A court in an action for patent infringement is without jurisdiction to proceed in the matter in the absence of *Indispensable Parties,* which includes all of the owners of the patent.

Exclusive patent licensee may not bring infringement action in his own name unless owner of patent is also named as a party and patent owner is therefore considered necessary party to such a suit; assignee of a patent, however, is considered to be a successor entitled to ownership of patent and may sue independently without being required to join assignor as indispensable party.

A patent suit involves issues of validity and infringement as well as damages or profits.

Jury may not find infringement of dependent claim after court has ruled that claim from which it depended was not infringed.

Invalidity of patent precluded consideration of claim for its infringement.

An invalid patent cannot be infringed.

In infringement suit, court may incidentally determine status of exclusive license agreement, but cannot adjudicate rights thereunder in no wise involved in question of infringement.

A later patent, for the same invention covered by a prior patent, but to a different patentee, is not void for priority of invention, being a matter to be determined in infringement suit.

In *infringement action the better practice is to treat both validity and infringement issues,* particularly in view of the public interest in the validity issue; however, where noninfringement is clear and invalidity is not plainly evident, it is appropriate to treat only the infringement issue.

Court may not pass upon validity of claims not put in issue, either by claim of infringement or counterclaim for declaration of invalidity.

Infringement is usually a question of fact, but where the facts are undisputed, and case can be determined by mere comparison of structures, and extrinsic evidence is not needed for purposes of explanation or of application of descriptions to subject matter, infringement *may be determined as a question of law.*

In patent infringement proceeding, *determination of range of equivalents* to be permitted *is question of law* which must be dependent upon state of the art, for an understanding of which the court must look to those skilled in the particular art.

Issue of patent infringement is a question of fact, while ultimate question of patent validity is one of law.

Equivalency is issue of fact, except of course where there is file wrapper estoppel which, as a matter of law, prevents giving patent claims interpretation sufficiently broad to cover accused devices.

While patent validity is question of law, it is to be decided on basis of factual inquiries.

Question of validity of patent being matter of law, grant of Judgment N.O.V. for defendant in infringement action did not deprive plaintiff of jury trial.

Although issues of validity and infringement of a patent involve questions of fact which may properly be considered by a jury, there is no right to a jury trial on such issues when the relief requested is wholly equitable.

The owner of a patent may bring either an action at law for damages for infringement or a *suit in Equity for Injunction,* with incidentally a right to an accounting for damages and profits.

The remedies available for patent infringement are wholly statutory.

A person may protect his ideas while his patent application is pending and before his exclusive rights under patent have vested by maintaining action for wrongful appropriation of *trade secrets.*

Where, in action for patent infringement and for wrongful misappropriation of patent holder's ideas and plans, evidence established that patents involved were not patentable in view of prior art and was not sufficient to establish the misappropriation, trial court, in granting judgment notwithstanding verdict for patent holder, did not invade jury's province or deny patent holder's constitutional right to a jury trial.

Even if a jury has found a patent to be valid, trial court can set aside the finding and enter a judgment for the defendant in a patent infringement action if there are no grounds for the verdict.

A mere contract to convey letters patent will not enable a party to maintain a suit for infringement.

Owner of patent must be the one who brings suit to recover for its infringement.

One having only a partial interest in a patent right cannot maintain an action for its infringement.

Equitable owner of patent may maintain equitable action for infringement.

Cause of action for patent infringement, failing to allege statutory conditions for grant of patents, was insufficient.

Generally, plaintiff in patent infringement suit is required to state what claims of patent he alleges to have been infringed.

Means or manner of the violation of the patent need not be set forth.

In suit involving a patent, plaintiff controls jurisdiction by allegations and prayer in his bill.

Plaintiff in infringement action should state on which of the claims in patents it would rely upon the trial, when it gave notice to the defendants of their acts of infringement, whether such notice was oral or written, and which of the defendants or their representatives were notified.

A bill for infringement had to state that the invention had not been in public use or on sale for more than two years before the application thereof and it was not sufficient to state that it was not in public use or on sale with the consent of the inventor.

A bill for an infringement of a patent in order to state a case had to allege the facts which were essential to the validity of the patent under this section, and negative those the existence of which would defeat it.

In patent infringement suit, defendant was entitled to a bill of particulars setting forth the claims which were alleged to have been infringed and on which plaintiff expected to rely.

A patent infringement suit should be dismissed where it is shown that the patent privilege has been misused in violation of the Sherman Antitrust Act, Sections 1 to 7 of Title 15, and Clayton Antitrust Act, Sections 12 to 27 of Title 15, or as a means of restricting competition.

While advertising claims alone may not be sufficient to make out a case of patent infringement, they may be relied on as admissions by the defendant of the infringing nature of the accused product.

To establish equivalency for purpose of showing infringement of a patent claim, patentee has burden of proving a real identity of means, operation, and result.

In case of product or composition patent, plaintiff may sustain his burden of establishing infringement by evidence as to physical item or its composition, but a far more difficult problem is encountered by a complainant alleging infringement as to a patented method of production.

Defendants in patent infringement action were required to prove invalidity by *clear and convincing evidence* but not beyond reasonable doubt.

In action for injunction and damages for infringement of patent, plaintiff had burden of proving by *preponderance of evidence* that his patent had been infringed by defendants; defendants had burden of proving by clear and convincing evidence that plaintiff's patent was invalid.

Neither patent applicants nor alleged infringers should normally be required to prove its case beyond a reasonable doubt in order to prevail.

In deciding issue of patent infringement, only permissible use of expert testimony is to enable judge to understand what the specifications say; when the judge has understood the specifications, it is for him to decide all questions of infringement, and testimony of such experts is inappropriate.

Court in patent infringement action need not be controlled by testimony or opinion which an expert may give, but opinion is evidence which a court may consider.

Infringement where structure is readily understandable is question for court to determine, and expert testimony on issue is not needed and is in fact superfluous.

As elements of patent cases are complex, necessitating good deal of explanation, court is not properly suited to act without benefit of expert testimony in most instances, and should apply summary judgment remedy only in clearest of cases.

Where crucial litigated question in patent infringement suit is that of infringement by accused structures, the only way that court can securely reach a decision is to be given at least an opportunity to consider and examine the matter that is disclosed in the file wrapper pertaining to the patent in suit.

In patent infringement suit, prior patents not specifically alleged cannot be considered for purpose of anticipation, but only as showing the state of the art.

Proof of prior knowledge and use cannot prevail when the answer merely alleges prior knowledge, and does not set forth where and by whom the invention had been used.

Evidence of prior use is inadmissible when such use is not set up in the pleadings.

Proof of the state of the art is admissible to show want of invention, regardless of whether the defense is pleaded.

Oral testimony, even if it deals with events and circumstances long past, is not excluded as a matter of law in a patent infringement action.

A *combination* is an entirety and, if one of its elements is omitted, the thing claimed is conclusively presumed to be material to the combination and no evidence to the contrary is admissible in any case of alleged infringement.

Decisions of Patent Office Examiner should not be lightly overruled.

Although determination of the United States Patent Office as to sufficiency of disclosure is not binding on District Court it is a factor to be considered in light of the expertise and competence that trained personnel of the Patent Office bring to bear on problems involved.

The decision on patent validity of another federal court, especially a higher one is entitled to be given great weight by federal courts but is not binding.

The determination of examiners, solicitors of patents, and CCPA [now CAFC] is not binding on District Court as to validity of a patent, but it is persuasive.

When a person charged with infringement seeks to establish

anticipation by oral testimony, he must do so by proof that leaves no reasonable doubt as to the fact.

Uncorroborated testimony of prior inventors or users should be evaluated with particular caution in patent infringement action as should oral testimony of an employee of a party to litigation recollecting long past events.

That method of accused machine reaches same result as that of patented machine is, while evidentiary, not conclusive that two methods are equivalent.

Where invalidity of patent has been urged and clearly established in an infringement action, the public interest is better served by a decision that the patent is invalid than by a decision that if it were invalid it would not be infringed.

Consent decree of validity of patent did not bar subsequent assertions of invalidity by party to decree.

Judgment of patent validity is no broader than the claims which were placed in issue by the parties, irrespective of the impact court's opinion may have on other claims not put in issue.

Letter which patent holder sent to certain members of trade after entry of judgment to effect that patent was being infringed did not constitute such a deliberate scheme of misrepresentation as to warrant vacating the infringement decree.

A decision by a district judge of another circuit that patent was invalid was not binding on Court of Appeals as a case of *stare decisis* and comity was not applicable.

A decision of the Court of Appeals of the District of Columbia reversing a decision of the Patent Office Examiner that there was no invention in application for patent added little, if any, weight to presumption arising from issuance of patent, and was not a precedent in suit for infringement of patent.

Noninfringement as a matter of law may be decided upon a motion for summary judgment when there is no genuine issue of material fact, and when it is possible to understand without extrinsic expert evidence the nature of the patented invention, and to determine that the alleged infringing device does not contain all the elements set forth in the patent claim, or the mechanical equivalents thereof.

Summary judgment is appropriate in patent cases where there is no genuine issue of fact to be resolved at trial or where evidence presented in support thereof would compel direction of verdict.

Summary judgment is an extreme and drastic measure and should be cautiously invoked in patent infringement cases.

Whether claims of patent read directly on defendant's alleged infringing device or whether such device is equivalent of plaintiff's patent device are questions of fact and will not be decided on motion for summary judgment.

Summary judgment on ground of *res judicata,* if otherwise proper, should be granted in patent cases.

In a patent action, as a matter of judicial administration, it is better to dispose of all claims and counterclaims at trial rather than to attempt a piecemeal disposition by the grant of partial summary judgment.

Declaratory Judgment Act, Sections 2201 and 2202 of Title 28, enables accused to secure judicial determination of charge of patent infringement without having to wait for patentee to institute proceedings.

Remedial nature of Declaratory Judgment Act, Section 2201 of Title 28, is particularly marked in patent area where such Act extended what had been the previously severely limited remedies afforded a party accused of patent infringement.

An *actual controversy,* for declaratory judgment purposes, exists if there has been a charge of patent infringement; however, such a charge need not be expressed and can be found in any conduct or course of action on part of the patentee which would lead a reasonable man to fear that he or his customers are facing an infringement suit or the threat of one if he continues or commences the activity in question.

In suit for declaratory judgment of noninfringement and invalidity of patents, the fact that the patentee learned for the first time that plaintiff is utilizing its patents when complaint is filed does not negative the existence of an actual controversy within Section 2201 of Title 28 if the patentee asserts publicly that use of its patents constitutes an infringement.

Where the manufacturer of the infringing machine was not joined as party to patent infringement suit, District Court would not make declaratory ruling as to the binding effect of the infringement decision upon the manufacturer since such ruling would be in the nature of an advisory opinion.

In patent infringement suit defendant was properly permitted to file a *counterclaim for declaratory relief.*

The *sine qua non* of appellate review of patent litigation is the notion that validity and interpretation are legal questions based on factual inquiries.

Factual matter in a patent case must be tried and decided by the trial judge in precisely the same manner as those of any other kind of lawsuit, and the functions of the appellate court of review are no different than they are in any other kind of case.

Nonexclusive licensee had no standing to appeal District Court judgment of patent invalidity.

Whether to exclude prior art patent was a matter resting within discretion of trial judge where notice of intent to rely thereon was given only nine days before trial of infringement case, and exercise of discretion would not be reversed without showing of abuse.

In patent infringement action, District Court's findings with respect to basic factual inquiries will be sustained *unless clearly erroneous,* and reviewing court will render an independent judgment on the issue of obviousness.

Findings of fact in patent cases are not to be set aside unless clearly erroneous; however, courts of appeals are not bound by this standard where evidence is documentary or where it involves actual examination of a product.

It was not reversible error for District Court to submit ultimate legal issue of patent validity to jury.

Because what was dealt with was such an integrated question of fact-made law, Court of Appeals could not say that it constituted reversible error for District Court to couch its conclusion respecting presumption of validity of patent in terms of proving patent invalidity, notwithstanding claim of defendant that District Court had attempted to set down a standard of proof for a question of law.

Finding by trial court in an infringement suit will not be disturbed in the absence of evidence decidedly, preponderating against such conclusion.

Jury findings on disputed matters of fact in patent cases will be upheld by the reviewing court if substantial evidence exists to support them.

Determination of District Court that claim of patent was invalid and not infringed was binding upon Court of Appeals on appeal, where supported by substantial evidence and not clearly erroneous.

The weight of evidence and the credibility of the witnesses in a patent infringement action are matters reserved for trier of fact and its decision in respect thereto must be respected by the court on appeal.

On appeal from judgment in patent infringement suit, Court of Appeals has right to interpret documentary evidence for itself.

Where art involved in patent infringement suit did not necessitate a technical expert, trial court's conclusion that there was no invention had even more weight on appeal than might have existed if expert testimony was a requisite to an understanding of the patent.

In determining propriety of granting a motion for directed verdict in an infringement action, the Court of Appeals may not weigh the evidence, pass on the credibility of witnesses, or substitute its judgment on the facts for that of the jury, but must view the evidence in the light most favorable to the party against whom the motion is made, giving him the benefit of all reasonable inferences from the evidence.

In patent infringement cases, in which construction of patent is main determinant, appellate court can consider infringement directly.

Where material facts in patent cases are undisputed or findings are based on documentary evidence which Court of Appeals is as competent to appraise as District Court, Court of Appeals does not hesitate to reject determination of validity either because significance of facts had not yet been fully perceived by trial court or there has been an error in application of legal principles.

It is not a proper function of reviewing court to try *de novo* the issue of patent validity.

The issue of patent validity cannot be determined by Court of Appeals in patent infringement case wherein issue of patent validity has not been litigated in the District Court; in such a case, the Court of Appeals has option to follow the District Court and decide only the issue decided by District Court or to remand for trial of validity or patentability issue when appropriate.

In patent infringement case, if evidence was incompetent or immaterial, presumption on appeal is that trial court disregarded the evidence in reaching its conclusion.

Rendition of advisory opinions as to what may amount to patent infringement in the future is not function of reviewing court.

Court of Appeals is court of review and not court for retrial of cases; and if there was adequate evidentiary basis for findings of trial judge in patent infringement case, and such findings were not induced by erroneous view of applicable law, judgment would have to be affirmed.

Where District Court passed on issues raised by counterclaim for declaratory judgment regarding validity of reissue patents but Court of Appeals improperly treated such issues as moot, the cause was remanded to the Court of Appeals for a review of the District Court's adjudication rather than to District Court for retrial of those issues.

In those comparatively rare patent infringement cases where patent is clearly invalid, and trial court has failed so to hold, an appellate court may do so without any remand for findings.

Patent infringement is fact issue, and findings of trial court will not be reversed unless clearly erroneous.

Trial court's decision as to validity of patent was to be reversed if induced by an erroneous view of the law.

Conflicting views of federal appellate courts concerning validity of same patent obliged United States Supreme Court to decide independently the factual issue of validity.

Concurrent findings of the courts below that new combinations, though they involved old mechanical constructions, combined them in a new way so as to produce an improved result which was patentable, were "findings of fact" which would not be disturbed by the Supreme Court where there was evidence to support them.

7

CONDUCT OF PATENT LITIGATION: JURISDICTION AND PROCEDURE

Patent rights may be enforced through negotiation, mediation, and through arbitration [in 1983 an amendment to the Patent Act (35 USC 294) dealing with arbitration of patent disputes went into effect]. These procedures depend either on the consent of the parties or of an arbitrator. In the absence of such consent, the primary procedure for enforcing patent rights and resolving other patent disputes is through litigation in the courts.

Three basic requirements govern whether a patent suit is filed in a proper court: (1) subject matter jurisdiction, (2) venue, and (3) jurisdiction over the person.

28 USC 1338: JURISDICTION

Federal courts are courts of limited subject matter jurisdiction. Thus, the party filing the suit must affirmatively show a statutory basis for the court's jurisdiction over the controversy. By statute (28 USC 1338), the federal courts have exclusive jurisdiction over all suits arising under any Act of Congress relating to patents. However, the courts distinguish between patent cases and patent questions. An example is a suit for breach of a patent license in which the validity of the underlying patent is raised as a defense. Such suits may be filed in a state court of general jurisdiction. They may be filed in a federal court only if some other basis for jurisdiction can be found, such as diversity of citizenship.

A separate jurisdictional requirement is that there be an actual ripe controversy between the parties. The "actual controversy" requirement arises most often in connection with actions for a declaratory judgment concerning patent rights.

In 1897, the Supreme Court embraced the position that state courts are competent to adjudicate the validity of a patent when that issue is raised "collaterally" in a case which does not arise under the patent laws. In a series of five cases spanning the years 1902 to 1926, the Supreme Court gave up completely any attempt to characterize the real nature of the action and let the issue of jurisdiction depend almost entirely on how the plaintiff chose to plead its action.

In a license situation where the licensee allegedly used the invention and exceeded or breached the terms of the license, a patent owner could choose between an infringement remedy in federal court and a contract remedy in state court.

> [T]he party who brings a suit is master to decide what law he will rely upon and therefore does determine whether he will bring a "suit arising under" the patent or other law of the United States by his declaration or bill.
>
> But when the patentee exercises his choice and bases his action on the contract and seeks remedies thereunder, he may not give the case a double aspect, so to speak, and make it a patent case conditioned on his securing equitable relief as to the contract.

The courts consistently hold that a claim of infringement, pleaded as such in the complaint, is within the exclusive jurisdiction of the federal courts under 28 USC 1338(a), and remains within this section even though the plaintiff in his complaint anticipates and avoids contract or other non-patent defenses by the defendant. On the other hand, when the plaintiff joins a claim ostensibly for infringement with other state law contract claims, some decisions find no "arising under" jurisdiction on the ground that the gravamen of the plaintiff's action lies other than on the patent. Federal law provides for the creation of patents as items of intangible personal property and defines what conduct constitutes infringement of that property right. Other legal relations concerning patents are left to state law.

The Declaratory Judgment Act of 1934 created a new remedy, which has been discussed above. While some cases recognize the availability of the declaratory judgment remedy to a patent owner, a number of courts have ruled against suits.

Federal court jurisdiction over actions arising under the patent laws is exclusive of state court jurisdiction. Nevertheless, the Supreme Court has emphasized that state courts are competent to adjudicate patent questions so long as the action itself does not arise under the patent laws. Thus, a state court in passing on a patent license suit for royalties may adjudicate the validity of a patent. Some state courts, however, have been reluctant to assume jurisdiction over patent-related disputes even when pleaded in contract or tort. In a 1978 North Carolina Court of Appeals case, it dismissed for want of jurisdiction a contract action on the ground that "the contract imposes no obligation other than those created by the patent law itself." It refused to believe that the Supreme Court "meant that a plaintiff, by calling a patent infringement something else, could avoid federal jurisdiction."

If a suit does not arise under the patent laws within the meaning of Section 1338(a), a U.S. District Court may nevertheless have jurisdiction over the suit under some other statute. Section 1332 confers jurisdiction over several types of suits between parties of diverse citizenship. Section 1330 confers jurisdiction over actions against foreign states. Some courts hold that a federal court has inherent jurisdiction or authority to enforce agreements between parties settling patent infringement suits.

It must be noted that the term *patent litigation* embraces different proceedings which are conducted in at least five fora as follows:

1. United States District Courts: These courts have original and exclusive jurisdiction of actions "arising under" the Patent Laws pursuant to 28 USC 1338(a).
2. State Courts: "not actions arising under" the Patent Laws, but actions which involve a patent.
3. United States Claims Court: If the U.S. government infringes a patent, the exclusive judicial remedy of the patent owner is an action against the government in the U.S. Claims Court for compensation under 28 USC 1498. There are two important distinctions from a normal patent infringement suit: An injunction against patent infringement cannot be obtained, either against the U.S. government, or against a supplier to the U.S. government in respect to the goods supplied to the government. The purpose of the statute is to protect a contractor from liability for the infringement of a patent when the contractor manufactured anything for the United States.
4. United States International Trade Commission: This is an administrative agency proceeding brought under 19 USC 1337 and 1337(a) for an order barring importation of products which infringe a U.S. patent. There is no provision for an award of damages or attorney fees.
5. United States Patent and Trademark Office: Strictly not litigation, this is an *inter partes* proceeding in patent interference arising under 35 USC 135 seeking to determine the priority between two persons claiming the same invention.

Nota bene: An applicant dissatisfied with the decision in an appeal to the BPAI (Board of Patent Appeals and Interferences) under 35 USC 134 may appeal the decision to the CAFC under 35 USC 141. By filing such an appeal, the applicant waives his right to file an appeal under 35 USC 145 for a civil action to obtain a patent.

THE U.S. FEDERAL COURT SYSTEM WITH RESPECT TO PATENTS

After a second or final rejection, an applicant may appeal within the PTO to the BPAI. Generally, the board's jurisdiction is over rejections of claims on the merits. Other objections, requirements, and restrictions imposed by an examiner are reviewed by petition to the commissioner. The decision of the BPAI represents the decision of the PTO. Further proceedings are adversarial in nature, in effect, pitting the commissioner (represented by his solicitor) against the applicant.

From an adverse ruling by the board, the applicant may either appeal on the record to the Court of Appeals for the Federal Circuit or file a *de novo* civil suit to obtain a patent against the commissioner in the District Court for the District of Columbia. An adverse decision in the *de novo* trial may be appealed by either the commissioner or the applicant, as a matter of right, to the CAFC. By going into court, it should be noted, an applicant loses his common law right to secrecy, since all court proceedings are a matter of public record, unless the court allows the proceedings to be conducted *in camera.*

The board's "statutory review power" is directed only to rejections of claims [35 USC 134]. The board has no jurisdiction to review claims allowed by the examiner, even though they may appear in the same application with claims rejected and appealed. It is the primary examiner who has the power to allow a case. Neither the BPAI nor the courts have the power to decree a patent's issuance. Usually, the application is returned to the primary examiner in charge of the application who then resumes *ex parte* examination of the application, allowing it if it is otherwise in condition for allowance.

After the second rejection, the applicant has the option of appealing a rejection. After a final rejection, the applicant must choose to appeal in order to avoid abandonment of the application. The board is not limited to review of grounds of rejection asserted by the examiner but may "originate, *sua sponte* [on his own] a truly new rejection of appealed claims."

A number of avenues of judicial review are open to the applicant dissatisfied with decisions by the PTO in the course of *ex parte* examination of an application:

1. From the BPAI to the CAFC, on the record;
2. From the BPAI to the District Court for the District of Columbia, *de novo;*
3. From the commissioner, by *writ of mandamus* or under the Administrative Procedure Act, to the proper U.S. District Court.

Prior to October 1, 1982, review under 35 USC 145 by civil suit and appeal to the Court of Customs and Patent Appeals (CCPA) were parallel modes of judicial review. Conflicting rules of law in the District of Columbia Circuit and the CCPA created problems for the PTO and influenced applicants' choice of forum on grounds other than the method of review. This conflict was ended by the formation of the CAFC by the merger of these two courts. Appeals to the former CCPA and now the CAFC make such an appeal a "waiver" of the applicant's right to file a civil action under 35 USC 145.

In a civil action to the District of Columbia Circuit, the court will only review claims rejected on the merits by the BPAI. Furthermore, the *de novo* character of the civil suit procedure is tempered by a number of doctrines. While the applicant may present new "evidence," he may not raise new "issues." The applicant may even be precluded from presenting new evidence if he was negligent in not presenting it to the PTO. The District of Columbia courts tend to defer to the expertise of the PTO. The CAFC has appellate jurisdiction over both direct appeals from the PTO and *de novo* actions in the District of Columbia Circuit.

Nonstatutory Judicial Review

The express "statutory avenues of judicial review" of PTO decisions are limited to rejections of claims on the merits by the BPAI. Decisions other than such rejections are either made by or reviewable on petition to the commissioner. There is as yet no fully consistent criteria with which to separate appealable decisions by examiners from petitionable decisions. Fortunately, however, the classification of most decisions is well settled by tradition, and borderline and unsettled cases are rare.

Early Supreme Court decisions recognized that such decisions may be reviewed by *writ of mandamus.* This right of "nonstatutory" judicial review is further emphasized in the Administrative Procedure Act [5 USC 702–704]. The district courts have subject matter jurisdiction over such review actions under 28 USC 1338, covering all actions arising under the patent laws, and 28 USC 1361, covering actions for *mandamus.* In 1962, Congress enacted Section 1361 and authorized service of process and venue in the district of the plaintiff's residence rather than solely being confined to the District of Columbia as previously.

Generally, nonstatutory review is available only as a final action as to which the applicant has exhausted his administrative remedies and has no adequate remedy under the statutory review procedure. Thus, for example, *mandamus* will lie to review whether the commissioner's decision not to revive an abandoned application or not to enter an amendment is arbitrary or capricious.

In District Court, one seeking review of a petitionable decision under the Administrative Procedure Act must overcome the "presumption of administrative correctness," which attaches to the decision in the PTO. The Federal Circuit has said that in reviewing such a decision during the course of an ordinary appeal, it will reverse only if an abuse of discretion is shown, and it never seems to find such an abuse.

A question of interest is whether District Court decisions in nonstatutory review cases lie within the exclusive appellate jurisdiction of the CAFC.

Court of Appeals for the Federal Circuit

Creation of the CAFC in 1982 was a landmark in the evolution of patent law and policy. Congress conferred on the CAFC exclusive appellate jurisdiction over most cases involving patent issues, including decisions by:

1. BPAI;
2. district courts in infringement and other patent suits;
3. the U.S. Claims Court including reasonable compensation suits against the United States for use of a patented invention; and
4. determinations of the U.S. International Trade Commission.

With the withdrawal of patent jurisdiction from the twelve regional courts of appeal, the CAFC becomes the court with primary responsibility for interpreting and developing the rules and principles of patent law. Existence of appellate jurisdiction in the CAFC will be clear in the typical case where an action is filed in a U.S. District Court by a patent owner claiming infringement by the defendant. Appeal from any judgment will go to the CAFC rather than to the regional Court of Appeals. In cases involving a mixture of patent law issues, nonpatent federal issues, and state law issues, jurisdiction may be less clear. The statute confers exclusive federal court jurisdiction over cases arising under the patent statutes, not every case in which a question of patent law is or may be raised. The existence of jurisdiction under 28 USC 1338 may turn on how the plaintiff chooses to plead his or her claim in the complaint.

A good example is a suit stemming from a dispute between the parties to a patent license: The licensee ceases paying royalties, and the licensor sues. If the licensor states the claim as one for breach of contract (the license), the case does not arise under the patent laws within the meaning of Section 1338(a) and may be brought in federal court only if there is an alternative basis for jurisdiction, such as diversity of citizenship between the parties. On the other hand, if the patent owner sues for patent infringement (treating the nonpayment of royalties as grounds for forfeiting the license without judicial declaration) the case does arise under the patent laws.

There is one difficult issue concerning appellate jurisdiction of the CAFC over patent matters emanating from the PTO. That relates to suits seeking judicial review of decisions by examiners and other PTO officials which are not appealable to the BPAI. Heretofore, aggrieved persons have sought judicial review by suit in a District Court with appeal to the appropriate regional Court of Appeals. The statute defining the jurisdiction of the CAFC makes no reference to such suits.

In its first reported opinion, the CAFC adopted as binding precedent "the holdings of our predecessor courts, the United States Court of Claims and the United States Court of Customs and Patent Appeals, announced by those courts before the close of business September 30, 1982." Proceedings before these various courts can be distinguished by their distinctive captions:

Ex parte—a case before the BPAI

In re—(in the matter of the application of) signifies an *ex parte* case before the CCPA or the CAFC appealed directly from the PTO

(Applicant's name) v. (commissioner's name)—signifies an *ex parte* case before the District Court or the Court of Appeals for the District of Columbia Circuit or from the CAFC appealed from the District Court where the commissioner prevailed in the District Court.

(Commissioner's name) v. (applicant's name)—where the applicant prevailed in the District Court and the commissioner has taken the appeal to the District of Columbia Circuit or to the CAFC, the order of the parties is reversed.

Court of Claims (1855) and the New U.S. Claims Court (1982)

Jurisdiction of all actions brought by owners of patent rights against the government of the United States, upon a contract express or implied for compensation for the use by the government of patent and patent rights owned by patentees or other owners and liability for such infringement, is specifically established by 28 USC 1498.

Without its consent, the United States may not be sued for infringement of a patent. The Congress has determined the conditions upon which the United States consents to be sued. By the applicable statute, Congress has permitted suit to be brought in the Court of Claims for reasonable compensation for the infringing use or manufacture (accomplished by the United States, or as U.S. contractor, without a license to practice the invention).

The findings, in order to be sufficient to sustain judgment for the plaintiff, must specifically decide questions of validity and infringement and also include circumstantial facts sufficient to warrant the court's conclusion in respect of the main issues.

International Trade Commission

Section 337 of the Tariff Act of 1930 [19 USC 1336] is concerned with the prevention of unfair practices in import trade in the United States. Under Section 337, products which infringe a U.S. patent can be excluded from importation into the United States. Also under Section 337, the sale of previously imported infringing products by the owner, importer, or consignee can be prevented. Because Section 337 actions must be completed within strict statutory time limits, these actions may well be favored by U.S. patent owners. The recent amendments to Section 337 (Omnibus Trade and Competitiveness Act of 1988), which were motivated in part by increasing U.S. trade deficits with many foreign countries, have made it substantially easier for U.S. patent owners to demonstrate violations of and obtain relief under Section 337.

As a result of the 1988 amendments, a suit based on patent infringement now requires proof of only two elements: (1) the import, or sale after import, of an infringing article, and (2) existence of a domestic industry.

The International Trade Commission (ITC) is the governmental agency authorized to investigate unfair import practices, including Section 337 actions. The commission is headed by six commissioners, none of whom are patent attorneys.

Section 337 actions encompass not only the importation or the sale after importation of products which infringe U.S. patents but also products which are manufactured abroad by a process which infringes a U.S. patent, and parts or components which can be assembled after importation or sale to produce an infringing product.

Prior to the 1988 amendments, it was necessary for the patent owner to show that the importation or sale had the effect or tendency to destroy or substantially injure an industry efficiently and economically operated in the United States, or to prevent the establishment of such an industry.

If, during a Section 337 investigation, the commission determines there is reason to believe the statute has been violated, it may issue a temporary exclusion order which prevents importation during the investigation of the accused articles. When a temporary exclusion order is issued, the commission usually will allow entry of the articles subject to payment of a bond by the owner or importer of the articles in an amount determined by the commission.

Once the commission has determined that a Section 337 violation has been established, several additional remedies are available to the complainant: First, the commission may grant a permanent exclusion order; and second, in addition to, or in place of, granting the above, the commission may also issue and serve on any person an order to cease and desist from engaging in the unfair acts which violate Section 337.

Patent-based Section 337 actions are usually initiated by the filing of a complaint by the U.S. patent owner. Upon filing a complaint, the commission votes on whether to institute an investigation. If an investigation is instituted, it is referred to an administrative law judge (who is not required to be and, with one exception currently, is not a patent attorney) who conducts discovery, presides at an evidentiary hearing and makes an initial determination concerning the Section 337 violation and the appropriate remedy. The commission then makes a final determination. Each determination must be concluded and a final order issued within twelve months, unless it is "more complicated," when a final order must be issued within eighteen months.

The federal courts have exclusive jurisdiction over patent claims, and therefore the commission may consider issues of patent validity only insofar as they impact its decision on unfair competition. Therefore, patent validity determinations by the commission are not accorded *res judicata* effect because the commission has no jurisdiction to determine patent validity except to the limited extent necessary to decide a case otherwise properly before it. The Federal Circuit has further stated that its appellate treatment of decisions of the commission does not estop fresh consideration by other tribunals.

Unlike a U.S. District Court, the ITC has nationwide subpoena power. In other words, witnesses can be compelled to attend a deposition or a hearing from anywhere in the United States. In addition, the ITC may impose incredibly short time constraints during the discovery phase. In some cases, discovery responses must be answered in five days. Soon after the commission votes to institute an investigation, the investigation will be assigned to one of the administrative law judges, from the "Office of the Administrative Law Judges," which is a government service that is independent of the ITC. These hearings may be less formal than a typical patent infringement trial held in a District Court. In a District Court, a plaintiff may obtain monetary damages, an injunction, and/or a declaratory judgment. However, in the ITC, a complainant may only obtain an exclusion order, or in some situations, a cease and desist order against a domestic receiver of the imported infringing goods. A complainant is not able to receive monetary damages.

Investigations at the ITC are conducted along a well-defined time schedule, while there is no fixed time schedule for completing trials in district courts. Within 70 days from publication of the Notice of the Investigation in the Federal Register, the administrative law judge will issue an initial determination as to whether temporary relief should be granted. Within seven days after service of the initial determination, the parties may file briefs concerning this determination. The full commission must then determine whether or not it will accept the initial determination within twenty days after issuance of it.

The commission opinion is published in the Federal Register and transmitted to the president. Exclusion Orders and Seizure and Forfeiture Orders are enforceable upon receipt of notice thereof by the secretary of the Treasury. The president rarely disapproves commission action. In the meantime discovery for the hearing on permanent relief continues. It is not uncommon for ITC investigations to be terminated by settlement. The fact that the complainant has the right to assert its U.S. patent rights both in the ITC and in U.S. district courts has been criticized as a violation of GATT. Decisions granting or denying exclusion orders under Section 337 may be appealed to the CAFC. Although a prior ITC determination of patent infringement on validity is not legally binding on a District Court in a parallel patent infringement action, the District Court may give preclusive effect to factual findings on patent validity.

PRELITIGATION CONSIDERATIONS

Introduction

Patent litigation is extremely expensive. Bringing suit merely on suspicion is rash. If the case is later dismissed for noninfringement, the party or his attorney runs the risk of being sanctioned with the defendant's litigation expenses, either under the "exceptional case" provision of 35 USC 285, or under Rule 11 of the Federal Rules of Civil Procedure. While it is not necessary for the patent owner to obtain proof to the degree of certainty required to prove infringement at trial before he can file his complaint, it is advisable that he have obtained the opinion of competent patent counsel before filing his complaint for patent infringement. Such opinion will go far to avoid sanctions.

In addition to the opinion of counsel, the patent owner should reassess the strength and enforceability of his patent. An updated patentability search would be a wise investment as well as a study of the prosecution history of the patent application; this is especially relevant where the patent owner is not the original inventor or assignee. Statutory bars, inequitable conduct in procurement, patent misuse, licensing practices should all be reevaluated, and this would best be done by a patent attorney other than he who prosecuted the original application.

During the above evaluation, should it be found that there is a defect in the patent, which arose without any deceptive intent, it is possible to have this defect corrected and have the patent reissued under 35 USC 251. Furthermore, if a prior patent or publication has recently come to light which raises a substantial new question of patentability about any claim, anyone, including the patent owner, can request reexamination of the patent under 35 USC 302. Some patent owners have sought reexamination of their own patents before bringing suit. If the patent is confirmed, it makes it more difficult for the challenger to carry its burden of proof as to obviousness. If not confirmed, the patent owner has found out with far less costs than in litigation and with no exposure to an adverse award of attorney fees.

The Proper Parties

The legal title holder of the patent is an indispensable party to a suit for the infringement of that patent or a suit to have the patent declared invalid and unenforceable. Where there is "joint" ownership, *all* must be joined. Where an assignee owns less than an entire interest in the patent, he cannot maintain a suit for infringement without joining the owners of the remaining interests. The owner of an equitable title to the patent may sue if the defendant is the patentee or his assignee. The United States is not liable to a suit for infringement of a patent.

The question sometimes arises whether a licensee can bring suit without naming the patent owner or should be named as a joint plaintiff with the patent owner; this depends on the nature of the license. An exclusive licensee has a substantial interest in the patent and is considered to be either indispensable or at least a necessary party. He can even be made an involuntary plaintiff in a suit for the patent's infringement. (Joining a party as an involuntary plaintiff will result in the decision being final against that involuntary plaintiff!) Even though a grant of an exclusive license is not a statutory assignment, on principle and authority, the patent owner ought to allow his name to be used as plaintiff in any action brought at the instance of the licensee to obtain redress for the patent's infringement. A right to bring suit for infringement is not afforded to a nonexclusive licensee, nor is he an indispensable party, although he may be allowed to intervene.

On the infringer's side, patent litigation offers an unusually large choice of defendants due to the pattern of distribution through which many products move. Members in the chain of distribution from a manufacturer to a distributor to a retailer to the end-user of an infringing product are joint tort-feasors and as such are jointly and severally liable for infringement. In such a chain, the manufacturer is likely to be the first choice in order to stop the infringement at its source, minimize litigation expense, and aim at the single defendant offering the largest potential damage award. For tactical reasons, others may be sued where the manufacturer is outside the country, for example, or where one wishes to control the place of suit.

With so many possible defendants one must be especially cautious. Where a manufacturer, for example, controls a customer's defense, a holding of infringement and validity against the customer may collaterally estop the manufacturer in a subsequent suit on the basis of *res judicata.* It should be noted that the CAFC has upheld the personal liability of a corporate officer for actively inducing infringement. Third parties may intervene in a suit under certain circumstances as a matter of right and under others by permission of the court [FRCP Rule 24].

A defendant in his answer may state as many defenses in the alternative, regardless of consistency, as the defendant deems essential to his defense and may in his answer set up any counterclaim against the plaintiff which might be subject of an independent suit against him. The court has the power to decide both a complaint and a counterclaim when those issues are the same, for example, validity and infringement.

Jurisdiction

Jurisdiction is the authority by which courts and judicial officers take cognizance of and decide cases; it is "power" conferred by Constitution and law. Jurisdiction is of three kinds:

1. Of the subject matter, i.e., jurisdiction of that class of cases to which a particular case belongs;
2. Of the person, i.e., power to subject parties in a particular case to decisions and rulings made in such case, the proper parties being present; and
3. To render particular judgment which was given, i.e., the point to be decided is within the issues.

Venue does not refer to jurisdiction at all. It is the place in which an injury is declared to have been done, or fact declared to have happened (in the common law). Jurisdiction of the court means the inherent power to hear a case; whereas venue designates the particular county or city in which a court "with jurisdiction" may hear and determine the case.

Subject Matter Jurisdiction. Federal courts have exclusive jurisdiction of all cases "arising under" the patent laws, but not of all questions in which a patent is the subject matter of the controversy. They are courts of limited jurisdiction having only the authority endowed by the Constitution and that conferred by Congress pursuant to the Constitution. 28 USC 1338 vests U.S. district courts with original jurisdiction of civil actions "arising under" any Act of Congress relating to patents, copyrights, and trademarks.

Patent matters primarily concerned with contractual matters, actions for royalties under a patent license, tortious wrongdoing, and so on, are properly brought in a state court unless there is "diversity of citizenship" among adverse parties and the requisite jurisdictional amount has been pleaded. In this latter case, a federal District Court has jurisdiction over the dispute even though such dispute may not arise under the patent laws. State courts may in these matters consider validity or infringement when incidental to an action based on contract or tort. Enforcement of a patent infringement settlement agreement which contains a patent license is more than a patent license, and is cognizable in a federal court even in the absence of diversity of citizenship.

The U.S. Supreme Court has determined that there is a distinction between patent issues raised by the case "as pleaded" and patent questions which are incidental to the case. The test is as follows:

> The state court had jurisdiction both of the parties and the subject matter as set forth in the declaration, and it could not be ousted of such jurisdiction by the fact that, incidentally to one of these defences, the defendant claimed the invalidity of a certain patent. To hold that it has no right to introduce evidence upon this subject is to do it a wrong and deny it a remedy.... There is a clear distinction between a case and a question arising under the patent laws. The former arises when a plaintiff in his opening pleading—be it a bill, complaint or declaration—sets up a right under the patent laws as ground for a recovery. Of such the state courts have no jurisdiction. The latter may appear in the plea or answer or in the testimony. The determination of such question is not beyond the competency of the state tribunals.

If a patent owner does not reside in the United States, 35 USC 293 (Nonresident Patentee; Service and Notice) provides that the District Court for the District of Columbia has jurisdiction and that a summons can be served by publication or otherwise as that court directs.

Venue [28 USC 1400(b)]. The situs of the District Court wherein a suit may be brought is subject to 28 USC 1400(b), which provides:

> Any civil action for patent infringement may be brought in the judicial district where the defendant resides, or where the defendant has committed acts of infringement and has a regular and established place of business.

This statute is exclusive of all other statutory provisions on venue. The only exception is infringement suits against aliens, which may be filed in any district.

The residence of an individual person is the place of domicile. Determining domicile is a recurrent problem in the law of jurisdiction and procedure. The residence of a corporation for purposes of Section 1400(b) is the state of incorporation even if the principal offices are in another state. The residence of an unincorporated association or partnership is its principal place of business.

To establish venue under the second option, the two events must occur in the district, that is; (1) possession by the defendant of a regular and established place of business, and (2) commission by the defendant of an act of infringement. Neither alone is sufficient; both must occur in order to establish venue under this option. Formal registration under state law for purpose of service of process does not as such constitute a regular and established place of business; nor would a mere sales office probably.

Numerous court decisions apply the regular-and-established-place-of-business concept to various fact patterns.

1. The Traveling Salesmen Cases: usually not, but if he operates out of his home, maybe.
2. The Sales Office Cases: The cases tend to find no place of business when the office or representative is shared, or when maintained at the salesman's expense. If the sales office can bind the principal, probably.
3. The Independent Sales Representative Cases: Even with an exclusive representation agreement, probably not.
4. Parent and Subsidiary, Separate Divisions: So long as the formalities of separate existence are respected, even with wholly owned subsidiaries, probably not a regular and established place of business. Venue is proper, however, if one division has a regular and established place of business in the district even though the infringing activity involves a division which has no such place.

The most common problem with the act of infringement element concerns the location of an act of sale. Other problems include the meaning of "use," the location of infringements involving processes, and the status of inducement and contributory infringement as acts of infringement for purposes of Section 1400(b).

1. Selling, The Consummated Sale Doctrine: In determining "if" and "when" a sale occurs for the purpose of determining patent infringement on the merits, the courts seem generally to follow common law and the Uniform Commercial Code definition of a sale. Whether these definitions should control for venue purposes under 1400(b) is a matter of some controversy.
2. Use: A number of decisions have held that the demonstration of the accused product for a prospective customer is a sufficient use. On the other hand, mere display of the accused device will not constitute a use.
3. Manufacture: Few problems arise as to the location of an act of making. The Supreme Court has held that an accused product is not "made" until it is fully assembled and is covered by a claim of the patent for purposes of the venue statute.
4. Contributory Infringement and Inducement: There are a number of split decisions as to where venue should be, depending on the location and impact of these acts.
5. Process Claims: In determining infringement on the merits, the courts find no infringement of a process claim of a patent by the sale or use of a product made by that process. In the venue context, the courts hold that sale in the district of an unpatented product made outside the district by the process does not constitute an act of infringement in the district, even when the sale is made by the same defendant who practices the process.

Where the defendant's activities provide a basis for more than one venue under 28 USC 1400(b), choice of venue used to be very important in patent litigation. Before the formation of the Court of Appeals of the Federal Circuit in 1982, forum shopping was commonplace due to the varying rates at which the district courts sustained validity actions. Today, venue contests are largely a thing of the past in patent litigation. However, even today, where alternative venues exist, there are a few judges whose prior records in patent cases demonstrate a pronounced bias pro- or anti-patent validity. The Supreme Court has ruled that the special patent venue statute, 28 USC 1400(b), is exclusive.

Timing

35 USC 286: Time Limitation on Damages

> Except as otherwise provided by law, no recovery shall be had for any infringement committed more than six years prior to the filing of the complaint or counterclaim for infringement in the action.

The only statute of limitations involving patent infringement suits limits period of recovery of damages to six years, not patentee's right to maintain an action. This is a condition on the right, not on the remedy, and is not subject to disabilities by which ordinary statutes of limitations could be avoided by plaintiff. This section provides the only limitation which can be invoked by an infringer to bar recovery.

Laches, as a defense, does not preclude a patent infringement action, it simply bars the recovery of all prefiling damages; it has no effect on post-filing damages or an injunction.

Alternatives

These prelitigation considerations provide a picture of whether there is infringement, who and where to sue, and the prospects of winning, before discovery has exposed possible flaws in the picture. Whether to sue requires balancing the harm experienced and the expected rewards of litigation against the expense and duration of litigation and the uncertainty of its outcome. Is the objective to obtain an injunction to maintain the patent owner's exclusivity in the marketplace, or is it primarily to force the infringer to accept a license and pay past damages?

Should one seek a preliminary injunction, or bifurcate so that an injunction may issue more quickly than during a trial? How much effort should be expended in discovery and many, many other matters?

There are several factors that require early attention: (1) the expense; patent lawsuits often take three to five years for resolution; (2) corporate management and technical time diverted to back up the trial efforts are substantial; and (3) how will the costs be financed; few law firms will take patent cases on a contingency.

There are alternatives to patent litigation. "Designing around" is actually encouraged by many court decisions. Where the defendant is willing to abandon the infringing product, it is often possible to negotiate a consent decree providing a permanent injunction in return for forgiveness of past damages. Licensing is a common method to terminate or avoid litigation.

Arbitration is specifically provided for under 35 USC 294 (Voluntary Arbitration); however, it has been rarely used. The main reason has been the unwillingness of parties not already bound by agreement (usually a license) to agree to arbitrate because of the absence of adequate provisions for obtaining and enforcing discovery and the desire of plaintiffs to retain the advantages of trial by jury.

Another Alternative Dispute Resolution (ADR) possibility is the so-called "minitrial," in which both sides present an abbreviated version of their case, over one or two days, to a jointly selected adjudicator, with management observers from both sides present. Minitrials have not gained more than isolated acceptance for resolving patent disputes, for which District Court litigation continues to be the conventional and generally preferred procedure. Arbitration in lieu of litigation can only come about voluntarily.

LITIGATION

Pleadings

Pleadings are allegations of fact made by parties to a case for the purpose of definitely presenting issues to be tried and determined between them. In modern civil practice, pleadings are generally two in number, namely, the plaintiff's complaint and the defendant's answer. The format of a complaint alleging patent infringement is set forth in Form 16 of the Federal Rules of Civil Procedure (FRCP) which have been judicially approved.

Form 16: Complaint for Infringement of Patent

1. Allegation of jurisdiction.

2. On May 16, 1934, United States Letters Patent No. ______ were duly and legally issued to plaintiff for an invention in an electric motor; and since that date plaintiff has been and still is the owner of those Letters Patent.

3. Defendant has for a long time past been and still is infringing those Letters Patent by making, selling, and using electric motors embodying the patented invention, and will continue to do so unless enjoined by this court.

4. Plaintiff has placed the required statutory notice on all electric motors manufactured and sold by him under said Letters Patent, and has given written notice to defendant of his said infringement.

Wherefore plaintiff demands a preliminary and final injunction against continued infringement, an accounting for damages, and an assessment of interest and costs against defendant.

The Federal Rules of Civil Procedure govern the practice and procedure in the U.S. district courts of all civil actions instituted and prosecuted in district courts. The purpose of the rules is to secure the just, speedy, and inexpensive determination of every civil action.

In patent litigation, one of the most frequent actions is a civil action for the infringement of a patent. However, other actions involving patents and patent questions and matters include those concerned with declaratory judgments, interfering patents, false markings, and appeals from decisions of the U.S. PTO Board of Patent Appeals and Interferences.

Discovery

The FRCP sanction the discovery of "any matter, not privileged, which is relevant to the subject matter involved in the pending action." This has been construed to include such matters as those reasonably calculated to lead to the discovery of admissible evidence and those useful merely for impeaching the credibility of a witness. A motion to compel discovery must be timely made.

The U.S. patent laws rely heavily for their enforcement on private infringement actions by patent holders. Pretrial discovery, under the FRCP, is an important part of the system of private enforcement; inadequate discovery frustrates the purposes of the patent laws and the Constitution.

Trade secrets are not immune from discovery. Disclosure may be had even of the content of pending patent applications, it having been held that 35 USC 122 does not render patent applications privileged for judicial purposes. A court will attempt to balance the competing policies, ordering discovery when the necessity outweighs the desirability of maintaining the secrecy of data, especially if "protective measures," for example, production of documents *in camera* or a "Protective Order" can be fashioned to minimize intrusion or to prevent excessive dissemination of revealed material.

While the work product of an attorney is privileged, it has been held that the attorney-client privilege does not extend to the work product of a patent "agent." If the communication relates merely to technical or prior art or research matters, even if prepared by an attorney, it is not privileged.

Because the federal courts have exclusive jurisdiction in patent infringement cases, discovery issues are normally resolved by interpreting the Federal Rules of Civil Procedure as applied in these courts. There are no special procedural rules which apply to discovery in patent cases. However, the most frequent, hard-fought discovery issues which arise seem to be in the area of discovery of confidential business information and trade secrets. This is undoubtedly due to the fact that parties in patent litigation are typically direct competitors who value both their confidential sales and marketing information and the technical developments they make to allow them to successfully compete.

In *Rosemount v. Beckman Instruments* (1984), the District Court ordered Beckman to identify its experts and permit their deposition. Although Beckman identified an expert, he was not proffered to answer questions about the *ex parte* tests. Rosemount indicated it would object to any testimony offered at trial in support of the tests. At trial, the testimony was excluded by the District Court. The Federal Circuit ruled that exclusion of the expert's testimony was within the possible sanctions provided by FRCP 26(e) and 37(b). The CAFC stated:

> One under a court order to identify its expert witnesses, and specifically requested by opposing counsel to identify who would testify on tests of the accused products, is ill advised to rely on his own characterization of the testimony as a basis for escaping the effects of Rules 26(e) and 37(b)(2)(b).

In *Minnesota Mining and Manufacturing v. Eco Chem* (March 1985), the District Court entered default judgment for failure to respond to interrogatories. The alleged infringer had engaged in dilatory tactics throughout the litigation including: (1) numerous extensions of time to answer the complaint, (2) failure to appear at hearings, (3) failure to schedule hearings on its own motions, and finally, (4) dissolution of the corporation in an attempt to avoid responsibility. The court found that under the unusual factual circumstances involved, granting the severest sanction possible was not an abuse of discretion.

In *American Standard v. Pfizer* (August 1987), American Standard sought discovery against nonparty Biomet, Inc. Biomet's outside counsel had shared a validity opinion on the patent in issue in confidence with inside counsel for the related distributor, and the distributor produced the opinion in discovery. The District Court granted Biomet's motion for a "protective order" finding that: (1) trade secrets existed; (2) there was substantial potential harm involved; and (3) some of the information was not sufficiently relevant to be made available. The District Court also found there was no waiver of Biomet's privilege by sharing the opinion. The Federal Circuit ruled that since there was no indication in the record that the opinion letter revealed the substance of a confidential communication, the District Court's decision was not clearly erroneous.

In conclusion, the court has issued few rulings relating to discovery issues in patent cases. It has consistently applied the law of the regional circuits in discovery disputes, and has applied the "abuse of discretion" standard of review in these matters.

Preliminary Injunction

A court, in its discretion, has the power to grant a preliminary injunction, also known as a Temporary or Interlocutory Injunction or an injunction *pendente lite,* that is, pending the outcome of the lawsuit. The CAFC has indicated that the criteria for granting a preliminary injunction in a patent infringement suit are no different from that in other litigation. These criteria are:

1. whether the patent owner will have an adequate remedy at law or will be irreparably harmed if a preliminary injunction does not issue;
2. whether the threatened injury to the patent owner outweighs the threatened harm that the injunction may inflict on the accused;
3. whether the patent owner has at least a reasonable likelihood of success on the merits; and
4. whether the granting of a preliminary injunction will disserve the public interest.

While the grant of a preliminary injunction does not require that infringement be proved beyond all question, or that there be no evidence supporting the viewpoint of the accused infringer, to demonstrate immediate irreparable harm, infringement must be clearly established.

The procedural requirements for the grant of a preliminary injunction set forth in Rule 65 of the FRCP require: (1) notice; (2) a statement of reasons for an injunctive order; and (3) the posting of security.

Trial

Patent cases have been said to be the best tried of all lawsuits.

Whether there exists a right to a jury trial (rather than a bench trial) depends essentially upon whether the relief sought is deemed to be of legal or equitable nature. The merger in 1938 of actions of law and suits in equity into a single "civil action" in the federal courts did not destroy the distinction between these two actions in determining the right to a jury trial. A civil action in the nature of an action at law is triable by a jury, while one in the nature of an action in equity is not triable by jury.

JURY	**BENCH**
Patent Rights	Injunction
Damages	Fraud

An Accounting
Obviousness

Declaratory Relief (neither)
Assessment of Damages (court-appointed master)

Expert witnesses play an important role in patent infringement litigation. Their chief function is to translate the patent specification from the arcane terminology understood by those skilled in the art to which the invention relates into terms comprehensible to courts. The patent examiner who examined a patent involved in litigation is subject to compulsory testimony as to factual matters that do not invade his decision-making mental processes. In the past, many members of the Patent Bar have wisely avoided jury trials in patent litigation; although today, much higher damages are found by juries.

Jury Decisions. Issues in jury trials are numerous and it will be several years before the CAFC establishes a pattern on most of the issues. Obviousness is one of the issues in jury trials that is still in flux in the court but a pattern is emerging. Another issue in patent jury trials on which the regional courts, prior to the creation of the Federal Circuit, were not uniform, was infringement.

The Seventh Amendment to the Constitution preserves the right to trial by jury and provides that courts shall not reexamine facts tried by jury except under the "rules of common law." Accordingly, a court must treat jury verdicts with great deference and may not substitute its view of the facts for that of the jury unless the jury's findings are clearly and unquestionably not supported by substantial evidence.

Obviousness under 35 USC 103 is a question of law. Like all legal conclusions, one on obviousness is reached after a series of fact questions have been answered. In the ordinary patent case, the trier of fact must answer the factual inquiries outlined in *Graham v. John Deere* (1966):

1. scope and content of the prior art,
2. differences between prior art and claims at issue,
3. level of ordinary skill in the art,
4. whatever objective evidence may be present as *indicia* of non-obviousness.

Submission of the obviousness question to the jury should therefore be accompanied by detailed special interrogatories designed to elicit responses to at least all the factual inquiries enumerated in *Graham* and based on the presentations made in the particular trial. Interrogatories to the jury should be directed to facts, not to questions of law such as obviousness, fraud, and claim interpretation. Those issues constitute the basis for jury instructions.

There is no question that the judge must remain the ultimate arbiter on the question of obviousness. He or she uses that rule first in exercising the duty of giving proper instructions on the law to the jury before considering its verdict and again when presented with a motion notwithstanding the verdict or a new trial.

Failure to submit detailed, factual interrogatories will not in every case require a new trial. When a party moves for a JNOV, the trial court must consider all of the evidence in: (1) a light most favorable to the nonmover; (2) must not determine credibility of witnesses; (3) must not substitute its choice for that of the jury between conflicting elements in the evidence. Following these guidelines, the trial court must then determine whether the evidence so viewed can constitute "substantial evidence" in support of the jury's findings and, if so, whether those findings can support the legal conclusions, drawn by the jury following the court's instructions *en route* to its verdict. Instructions must be meaningful and can be understood and given effect by the jury.

The court recommends resort to special verdicts; these eliminate the necessity of complicated instructions on the law and allow the trial court to give the jury only such explanation and instructions necessary to enable the jury to make intelligent findings upon the issue of facts submitted to them. *All* fact findings of a jury are nonadvisory, unless made in an area expressly removed from jury verdict.

35 USC 282 creates a presumption that a patent is valid and imposes the burden of proving invalidity on the challenger by clear and convincing evidence. That burden is permanent and does not change.

The court has firmly established that obviousness under Section 103 is a question of law reached after a series of fact questions (*Graham*) have been answered by the jury with proper instructions, the court prefers special rather than general verdicts.

In *Data Line v. Micro Technologies* (March 1987), an accused infringer cannot argue that the claim must include a limitation found in the specification. The Federal Circuit also set out the standard for review of a JNOV. Appellant contesting the JNOV must show there was "substantial evidence" to support the jury findings. Substantial evidence is defined as such relevant evidence from the record taken as a whole as might be accepted by a reasonable mind as adequate to support the finding under review.

In *Newell Companies Inc. v. Kenney Manufacturing Company* (1988), the Federal Circuit affirmed JNOV where the facts underlying the jury's determination of nonobviousness were not in dispute. Because the application of the statutory standard of obviousness to an established set of facts is solely a question of law, the majority subjected the trial court's conclusion on obviousness to full and independent review. "A party has a right to a *jury trial* in an action at law, not a right to a *jury verdict.*" Judge Newman filed a lengthy dissent stating that "the full weight of Supreme Court and Federal Circuit decisions [were] contrary to their ruling, as are the traditions and laws governing jury verdicts and the constitutional guarantee."

In summary, the dissent pointed out that the question of obviousness is a mixed question of law and fact; the law/fact distinction is both difficult and unnecessary in the context of a jury verdict because the jury necessarily applies the law to the facts.

Consent Judgments and Settlement Agreements

Consent judgments have many of the attributes of ordinary contracts and should be construed as such. Settlement agreements are highly favored in the law and will be enforced whenever possible as a fair means of resolving disputes without litigation.

Summary Judgment

Suits involving patent validity are not immune from disposition on Motion for Summary Judgment, where there is no material issue of fact requiring a trial to resolve and the facts of record require a holding of patent validity.

Class Actions

Courts seem reluctant to allow actions against a "class" of infringers, primarily because of the diverse issues and adverse interests among the members of the would-be class. The class action was an invention of Equity to enable it to proceed to a decree in suits where the number of those interested in the litigation was too great to permit joinder.

APPELLATE REVIEW

A party dissatisfied with the decision of the District Court has a right of appeal. For any patent infringement suit or any declaratory judgment action involving patent validity and/or infringement in which a Notice of Appeal was filed in a U.S. District Court on or after October 1, 1982, the forum is the U.S. Court of Appeals for the Federal Circuit (CAFC). The CAFC is charged with the duty of increasing "doctrinal stability" in the field of patent law.

The CAFC has the power, under the All Writs Act, to issue a *Writ of Mandamus* directing a district judge to perform a ministerial act, such as to grant summary judgment of patent validity where, in a previous action, the patent owner had a full and fair opportunity to litigate that issue. A frivolous appeal filed or proceeded with the CAFC will result in the imposition of damages and costs, a definition of what is a "frivolous appeal" is difficult. Access to the Supreme Court for review on the merits is at the discretion of that Court. To obtain such review, application must first be made to it for a *Writ of Certiorari,* a screening process.

Two additional sections of the Patent Law should be at least mentioned:

35 USC 288: Action for Infringement of a Patent Containing an Invalid Claim

> Whenever, without deceptive intention, a claim of a patent is invalid, an action may be maintained for the infringement of a claim of the patent which may be valid. The patentee shall recover no costs unless a disclaimer of the invalid claim has been entered at the Patent and Trademark Office before the commencement of the suit.

35 USC 290: Notice of Patent Suits

> The clerks of the courts of the United States, within one month after the filing of an action under this title shall give notice thereof in writing to the Commissioner. . . . The Commissioner shall, on receipt of such notices, enter the same in the file of such patent.

EPILOGUE

The *Hilton-Davis* case, mentioned several places in the text as well as in the Preface of this work, is a most important case before the Court of Appeals for the Federal Circuit. It was hoped that critical guidance in the application of the Doctrine of Equivalents would be provided by the *en banc* decision of the CAFC before this work went to press. Unfortunately, at this time, though arguments have been heard, no decision has as yet been issued.

On another subject, significant changes in our patent laws have been enacted arising from the GATT Uruguay Round, implementing legislation signed by the president on December 8, 1994. Most of the provisions of this legislation will take effect on January 1, 1996. However, there is a very significant part of the legislation—the provisions relating to patent term and provisional applications—that will take effect six months after the signing of the bill, on June 8, 1995. The changes and their effective dates are discussed below.

TREATMENT OF INVENTIVE ACTIVITY

In accordance with the GATT Uruguay Round agreement that patents be available without discrimination as to the place of invention, Section 104 of the Patent Law has been amended to provide that evidence of inventive activity in the territory of a World Trade Organization (WTO) member country may be treated the same as inventive activity in the United States. Should discovery procedures in a WTO member country be unable to produce information to the extent it could be obtained in the United States, the commissioner, court, or other authority is to draw appropriate inferences in favor of the party that requested the information. These changes parallel those made to implement the NAFTA agreement. Since the WTO agreement entered into force for the United States on January 1, 1995, these changes apply to all applications filed on or after January 1, 1996. However, a date of invention may not be established in a WTO member country, other than the United States, Canada, or Mexico, that is earlier than January 1, 1996, except as provided in sections 119 and 365 of the Patent Law.

NEW INFRINGING ACTIVITY UNDER 35 USC 271

At the present time, infringment of a U.S. patent involves the making, using, selling, or importing of the patented invention into the United States. Effective January 1, 1996, a patent will also be infringed by "offering for sale" the patented invention in the United States.

PATENT TERM

The current term of protection of a U.S. patent is seventeen years measured from the grant of the patent, provided that required fees for maintaining the patent in force are paid. The implementing legislation changes Section 154 of the Patent Law to provide that the term of protection begins on the date of grant and ends twenty years from the filing date of the application for the patent. If priority of an earlier application(s) is claimed under sections 120, 121, or 365(c) of the Patent Law, the twenty-year period is measured from the date of the earliest of such early applications.

The twenty-year term may be extended for a maximum of five years for delays in the issuance of the patent due to interferences, secrecy orders, and/or successful appeals to the Board of Patent Appeals and Interferences or the federal courts.

All patents that are in force on or that will issue on an application that is filed before June 8, 1995 will automatically have a term that is the greater of the twenty-year term provided above or the seventeen years from grant. This provision affects all patents that are in force on June 8, 1995 and all patents issued thereafter on applications filed prior to June 8, 1995. The terms of these patents are, of course, subject to any applicable terminal disclaimers. The remedies for infringement are limited in any term extended as a result of the automatic seventeen- or twenty-year term provision.

PROVISIONAL APPLICATIONS

Sections 111 and 119 of the Patent Law have been amended to establish a domestic priority system. The Paris Convention for the Protection of

Industrial Property requires that the terms of protection of patents for the same invention granted by different countries should generally be independent of one another. This precludes the United States from measuring, in a foreign origin application, the term of protection from the filing date of a foreign-filed application, even though the benefit of that foreign filing is subsequently claimed in the United States. To give U.S. inventors a similar opportunity, in the United States, of having an initial application filing which does not serve as a basis from which the term of protection is measured, a domestic priority system has been established that provides for provisional filing in the United States.

A provisional application requires only the filing of a specification in compliance with the first paragraph of Section 112 of the Patent Law and drawings where necessary for the understanding of the invention. It does not require a claim or an oath or declaration. It cannot mature into a patent, it is not examined, and it cannot claim priority of an earlier application. A provisional application is kept in confidence by the Patent Office. It is, however, a regular application that starts the Paris Convention priority year.

The provisional application has several important benefits. It places domestic applicants on an even footing with foreign applicants because the filing of a provisional application does not trigger the start of the twenty-year patent term. It has minimum legal and formal requirements whereby applicants can quickly and inexpensively establish an early effective filing date in a patent application which establishes a constructive reduction to practice for any invention described therein. The filing of a provisional application also provides up to twelve months to further develop the invention, determine marketability, acquire funding or capital, seek licensing, or seek manufacturing.

The effective date for all of the patent term and provisional applications provisions is June 8, 1995. The provisions do not apply to applications for design patents.

It should be pointed out that bills may soon be introduced into the Congress to (1) require publication of patent applications after eighteen months, (2) expand rights of third parties to participate in reexamination proceedings, and (3) clarify rights of patent prior users.

SELECTED BIBLIOGRAPHY

U.S. GOVERNMENT PUBLICATIONS

Manual of Patent Examining Procedure. Original fifth edition, August 1983; latest revision 16, March 1994.

The *Official Gazette* of the United States Patent and Trademark Office.

Patent and Trademark Office Notices.

Patent Laws. United States Code, Title 35, Patents (MPEP Appendix L).

Patent Rules. Title 37, Code of Federal Regulations, Patents, Trademarks, and Copyrights (MPEP Appendix R).

TREATISES AND TEXTS

Aisenberg, Irwin M. *Attorney's Dictionary of Patent Claims.* 2 vols. New York: Matthew Bender & Company, Inc., 1988.

Chisum, Donald S. *Patents.* 6 vols. New York: Matthew Bender & Company, Inc., 1978–1994 with supplements.

Deller, Anthony W. *Patent Claims.* 2d ed. Rochester, N.Y.: The Lawyers Cooperative Publishing Company, 1971 with supplements.

Kayton, Irving, ed. *Patent Practice.* 7 vols. Washington, D.C.: Patent Resources Institute, 1985.

Kramer, Barry, and Allen D. Brufsky. *Patent Law Practice Forms.* New York: Clark Boardman Company, Ltd., 1988.

Landis, John L. *Mechanics of Patent Claim Drafting.* 2d ed. New York: Practicing Law Institute, 1974.

Lipscomb, Ernest Bainbridge, III. *Walker on Patents.* 3d ed. 11 vols. Rochester, N. Y.: The Lawyers Cooperative Publishing Company, 1984.

Rosenberg, Peter D. *Patent Law Fundamentals.* 2 vols. New York: Clark Boardman Company, Ltd., 1989 revision.

United States Code Annotated. Title 35, Patents. 3 vols. St. Paul, Minn.: West Publishing Co., 1984.

PERIODICALS

AIPLA Bulletin. Published 4/5 times a year by the AIPLA.

AIPLA Quarterly Journal. American Intellectual Property Law Association, 2001 Jefferson Davis Hwy., Arlington, Va. 22202.

Journal of the Patent and Trademark Office Society. The Patent and Trademark Office Society, 2021 Jefferson Davis Hwy., Arlington, Va. 22202, monthly.

United States Patents Quarterly, and *BNA's Patent, Trademark & Copyright Journal.* The Bureau of National Affairs, Washington, D.C. 20037.

OTHER SOURCE MATERIAL

AIPLA, Special Publications.

American Bar Association, Section of Patent, Trademark and Copyright Law, Chicago, Ill. 60611.

Patent Resources Group, Special Publications.

Practicing Law Institute, Special Publications.

TABLE OF CASES

INDEX

About the Author

RICHARD T. HOLZMANN is a registered patent attorney. He has his own patent practice specializing in international matters and prosecuting cases before the U.S. Patent Tribunal. Dr. Holzmann was counsel to the Koreana Patent & Law Firm in Seoul, Korea, and earlier, president of an electronic specialty chemical company, Dynachem Corporation.

www.ingramcontent.com/pod-product-compliance
Ingram Content Group UK Ltd.
Pitfield, Milton Keynes, MK11 3LW, UK
UKHW021908150926
475560UK00003B/243

9 780899 308647